COUNTERING TERRORIST FINANCING

T0326623

MARK PIETH /
DANIEL THELESKLAF /
RADHA IVORY (EDS.)
BASEL INSTITUTE ON GOVERNANCE

COUNTERING
TERRORIST
FINANCING

THE PRACTITIONER'S POINT OF VIEW

PETER LANG
Bern · Berlin · Bruxelles · Frankfurt am Main · New York · Oxford · Wien

Bibliografische Information Der Deutschen Bibliothek
Die Deutsche Bibliothek verzeichnet diese Publikation in der Deutschen Nationalbibliografie;
detaillierte bibliografische Daten sind im Internet über ‹http://dnb.ddb.de› abrufbar.

British Library and Library of Congress Cataloguing-in-Publication Data: A catalogue record for this
book is available from The British Library, Great Britain, and from The Library of Congress, USA

Library of Congress Cataloging-in-Publication Data

Countering terrorist financing : the practitioner's point of view / Mark Pieth,
Daniel Thelesklaf, Radha Ivory (eds.).
p. cm.
Includes bibliographical references.
ISBN 978-3-03911-731-4 (alk. paper)
1. Terrorism—Finance. 2. Terrorism—Prevention. 3. Money laundering—Prevention.
4. Transnational crime—Prevention. I. Pieth, Mark. II. Thelesklaf, Daniel. III. Ivory, Radha.
HV6431.C69184 2009
363.325'16—dc22

                          2009017457

Cover Design: Eva Rolli, Peter Lang Bern

ISBN 978-3-03911-731-4

© Peter Lang AG, Internationaler Verlag der Wissenschaften, Bern 2009
Hochfeldstrasse 32, CH-3012 Bern
info@peterlang.com, www.peterlang.com, www.peterlang.net

Printed in Germany

Contents

MICHELINE CALMY-REY
Preface vii

Contributors ix

About the Basel Institute on Governance xv

Acknowledgements xvii

Abbreviations ixx

GUIDO STEINBERG
Al-Qaida and Jihadist terrorism after 2001 1

KRISTEL GRACE POH
Measures to counter the financing of terrorism 11

BOB UPTON
The financing of terror: a private sector perspective 25

YEHUDA SHAFFER
Detecting terrorist financing through financial intelligence:
the role of FIUs 41

HENRIETTE HAAS
Systematic Observation as a tool in combating terrorism 59

GIUSEPPE LOMBARDO
Terrorist financing and cash couriers:
legal and practical issues related to the implementation of
FATF Special Recommendation IX 95

KILIAN STRAUSS

Combating terrorist financing:
are transition countries the weak link? 109

MARCO GERCKE

Cyberterrorism: how terrorists use the Internet 127

STEPHEN BAKER

The misuse of offshore structures so as to assist
the financing of terrorism 151

MARK PIETH AND STEPHANIE EYMANN

Combating the financing of terrorism:
the 'Guantanamo Principle' 163

JACQUES RAYROUD

The UN listing system:
challenges for criminal justice authorities 181

YARA ESQUIVEL SOTO

An autonomous offence for the financing of terrorism:
notes from an Ibero-American perspective 195

SCOTT VESEL

Combating the financing of terrorism while
protecting human rights: a dilemma? 205

RADHA IVORY

Recovering terrorist assets in the United Kingdom:
the 'domestication' of international standards
on counter-terrorist financing 243

MARK PIETH, DANIEL THELESKLAF AND RADHA IVORY

The international counter-terrorist financing regime
at the cross-roads 277

Preface

There appears to be widespread consensus concerning what a terrorist act actually is, the most common definition being a deliberate attack on civilians or civilian property with the aim of intimidating ordinary people or pressurising a state or international organisation into acting in a certain way or refraining from action. The urgency and intensity of the terrorist threat is evident for all to see and states are regularly reminded of the need for counter-terrorism measures and international cooperation in this field.

Concerns about terrorism have generated concerns about the financing of terrorism. The financing of terrorism is a global phenomenon that not only threatens security but also compromises the stability, transparency and efficiency of financial systems, thus undermining economic prosperity. The fight against terrorism and its causes and financing is now viewed as a collective responsibility on the part of all members of the international community and participants in the public and private sectors.

The global agenda to curb the financing of terrorism calls for a cooperative approach among many different international bodies. Efforts to standardise the international response to the financing of terrorism have been led by the Financial Action Task Force on Money Laundering (FATF). Its 9 Special Recommendations on Terrorist Financing serve as the international framework for efforts in this area.

In its efforts to counter terrorism, the United Nations Security Council has imposed a number of obligations on UN member states. These include targeted financial sanctions against individuals and entities that are known to have, or are suspected of having, connections with al-Qaida or the Taliban. To date, the criteria governing delisting have not been adequately defined and there is no independent review mechanism in place. This shortcoming has led to legal action in Europe and elsewhere, which in turn has raised questions concerning the legitimacy of the UN system of sanctions. Recently, the European Court of Justice overturned the European sanctions programme targeting Usama Bin Laden, al-Qaida and the Taliban. These court cases may threaten the system of sanctions. In order to strengthen sanctions that are crucial for countering terrorism, it is important that they are applied consistently by the international community.

Therefore, in summer of 2005, Switzerland, together with Sweden and Germany, launched an initiative to improve sanctions. The aim was to strengthen the UN sanctions and to ensure that greater consideration be given to human rights in sanctions proceedings. In summer 2008, Switzerland and its partners (Sweden, Germany, Liechtenstein, Denmark and The Netherlands) followed up the initiative by submitting to the Security Council a discussion paper containing proposals for establishing an independent panel of experts which would be authorised to submit recommendations concerning delisting to the Security Council's Sanctions Committee. In essence, the discussion paper proposes the establishment of a Review Panel within the Security Council that would be mandated to issue non-binding recommendations on individual delisting requests. The proposal is modest and, in some important respects, does not fully satisfy all requirements from a human rights perspective. However, it aims to find a balanced solution, which increases fairness and transparency in procedures - thus strengthening individual human rights - without infringing upon the authority and integrity of the Security Council.

It is now up to the UN Security Council to make a decision regarding these reform proposals. In the meantime, the cases show that European countries (and also the UN) need to act to develop a system capable of effectively balancing the interests in financial security and individual rights. A new system needs to be developed to provide an efficient, effective, and legally sustainable way of countering the financing of terrorism on a global basis.

Terrorism and its financing must be countered by efficient means by all states. For this to happen, and to avoid playing into the hands of terrorists, these instruments must be compatible with human rights.

Micheline Calmy-Rey
Federal Councillor
Head of the Swiss Federal Department of Foreign Affairs

Contributors

STEPHEN BAKER is a member of both the English and Jersey Bars. Between 1990 and 2007, he has specialised in cases involving complex fraud, money laundering and asset recovery, particularly those with an international and political dimension. He acts regularly for foreign governments in asset recovery actions. He has considerable experience in terrorist financing matters, having formerly been responsible for dealing with suspicious activity reports and subsequently investigating them for the Attorney General of Jersey. He regularly speaks abroad on the subject matters of corruption and asset recovery.

YARA ESQUIVEL SOTO worked as a Public Prosecutor in Costa Rica, where she was in charge of the investigation and trial of several high-profile corruption cases involving high-ranking government officials and private entrepreneurs. In October 2006, she took a position as a regional investigator in the Office of Internal Oversight Services of the United Nations (UN) and moved to Kenya, where she was posted for one year to investigate fraud, corruption and malfeasance within the UN organisation. Currently, she works as an Asset Recovery Specialist for the International Centre for Asset Recovery at the Basel Institute on Governance, helping developing countries recover stolen assets. She is also pursuing a Master's Degree at Oxford University in the field of International Human Rights Law.

STEPHANIE EYMANN studied law at the University of Basel from 1999–2004, taking her degree in 2004. She has worked as an academic assistant to Prof. Mark Pieth since 2005 and handed in her PhD thesis, 'Freezing of Swiss Bank Accounts', in March 2009.

MARCO GERCKE, Attorney-at-Law, has a PhD in Criminal Law from the University of Cologne, Germany. He is a Lecturer in Law at the University of Cologne and a Visiting Lecturer for International Criminal Law at the University of Macau, China. Since 2001, he has published widely in the areas of cybercrime (including on the Council of Europe Cybercrime Convention), international criminal law and media law. He is a regular organiser and speaker at national and international training events. Dr. Gercke is a member of the Financial Integrity Network.

HENRIETTE HAAS is a senior lecturer in Forensic Psychology at the University of Zurich. She holds a PhD in clinical and consulting psychology and a licentiate (MSc) in clinical and consulting psychology, psychopathology and mathematics from the University of Zurich. She has been a scientific consultant and Head of the Analysis Division at the Service for Analysis and Prevention (SAP) of the Federal Office of Police and a Professor of Criminology and Forensic Psychology at the School of Criminal Justice (ESC) at the University of Lausanne.

RADHA IVORY is a research fellow at the Basel Institute on Governance. A graduate with honours in law, international relations and German from the University of Queensland, Australia, she practiced in employment law and litigation at top-tier Australian firm, Freehills, before relocating to Geneva, Switzerland, in 2006. There, she advised on preventing and responding to cases of abuse and exploitation by humanitarian workers at the Humanitarian Accountability Partnership. At the Basel Institute on Governance, she specialises in anti-corruption and counter-terrorism law, particularly, the compatibility of multilateral asset recovery regimes with international human rights standards.

GIUSEPPE LOMBARDO has a degree in law and is currently a consulting counsel in the Financial Integrity Group of the International Monetary Fund's (IMF) Legal Department. He worked as a lawyer in Italy's Financial Intelligence Unit for five years. He was Project Leader of the PHARE project 'Strengthening the Capacity of the Romanian Institutions for the Prevention and Control of Money Laundering'. He was a lecturer in AML/CTF within the Masters programme in International Economy and Finance at the Università degli studi Tor Vergata, Rome. He was also National Legal Expert for the European Commission for Justice and Home Affairs. He conducted the AML/CTF assessment of Hungary in 2005 and Denmark in 2006.

MARK PIETH is Professor of Criminal Law and Criminology at the University of Basel, Switzerland, and co-founder and Chairman of the Board of the Basel Institute on Governance. From 1989 to 1993, he headed the section on Economic and Organised Crime in the Swiss

Federal Department of Justice and Police. Since 1990, he has been Chairman of the OECD Working Group on Bribery in International Business Transactions. From 2003 to 2005, he was a Member of the Independent Inquiry Committee into the Iraq Oil-for-Food Programme by the UN Secretary General. Prof. Pieth is also a Member of the Wolfsberg Anti-Money Laundering (AML) Banking Initiative and a Board Member of the World Economic Forum's Partnering against Corruption Initiative (PACI).

KRISTEL GRACE POH is Head of the Anti-Money Laundering and Counter-Terrorist Financing (AML/CFT) Unit at the Basel Institute on Governance. Prior to joining the Basel Institute, she worked as Head of Financial Services Cooperation and Co-Head of the AML/CFT policy unit at the Monetary Authority of Singapore. From 2003 to 2006, she worked with the Financial Stability Forum and Bank for International Settlements in Basel, Switzerland, on a range of issues relating to financial stability and financial regulation. She has extensive experience with the work of the Financial Action Task Force (FATF) and has worked closely with the Asia Pacific Group on Money Laundering (APG). She is also actively involved in the work of the Wolfsberg Group on AML/CFT industry standards. Ms. Poh has a Masters degree in Banking and Finance from the Nanyang Technological University of Singapore.

JACQUES RAYROUD joined the Office of the Attorney General of Switzerland in Bern as a Federal Attorney on 1 July 2003, having worked as a magistrate for more than twelve years, including nine years as Examining Magistrate in the region of Fribourg, Switzerland. Now specialising in passive mutual legal assistance, he deals with international cases, especially in the fields of money laundering, organised crime, the financing of terrorism and corruption. From 1990 to 1992, he completed his articles and passed his final bar exams in 1994. In the meantime, he worked as assistant lecturer at the University of Fribourg, in the civil code section. He received his law degree from this University in 1990.

YEHUDA SHAFFER is the founder and director of Israel's Financial Intelligence Unit (FIU), the Israel Money Laundering and Terror Financing Prohibition Authority (IMPA), located in the Ministry of Justice. A lawyer with a Masters in Public Administration (MPA) from the Kennedy School of Government at Harvard University (2000), he served for 10 years from 1992 to 2002 as Senior Deputy to the State Attorney in the High Court of Justice Department of the Israeli Ministry of Justice. Mr. Shaffer received his LLB in 1987 and LLM in 1989 from the Faculty of Law of the Hebrew University in Jerusalem.

GUIDO STEINBERG is a research associate specialising in Middle East and Gulf Affairs at the German Institute for International and Security Affairs (Stiftung Wissenschaft und Politik, SWP) in Berlin. By training an Islamicist and historian of the Middle East, he has worked as a research coordinator at the Free University Berlin and as an advisor on international terrorism in the German Federal Chancellery. He is a frequent expert witness in German terrorism trials and has published widely on the Middle East, the history and politics of Saudi Arabia and Iraq, the Wahhabiya, Islamism and terrorism.

KILIAN STRAUSS is an expert on Eastern Europe and economies in transition. He studied economics, international relations and law in France, Germany and Russia and is an alumnus of the Institut d'Etudes Politiques in Paris. He is currently Senior Programme Officer at the Office of the Co-Ordinator of Economic and Environmental Activities of the Organisation for Security and Cooperation in Europe (OSCE) in Vienna, where he is in charge of project development and management, with a particular focus on activities aimed at combating corruption, money laundering and terrorist financing.

DANIEL THELESKLAF is a lawyer by profession. After a career in the private sector at Swiss Life and Dresdner Bank, he joined the Swiss Federal Office of Police in 1998 to become the first Director of Switzerland's FIU. In 2002/2003, he led the Due Diligence Unit (the AML regulator) in Liechtenstein and, since 2000, he has been a board member of Transparency International, Switzerland. He is now engaged in various anti-money laundering, counter-terrorist financing and anti-corruption projects and technical assistance missions for the OECD, the UN, the Council of Europe, the OSCE and the IMF. In 2008, he became Co-Director of the Basel Institute on Governance.

BOB UPTON joined Lloyds Private Banking 34 years ago, specialising is personal taxation and asset management. He subsequently undertook a number of specialist roles, including that of Head of Technical Training for the bank's Life Insurance and Investment Division. Mr. Upton was in a compliance role for 17 years, being appointed Head of Financial Crime Prevention and Monitoring in September 2001. He ended his career as Deputy Group Money Laundering Reporting Officer. Mr. Upton is a member of the Financial Integrity Network.

SCOTT VESEL is currently Human Rights and Anti-Terrorism Project Officer at the OSCE Office for Democratic Institutions and Human Rights in Warsaw. He previously worked as Deputy Director of the programme on security and good governance at the EastWest Institute in Prague and as a lawyer in the international arbitration practice group of law firm, Shearman & Sterling, in Paris. He holds advanced degrees in law and political science from Yale University and in international relations from Princeton University. He has authored and edited several publications in the fields of security sector reform, international relations and international law.

.

The Institute and its dedicated AML/CTF and asset recovery units

The Basel Institute on Governance is an independent non-profit think tank conducting research, policy development and capacity building in the areas of corporate and public governance, anti-corruption, anti-money laundering/counter-terrorist financing (AML/CTF) and asset recovery. Based in Basel, Switzerland, and associated with the University of Basel, the Institute cooperates with governments and non-government organisations around the world.

The Institute's dedicated AML/CTF unit specialises in the provision of advisory and capacity building services in the areas of AML and CTF, including the delivery of training. It aims to assist countries implement AML/CTF systems that are effective, workable and in compliance with international standards. In the delivery of training and advisory services, the Institute adapts its programmes to fit the specific needs and priorities of client countries and their respective financial institutions. These programmes may be delivered in the form of short-term engagements or longer-term commitments; they may consist of desk-based policy advice, short-term on-site advisory missions, the longer-term assignment of experts or resident advisors and/or national or regional seminars and workshops.

Advisory services and trainings are based on international AML/CTF standards, best practices and national legislation. The unit's experts are experienced professionals specialising in FIU related work, financial sector AML/CTF supervision and private sector AML/CTF. They combine their experience with proficiency in issues relating to legal and institutional reform, financial intelligence, financial sector supervision for banks, securities, insurance and trust companies, the implementation of AML/CTF measures in financial institutions, mutual legal assistance and international cooperation.

The Basel Institute on Governance's International Centre for Asset Recovery (ICAR) was founded in July 2006 and assists authorities in enhancing their capacities to seize, confiscate and recover the proceeds of crime. To this end, ICAR delivers trainings in the theory, techniques and practices of mutual legal assistance and asset recovery. It also provides analytical and strategic case assistance and facilitates cooperation between law enforcement agencies of different jurisdictions. To support these activities, ICAR operates a web-based knowledge-sharing and training tool, the Asset Recovery Knowledge Centre (www.assetrecovery.org).

Basel Institute on Governance
Steinenring 60, 4051 Basel, Switzerland
Phone +41 61 205 55 11, Fax +41 61 205 55 19
www.baselgovernance.org, info@baselgovernance.org

MARK PIETH / DANIEL THELESKLAF / RADHA IVORY

Acknowledgements

We would like to extend our warm thanks to the authors for their expert contributions. Without their generous assistance, this book would not have been ready for the 17th Plenary of the Egmont Group in May 2009 in Doha, Qatar. The dedicated work of Nina Schild and Katrin Aegler from the Basel Institute on Governance was equally crucial to finalising this unique publication.

We would also like to express our gratitude to the co-sponsors of the International Seminar on Combating Terrorist Financing in Davos, Switzerland, in October 2008 (Giessbach II). The seminar received important contributions from such organisations as the Council of Europe, the OSCE and the IMF, as well as significant financial support of World-Check, Netbreeze, Cellent and IMPAQ.

Further, the Basel Institute on Governance would not be able to operate without funding from the Swiss Agency for Development and Cooperation (SDC), the Government of Liechtenstein and the United Kingdom's Department for International Development (DFID).

Mark Pieth
Daniel Thelesklaf
Radha Ivory

Basel Institute on Governance

Abbreviations

ATCS Act	Anti-Terrorism, Crime and Security Act 2001 (UK)
AIVD	Algemene Inlichtingen- en Veiligheidsdienst (The Netherlands)
AML	Anti-Money Laundering
AQO	The Al-Qaida and Taliban (United Nations Measures) Order 2002 and 2006 (UK)
AP	Additional Protocol
ATF	Bureau of Alcohol, Tobacco, Firearms and Explosives of the US Department of Justice
CAIA	Centre for Advanced Internet Architectures
CDD	Customer Due Diligence
CFI	European Court of First Instance
CIS	Commonwealth of Independent States
CoE	Council of Europe
CRS	Congressional Research Service (US)
CT Act	Counter-Terrorism Act 2008 (UK)
CT Bill	Counter-Terrorism Bill 2008 (UK)
CTF	Counter-Terrorist Financing
DoS	Denial-of-Service
EBI	Enterprise Business Intelligence
EBRD	European Bank for Reconstruction and Development
EC	European Commission or European Community
EEC	European Economic Community
ECJ	European Court of Justice
ECMA	European Convention on Mutual Assistance in Criminal Matters
ECtHR	European Court of Human Rights
ECHR	Convention for the Protection of Human Rights and Fundamental Freedoms (CoE)
EU	European Union
EUR	Euro

FATF	Financial Action Task Force
FBI	Federal Bureau of Investigation of the US Department of Justice (US)
FCD	Federal Court Decision (Switzerland)
FIU	Financial Intelligence Unit
FSRB	FATF-Style Regional Body
GAFISud	Grupo de Acción Financiera de Sudamérica
GPML	Global Programme against Money Laundering of the UNODC
HSBC	Hongkong and Shanghai Banking Corporation
ICAR	International Centre for Asset Recovery at the Basel Institute on Governance
ICCPR	International Covenant on Civil and Political Rights (UN)
ICTs	Internet Communication Technologies
ITU	International Telecommunications Union
ID	Identification
IMF	International Monetary Fund
IMPA	Israel Money Laundering and Terror Financing Prohibition Authority
IRTPA	Intelligence Reform and Terrorism Prevention Act of 2004 (US)
IT	Information Technology
IVTS	Informal Value Transfer System
KYC	Know Your Customer
MENA	Middle East and North Africa
ML	Money Laundering
MLA	Mutual Legal Assistance
MSB	Money Service Business
MVT	Money and Value Transfer Mechanism
NAFTA	North American Free Trade Agreement
NATO	North Atlantic Treaty Organisation
NCCTs	Non-Cooperative Countries and Territories
NCRI	National Council of Resistance of Iran
NGO	Non-Government Organisation
NPO	Non-Profit Organisation
OAG	Office of the Attorney General

OFAC	Office of Foreign Assets Control of the US Treasury (US)
OMPI	Organisation des Modjahedines du people d'Iran (see also, People's Mojahadeen Organisation of Iran)
OSCE	Organisation for Security and Cooperation in Europe
PACE	Parliamentary Assembly of the Council of Europe (EU)
PEP	Politically Exposed Person
PMOI	People's Mojahadeen Organisation of Iran (see also, Organisation des Modjahedines du people d'Iran)
POCA	Proceeds of Crime Act 2002 (UK)
POAC	Proscribed Organisations Appeal Commission (UK)
PRADO	Public Register of Authentic Identity and Travel Documents Online (Council of the EU)
RBA	Risk-Based Approach
RIPA	Regulation of Investigatory Powers Act 2000 (UK)
SAR	Suspicious Activity Reports
SDN	Specially Designated National
SRIX	Special Recommendation IX
STR	Suspicious Transaction Report
SWP	Stiftung Wissenschaft und Politik (German Institute for International and Security Affairs)
SWIFT	Society for Worldwide Interbank Financial Telecommunications
TACT	Terrorism Act 2000 (UK)
TACT 2006	Terrorism Act 2006 (UK)
TF	Terrorist Financing
TO	The Terrorism (United Nations Measures) Order 2006 (UK)
UAE	United Arab Emirates
UK	United Kingdom of Great Britain and Northern Ireland
UN	United Nations
UNCCPR	United Nations International Covenant on Civil and Political Rights (see also ICCPR)
UNGA	United Nations General Assembly

UNGAOR	United Nations General Assembly Official Records
UNODC	United Nations Office for Drug Control and Crime
UNSC	United Nations Security Council
US or USA	United States of America
USD	United States Dollar
USIP	United States Institute for Peace
VoIP	Voice over Internet Protocol
WB	World Bank
9/11	The attacks on the US of 11 September 2001

GUIDO STEINBERG*

Al-Qaida and Jihadist terrorism after 2001

Since 2001, the term 'al-Qaida' has become widely synonymous with international Islamist terrorism. Whenever Islamist terrorists perpetrate an attack – in Europe, the Middle East, South or Southeast Asia – al-Qaida is the prime suspect. Nevertheless, the Jihadist movement is a much more diverse and diffuse phenomenon than the interest in al-Qaida would suggest. Al-Qaida might be the most successful and most well-known organisation but it is only one among a larger spectrum of different actors. Groups like the Jemaah Islamiyah in Indonesia, Lashkar-e Tayyiba in Pakistan or Ansar al-Islam (Supporters of Islam) in Iraq might maintain relations with al-Qaida and follow broadly similar goals but they are not part of the al-Qaida organisation. In general, the networked character of al-Qaida has been overstated.

During their years in Afghanistan, Usama Bin Laden and his supporters tried, rather, to build a hierarchical organisation with a well-controlled infrastructure of training camps and guest houses. Like terrorist groups of the past, al-Qaida profited from the support given to it by a state actor, namely, the Taliban. In some cases, al-Qaida did in fact rely on more networked forms of organisation, e.g., when it financed operations by non-members. However, this was only for the sake of more effectively targeting its enemies and not because of a particular preference for loose organisational structures. To the contrary, on a global scale, al-Qaida instigated a centralising process among Islamist militants in the 1990s.

In the early 1990s, most Islamist terrorist groups operated independently from each other, Egyptians against the Egyptian regime, Saudis against the Saudi monarchy and so on. This changed, begin-

*   A former advisor on international terrorism in the German Federal Chancellery, Dr. Guido Steinberg is a senior fellow at the German Institute for International and Security Affairs (Stiftung Wissenschaft und Politik, SWP) in Berlin.

ning in the mid-1990s, when al-Qaida attracted a rising number of recruits who aimed at fighting the West in general and the US in particular. Its internationalist ideology proved attractive to young men
from all over the Arab world. However, even in 2001, al-Qaida was an
Arab organisation, dominated by Egyptians and Saudi Arabians whose
influence was resented by other smaller national groups within al-
Qaida. In all, al-Qaida was far from a highly integrated global network
– it was better described as a joint venture of Egyptian and Saudi
Arabian militants.

I. The demise of Usama Bin Laden's al-Qaida
in 2001 and 2002

The attacks on the United States (US) of 11 September 2001 (9/11),
which began al-Qaida's rise to prominence, also endangered the very
existence of the organisation. During 2002 and 2003, it first lost its
head-quarters in Afghanistan and then was nearly destroyed entirely in
US reprisals. In late 2001, al-Qaida was still in the process of centralising and professionalising its terrorist activity, so that the organisation disintegrated in the following years and developed into a rather
loose network, quite unlike what Bin Laden and Zawahiri seem to
have envisaged before 2001.

The American attacks in Afghanistan, which began in October
2001, were catastrophic for al-Qaida. Just as the organisation's alliance
with the Taliban had enabled it to build a unique infrastructure, the loss
of its retreat in Afghanistan suddenly threatened the organisation's very
survival. Al-Qaida's leadership managed to flee to Pakistan, where it
has been hiding in mountain refuges ever since. Most of its medium
level operational chiefs also escaped; they too continue to organise
terrorist attacks from their hideouts in Pakistani cities. Most importantly, Khalid Shaikh Mohammed, the chief planner of the 9/11
attacks, fled to Pakistan and continued plotting attacks. The attacks on
an Israeli airplane and a hotel frequented by Israeli tourists in Mom-

basa in November 2002 were one result of the activities of the al-Qaida diaspora.

These spectacular escapes aside, 2002 and 2003 also saw the arrests of al-Qaida's most important medium-level planners: Abu Zubaida in March 2002, Abdarrahim al Nashiri in November 2002 and Khalid Shaikh Mohammed in March 2003. These successes were so spectacular that in 2003 and 2004 it seemed as if Usama Bin Laden's al-Qaida was on the verge of collapse. The organisation survived by splitting up into the main elements of its structure, namely the single national groupings. These splinter groups then dominated the terrorist scene between 2003 and 2005.

II. Trends in the development of al-Qaida after 2001

Three main developments have characterised the development of international Islamist terrorism after 2001:

- The return of Jihadists from South Asia to the Arab world
- The emergence of new Jihadist organisations
- The development of al-Qaida from organisation to ideological clearing house

1. The return of Jihadists to the Arab world

In winter 2001/2002, most surviving al-Qaida members fled from Afghanistan to Pakistan. Only some militants were given detailed instructions on where to go and what to attack. Most received rather vague orders to return to their home countries, or other places that they were familiar with, and plan, organise and perpetrate terrorist attacks there. This move led to a serious deterioration of internal security in a number of Middle Eastern states. In 2003 and 2004, local and regional groupings, mainly made up of returnees from Afghanistan who had retained their independent logistic capabilities, hit targets in Saudi Arabia and Turkey.

After the battle of Tora Bora in December 2001, dozens of Saudi Arabian militants fled from Afghanistan back home. The war in Iraq in March and April 2003 triggered their decision to attack in Saudi Arabia as well. This was surprising because Saudi Arabia had been the main logistical and financial hub of al-Qaida since the 1990s. Businessmen from the Gulf were the main financiers of al-Qaida and a direct attack on Saudi Arabia might have threatened this line of support. Nevertheless, al-Qaida unleashed a ferocious campaign against Westerners and state institutions in Saudi Arabia, which lasted until 2005. For a short while in 2004, it even seemed as if the stability of the Kingdom itself was at threat.

The terrorist campaign in Saudi Arabia did not remain an isolated development. Many fighters from Afghanistan returned to the Middle East and North Africa, leading to an overall increase in terrorist activity in the Arab world from 2002 onwards. However, Iraq was the country that suffered most from resurgent Jihadism.

2.   The emergence of new Jihadist organisations

After al-Qaida partly lost its ability to plan and organise attacks from Pakistan, new organisations emerged, primarily, but not exclusively, in connection with the insurgency in Iraq. The most important of these was the group known as Jamaat al-Tawhid wa-l-Jihad (The Monotheism and Jihad Group) until autumn 2004 and headed by the Jordanian, Abu Musab al-Zarqawi. From 1999, Zarqawi had built up a training camp exclusively for Palestinians, Jordanians, Syrians and some Lebanese, close to the Afghan city of Herat. He did not join al-Qaida because he rejected al-Qaida's program of global jihad. Rather he stuck to his original goals, namely, toppling the Jordanian monarchy and 'liberating' Palestine.

After coalition forces evicted al-Qaida and its affiliates from Afghanistan, Zarqawi fled via Pakistan and Iran to Northern Iraq. For several months, he found refuge with the Iraqi-Kurdish group Ansar al-Islam (Supporters of Islam) and rebuilt his organisation. From

2003, he redirected it to fight American forces and their allies in Iraq. He integrated large numbers of Iraqis into his organisation but also relied heavily on volunteers from neighbouring Arab countries, in the majority Syrians and Saudis. Zarqawi adjusted his goals to reflect the group's new social support base: from 2004, Zarqawi called for the establishment of an Islamic state in Iraq, next, he declared his intention to fight a 'holy war' in neighbouring Syria, Jordan, Kuwait and Saudi Arabia and, finally, he described his ultimate goal as the 'liberation' of Jerusalem. The re-defined goals thus reflected the changed national composition of the organisation.

Zarqawi's organisation was responsible for most of the major suicide bombings in Iraq after 2003. In order to destabilise Iraq, Zarqawi developed a strategy of provoking civil war between the Shiites and Sunnis, attacking Shiite religious leaders, politicians, officials and civilians. After Shiite and Kurdish parties won the elections in January and December 2005, some Shiite militia did indeed fight back and a civil war ensued. However, his organisation's use of indiscriminate violence eroded popular support and even endangered its relations to al-Qaida. In a gesture of reconciliation in October 2004, Zarqawi swore allegiance to Usama Bin Laden and changed the name of his organisation to 'Qaidat al-Jihad in Mesopotamia', establishing a theoretically subordinate branch of al-Qaida in Iraq. The al-Qaida leadership accepted Zarqawi's oath of allegiance, though it publicly rejected his anti-Shiite strategy and demanded a more circumspect use of violence against Muslims. Zarqawi refused and his organisation, al-Qaida in Iraq, stuck to his strategy even after his death in an American air strike in July 2006. As a result, al-Qaida in Iraq remained an independent organisation, structurally and strategically.

3. The development of al-Qaida from organisation to ideological clearing house

From late 2001, the al-Qaida leadership was increasingly isolated in its hideouts in the Pakistani mountains. Therefore, it began to issue ideological guidance through video- and audiotapes. During the first years, the files were published by the Qatar-based satellite television channel, al-Jazeera; later, al-Qaida relied on the Internet to spread its propaganda. In some cases, it seems as if Usama Bin Laden even sent direct orders in these messages. For example, in a tape published in October 2003, Bin Laden identified Spain, Italy and Great Britain as the main allies of the US in Iraq and demanded attacks on Spanish, Italian and British targets. By November 2003, the British HSBC bank had been targeted in Istanbul, Italian troops had been attacked in Southern Iraq and Spanish intelligence agents had been killed in an ambush south of Baghdad. Most importantly, a North African cell targeted commuter trains in the Spanish capital, Madrid, on 11 March 2004. Catastrophic crisis management by the conservative Aznar government contributed to its defeat in parliamentary elections three days later and a victory for the opposition party, the Socialists. The latter stuck to their promise to withdraw Spanish troops from Iraq and thereby conformed with al-Qaida's expectations.

Still, the extent to which al-Qaida played a more direct role in the Madrid bombings has not been established. Although many specialists suspect some influence from al-Qaida, al-Qaida in Iraq or other groups, there is no hard evidence of this as yet. Similarly, in several recent terrorist attacks or foiled plots, the perpetrators seem to have planned, organised and perpetrated their activities on their own. In view of this, European counter-terrorism officials have established a new category of 'home-grown terrorists': cells and groups (mainly in Europe) which need less direction from larger organisations. Cases frequently cited as examples of 'home-grown terrorism' include the murder of the Dutch filmmaker van Gogh in Amsterdam in November 2004 and the failed attacks by the so-called 'suitcase bombers' on two German regional trains in July 2006.

However, there may be other explanations for the failure of security services to establish links between terrorist cells and larger organisations. The terrorists might simply have become more sophisticated in covering their links or the services may be insufficiently effective in tracking down links – or both. Moreover, in all cited cases of 'home-grown terrorism', there are indications that links existed to larger organisations or, at least, to masterminds with a history of militant activity. As a consequence, the term 'home-grown terrorism' better describes an ideal type and a trend than it does a current reality.

Hence, Europe should focus on the growing importance of al-Qaida's ideology and what has been labelled al-Qaida's development from organisation to ideology. Through the Internet and through affiliated preachers, al-Qaida's ideology has gained ground among Muslim youth worldwide – even at times when the organisation itself has had difficulties keeping up its activities in Pakistan. Its ideological capital enabled it to re-emerge as a major actor after 2005, broadening from an Arab organisation in 2001 to an organisation with members and supporters from other places, especially Europe. In England, for example, it is recruiting more ethnic Pakistanis and, in Germany, there is an apparent Jihadist radicalisation of young people of Turkish and Kurdish descent.

III. Al-Qaida's resurgence since 2005

The years between 2005 and 2007 have witnessed a spectacular resurgence of 'al-Qaida proper', i.e., the core of the organisation under the command of Usama Bin Laden and his deputy, Aiman al-Zawahiri especially in Pakistan and Afghanistan.

Although it might be argued that al-Qaida never disappeared, it is beyond doubt that it was seriously weakened in 2003 by the military campaign in Afghanistan, the fall of the Taliban and Western, Arab and Pakistani counter-terrorism measures. However, the most important blow to al-Qaida was the arrest and killing of its mid-ranking operatives who were responsible for planning and supervising actual operations. Only the shift of American focus to Iraq allowed al-Qaida to regain its strength. From 2002, US military and intelligence resources were withdrawn from Pakistan and Afghanistan and used in or on Iraq, reflecting the growing importance of that war and, subsequently, the counter-insurgency to the US administration.

Al-Qaida's remarkable resilience is also based on its ability to recruit new fighters and to train replacements for the operational commanders who were caught or killed. In fact, the replacement of its former chiefs of operations might be considered al-Qaida's greatest success of recent years: field commanders like the Libyan Abu Laith al-Libi, the Egyptians Abu al-Yazid and Abu Ubaida al-Masri, the ideologist Abu Yahia al-Libi, took over the operational functions along with other, less well-known, figures.

There is an increasing amount of evidence that these new mid-level leaders have indeed planned and organised terrorist activities. Although, in most cases, their projects have been restricted to Afghanistan and Pakistan, two of the new commanders, Abu Laith and Abu Ubaida, seem to have led operations abroad. One example of Abu Laith al-Libi's work may be an aborted plot against Germany in September 2007. Abu Laith al-Libi planned the attack in conjunction with Uzbeks belonging to an organisation called the 'Islamic Jihad Union in Pakistan'. This pattern fits what has been established about al-Qaida's role in the London bombings in July 2005 and shows that al-Qaida is able to plan attacks in Europe again.

IV. Financial dimensions of al-Qaida's resurgence

Al-Qaida's new strength seems also to have a financial dimension. Reports about Bin Laden's wealth have always been more of a myth than reality. What money he might have had he invested in the Afghani jihad of the 1980s and later in his career in Saudi Arabia, Sudan and again Afghanistan. As a consequence, al-Qaida has always been highly dependent on external finance.

Before 2001, al-Qaida might have received some form of protection money from the Saudi state, however, most financial contributions to al-Qaida's budget came from private donors in the Gulf region, especially Saudi Arabia, Kuwait and the United Arab Emirates. Some wealthy businessmen may well have figured it was wise to support the Jihadists just in case they should one day play a more important role in Saudi politics, others might simply have sympathised with Bin Laden's 'war against the West'. In any case, their financial support dried up during 2003. After the terrorist campaign in Saudi Arabia, the Gulf States introduced stricter measures against terrorist financing and, more importantly, al-Qaida lost support among the people of the Gulf when it began attacking Saudi civilian targets in November 2003. Furthermore, Gulf money increasingly ended up in Iraq, the insurgency having caught the attention of Islamist sympathisers all over the region. So, for some time during 2004 and 2005, the al-Qaida leadership seems to have had serious financial difficulties.

In response to these developments, al-Qaida reorganised its financial flows between 2005 and 2008. Most of its money still seems to come from wealthy donors in the Gulf and to be transferred via Pakistan. However, due to increased control of legal financial channels, al-Qaida and its supporters increasingly rely on couriers travelling with cash. (The physical transportation of money is still the means by which funds finds their way from Kuwait and Saudi Arabia to the theatres of conflict.) As a consequence, measures from the G8 states against terrorist financing often do not address the core issue, namely, informal money flows from the Gulf to Pakistan, Afghanistan and Iraq. That said, now that al-Qaida has regained strength, banking channels might again play a larger role in terrorist financing.

V. The future

If al-Qaida and its headquarters in Pakistan continue to grow stronger, we should expect more and better attacks to follow. Al-Qaida might have accepted that, under current conditions, it is only able to perpetrate attacks on softer targets, such as commuter trains in Europe. But the organisation still aims at maximum-impact terrorist attacks on the United States and other Western states, possibly coordinated between different continents. A resurgent al-Qaida might obtain the ability to plan, organise and perpetrate such attacks again. In the foreseeable future, it is rather unlikely that al-Qaida will be capable of attacking within the US. Therefore, it may choose to attack in Europe as an especially effective means of weakening the West's resolve in Iraq and Afghanistan. Moreover, since al-Qaida has won a large number of new recruits from Europe, it is highly likely that attacks along the lines of Madrid and London will continue.

That said, some of the more important mistakes in American strategy have been corrected since 2007. There is a heightened awareness that the loss of focus on Pakistan and Afghanistan was a reason for the re-emergence of al-Qaida after the near-fatal US and allied campaign immediately after 9/11. Since October 2007, the US has intensified attacks on al-Qaida and Taliban hideouts in the Pakistani tribal areas and killed many senior al-Qaida operatives. Nevertheless, the US fight against al-Qaida depends on Pakistani cooperation and Islamabad has been unwilling to effectively combat al-Qaida's presence on its territory. Unless Pakistan fundamentally changes its behaviour, al-Qaida and affiliated groups will continue to find refuge in the Pakistani tribal areas.

Al-Qaida's resurgence is also important for those concerned with the issue of counter-terrorist financing. As al-Qaida's organisational structures become more sophisticated, so its needs for money increase. Furthermore, as it prepares for more sophisticated attacks in Europe and elsewhere, so it will again demand the transfer of money across continents via banking channels.

KRISTEL GRACE POH[*]

Measures to counter the financing of terrorism

I. Introduction

The term 'financing of terrorism' is set out in the International Convention for the Suppression of the Financing of Terrorism.[1] In simple terms, it means the financial support of terrorism or of those who encourage, plan or engage in terrorism. The term 'terrorism', however, is not so clear cut and may vary from country to country as it has social and political implications.

For financial institutions, the financing of terrorism is often difficult to detect not only because of the different definitions of 'terrorism' but also because terrorist financing follows few hard patterns. For instance, an investigation into the financial transactions of some high profile terrorists and hijackers showed that most of the individual transactions were not unusual. The account holders appeared to be foreign students receiving money to fund their studies.[2] The transactions would not have been flagged out as suspicious transactions needing special scrutiny by the financial institutions involved. In addition, terrorist finance may originate from legitimate sources, criminal sources or both. This represents a significant difference between

---

*   Kristel Grace Poh is Head of AML/CTF at the Basel Institute on Governance. Prior to her appointment at the Basel Institute, she was head of Financial Services Cooperation and co-head of AML/CTF unit at the Monetary Authority of Singapore.
1   International Convention for the Suppression of the Financing of Terrorism, adopted by the General Assembly of the United Nations on 9 December 1999, available at http://untreaty.un.org/English/Terrorism.asp.
2   Financial Action Task Force (FATF), *Guidance for Financial Institutions: Detecting Terrorist Financing*, FATF/OECD, 2002: 6, available at http://www.fatf-gafi.org/dataoecd/39/21/34033955.pdf.

money laundering and terrorist financing. Terrorist financing may involve funds from legitimate sources, such as charitable donations, that are in turn funnelled to terrorist organisations or terrorists. The donors may or may not know that the funds are being utilised to support terrorist activities.

Terrorists and terrorist financiers also use ways to disguise and conceal the source of terrorist financing so that their financial activities go undetected. Further, given their efforts to use the informal sector, the focus on targeting terrorists' financial support networks may not be effective. For example, if terrorists just carry USD 5,000 to USD 10,000 cash and do not route it through the formal financial system, they would avoid standard counter-terrorist financing (CTF) measures and detection systems. In such cases, one might ask whether it would be more effective to directly target terrorist activities than to go after the financing of terrorism.

II. CTF measures and their impact on financial institutions

Notwithstanding the difficulties involved, national authorities often have high expectations of financial institutions and have assigned them an important role in the detection and disruption of terrorist financing. Policy makers often view money as indispensable to terrorists, the planning of their attacks, training of their operatives and maintenance of their organisations. They have reasoned that, without money, no terrorist organisation or network can survive; money is routed through the financial system; terrorist financiers are likely to continue using the formal financial sector as a speedy and secure means of transmitting their funds to their network and operatives; therefore, financial institutions should take steps to identify and stop terrorist transactions. Certain sectors have been shown to be vulnerable to exploitation by terrorist financiers. For instance, the typologies and case studies submitted by national jurisdictions to the Financial Action Task Force (FATF) showed that money and value transfer mechanisms (MVT) are particularly attractive to terrorists. MVT operations range from large-scale and regulated funds transfer mechanisms available in the formal financial sector, to small-scale alternative remittance systems.

Even though there are difficulties in detecting financing of terrorism, it remains a high priority for financial institutions because any institution that is found to have violated CTF regulations stands to suffer severe consequences. Violation of CTF compliance standards can have a real financial impact on institutions, in the form of hefty fines, legal fees and other regulatory sanctions, even the suspension or revocation of a licence. An apparent 'involvement' in terrorism may also cause significant harm to the institution's reputation. In the extreme case, such reputational damage may affect public confidence and endanger the financial institution's stability.

Financial institutions thus shoulder a heavy responsibility with respect to CTF and devote considerable energy to CTF measures. Their fundamental means of control is the screening of customer accounts and transactions against name lists from sanction databases. Some institutions supplement the official sanction lists with commercial sanction databases for more comprehensive checks. Commercial intelligence companies, such as World Check, have indicated that there is a wide gap between the number of terrorists officially sanctioned by the world's key sanctioning bodies and the number of individuals and organisations who are actually involved in terrorism. For instance, the four lists issued by the UN Security Council (UNSC), the US Office of Assets Control (OFAC), the UK Treasury and the European Union (EU) designate some eight hundred terrorists; conservative estimates put the number of operatives trained in al-Qaida camps alone at between 50,000 and 100,000.[3] In any case, even if authorities and financial institutions knew the exact number of terrorists, they would not know all their names.

Financial institutions also use technologies and software that provide link analysis. These systems analyse and connect data based on parameters fed into the system by financial institutions to identify potentially suspicious transactions from a CTF perspective. These

---

3   Jay Jhadveri, Director of World Check, at a seminar on 'Countering the Financing of Terrorism' held on 12 February 2008 in Singapore.

transactions are then flagged out for reporting to the local Financial Intelligence Unit (FIU). In addition, banks use and incorporate knowledge gleamed from available typologies and case studies to design detection rules for identifying off-market or suspicious transactions.

III. Contributions by the financial sector

1.   *Generating leads by reporting suspicious transactions*

As terrorists do not follow fixed patterns in moving their money, financial institutions cannot develop and apply generic indicators to detect terrorist money as such. However, they can see when a designated person or organisation has opened an account and they can detect unusual or suspicious transactions that may later prove to be related to terrorist financing. In this respect, the financial sector makes an important – if indirect – contribution to CTF by performing customer due diligence and monitoring transactions. With the knowledge they have of their customers, financial institutions can see when transactions are out of line with the customer's profile or transaction history and report them to the FIU for further investigation. According to the FATF, the most frequently reported suspicious activities from a CTF perspective are:

–   Unusual business activity
–   Funds for which the source cannot be ascertained
–   Multiple deposits at different branches
–   Third party deposits in US cash
–   Wire transfers following cash deposits
–   Regular wire transfers to specific locations or accounts
–   Large cash deposits[4]

---

4   FATF, *FATF Terrorist Financing Typologies Report*, FATF/OECD, 2008: 31, available at http://www.fatf-gafi.org/dataoecd/28/43/40285899.pdf.

While the indicators contain little actionable intelligence from the CTF perspective, this can be viewed in the context that financing of terrorism comes with few hard patterns and it is difficult to generate indicators that can help financial institutions detect the financing of terrorism outright.

These suspicious transaction reports may be instrumental in assisting law enforcement agencies to initiate or supplement major terrorist financing investigations and other criminal cases.

The foiled bomb plot against flights between the UK and the US in August 2006 demonstrates how financial institutions can play an important role in flagging suspicious transactions and providing information to law enforcement agencies. Rashid Rauf, the key player in the plot, was placed under police surveillance, along with a number of others, after banks reported that his account had received very large wire transfers as 'earthquake relief' from a charity. The arrest of the terrorist operatives helped to disrupt the terrorists' plot. Had it succeeded, Rauf and his accomplices would have destroyed as many as ten aircraft in transit from the UK to the US using liquid explosives brought on board as hand luggage.

2. Using financial customer and account information to assist investigations

Financial institutions also store financial information about individuals, which can be valuable to intelligence and law enforcement agencies in counter-terrorism investigations. The information includes, for example, financial reports of large cash transactions, wire transfers and cross-border currency movements. This information can significantly increase the pool of financial information available to investigators in uncovering the operational infrastructure of a terrorist organisation. For instance, in the aftermath of the London bombings of 2005, financial institutions worked around-the-clock to provide financial records relating to a credit card fragment belonging to one of the bombers. The records were voluminous and ongoing cooperation was necessary to resolve the inquiry. But the financial institution could provide crucial leads as to the financial profile of the terrorist, his connection with other members of the terrorist group, their spending patterns and training expenses.

3.   *Using other compliance systems to detect terrorist activity*

There also appears to be a growing nexus between terrorism and money laundering. Terrorists increasingly turn to criminal activities to fund their terrorist activities and to money laundering to move these funds. In this context, some financial institutions have been able to use their anti-money laundering (AML) capacities to detect suspicious transactions. Reports filed with the FIU can produce crucial leads on terrorist activities. A case highlighted by the FATF[5] illustrated how a financial institution queried a customer whose account was credited with significant cash deposits. It was able to flag out transactions which were not in line with the customer's profile. The information was forwarded to the FIU and then combined with counter-terrorist intelligence and investigations and eventually assisted authorities to link the funds to terrorist activities.

IV. Collaborative efforts between the private
and public sectors

Combating the financing of terrorism cannot be viewed as a task solely for the financial sector or solely for intelligence and law enforcement agencies. As different institutions and stakeholders hold different pieces of information, and all of it is necessary to combat terrorism, a collaborative response is essential.

To detect the financing of terrorism, financial institutions need intelligence. Sharing intelligence is particularly important given the changing face of global terrorism. It is to be expected that terrorists

---

5   FATF, *Terrorist Financing*, FATF/OECD, Paris 2008: 12, available at http://www.fatf-gafi.org/dataoecd/28/43/40285899.pdf.

and terrorist groups will be innovative, that they will look for new sources of funds, new ways to move money and new ways to recruit operatives and carry out operations. Already, some terrorist operatives do not rely on external sources of money but are funding themselves through legitimate business activities or employment. Likewise, we should expect that terrorists will react quickly to new legislation, law enforcement interventions and technological developments. They may be younger individuals, who are quite capable of making bombs by themselves using information on the Internet.[6]

Therefore, it is particularly important that national authorities share intelligence that would help financial institutions identify new forms of terrorist financing. It is important that intelligence agencies provide timely information to the financial sector and assist financial institutions to gain a good understanding of the evolving nature and scope of the national, regional and global threats.

V. Other challenges in implementing CTF standards

There is another reason why the financial sector cannot carry the full burden of detecting and preventing the financing of terrorism: there are many other sectors which are vulnerable to exploitation by terrorist financiers.

1. *Other vulnerable industries and professions*

The FATF has identified casinos, lawyers, accountants, trust companies and service providers, real estate agents and jewellers as vulnerable to money laundering and terrorist financing and in need of proper controls. In terms of terrorist financing, cash couriers, money

---

6 Counterterrorism Threat Assessment and Warning Unit, Counterterrorism Division, *Terrorism in the United States*, Federal Bureau of Investigation, Washington (DC), 1999: 40, available at http://www.fbi.gov/publications/terror/terror99.pdf.

value services providers and non-profit organisations have been identified as particularly high-risk actors in the economy.

2. *Common vulnerabilities in developing countries*

Developing and low-income countries face major challenges in implementing CTF standards, such as a lack of legislative frameworks, predominantly cash-based economies and capacity and resource constraints. The absence of the required legislative framework, the lack of effective criminalisation of money laundering and terrorist financing, and the capacity constraint of financial sector supervision are all factors which render financial sectors in a number of developing countries vulnerable. These challenges are discussed in more detail below.

Lack of CTF and AML legislation

Of particular concern are countries which have yet to make the financing of terrorism a criminal offence. The problem is especially acute in developing and low-income countries.

Lack of capacity and tools to implement CTF standards

Even if the required legislative framework is in place, financial institutions in developing and low-income countries frequently lack the awareness and the information technology tools needed to carry out basic controls, such as the screening of customer names against international lists of designated persons and entities. In most cases, customer records are retained in paper and interspersed among a bank's branches. To screen for a name, bank staff will have to check through the whole volume of customer records, to identify whether a designated person or entity has an account with the bank. This is an enormous task and its enormity often means that the name screening measure is not being carried out at all. This is a significant loophole and a serious threat to the international effort to tackle the financing of terrorism.

Competition from the informal financial sector

Another complication for developing countries in attempting to reduce their vulnerability to money laundering and terrorist financing is competition from outside the financial sector. If they are at all successful in protecting their financial sectors, they can expect some money laundering and terrorist financing business to be displaced into the non-financial sector or parallel economies, underground 'banks' and alternative remittance systems. For this reason, one of the FATF Special Recommendations on Terrorist Financing (Recommendation VI) deals with informal money or value transfer systems. It requires that each country,

> [...] take measures to ensure that persons or legal entities, including agents, that provide a service for the transmission of money or value, including transmission through an informal money or value transfer system or network, [are] licensed or registered and subject to all FATF Recommendations that apply to banks and non-bank financial institutions. Each country should ensure that persons or legal entities that carry out this service illegally are subject to administrative, civil or criminal sanctions.

For many developing countries, however, it is doubtful that the vast efforts that would be required in order to identify, register, regulate and monitor informal value transfer services are an immediate priority.

High proportion of cash transactions

Another issue for developing countries is the predominance of cash in their economies. Cash transactions are the norm, rather than the exception, in most of the developing world. These cash movements and transactions are neither documented nor traceable. It is often suggested that jurisdictions should introduce a requirement for individuals and businesses to report all cash transactions that exceed a certain threshold to the authorities. These transactions would then be subjected to the usual AML/CTF controls. One also hears that the use of cash should be reduced, as part of the 'best way forward' in strategies to combat money laundering and the financing of terrorism. Others still have suggested that states should outlaw cash payments for transactions above a certain threshold altogether. Such proposals hold some appeal in the abstract and could perhaps be encouraged in certain instances. Nonetheless, it is hard to imagine that they could form a realistic basis for action in most developing countries. Assistance is needed to help these developing countries find workable alternatives and, in the long-term, promote comprehensive financial sector reform, which will begin to address the issues.

Cross-border transportations of cash

A related issue is the cross-border transportation of cash by terrorists and other criminals. In countries without proper controls, it is relatively easy for criminals, money launderers and terrorist groups to move money and other valuable assets across borders without drawing the attention of authorities. Criminals and traffickers use cash couriers to move criminal proceeds and engage in illicit trafficking transactions. The FATF's Special Recommendation IX creates new obligations for countries to prevent terrorists and criminals from using cash couriers to finance their activities and launder their funds. A best practice paper issued by the FATF in 2005[7] proposes a number of methods that may help alleviate cash smuggling. A central element of the approach is compulsory declaration or disclosure systems, in which everyone crossing a border with currency, bearer negotiable instruments or an item of value above a certain threshold must declare or disclose the cash or equivalent to border officials. Countries must also develop effective measures to detect, stop or restrain and (where appropriate) confiscate the currency or value.

The efforts and resources required to implement such official declaration and interdiction systems are quite significant, especially for developing countries. It is crucial that assistance be extended to these countries to help them implement effective systems to monitor the movement of cash across borders.

---

7   FATF, *Detecting and Preventing the Cross-Border Transportation of Cash by Terrorists and Other Criminals: International Best Practices*, FATF/OECD, Paris, 2005, available at http://www.fatf-gafi.org/dataoecd/50/63/34424128.pdf.

VI. Efforts by the international community

At the international and national levels, it is important that countries adopt the international standards on CTF and that capacity building and technical assistance be given to countries struggling with the challenges of putting the basic components of a CTF strategy in place.

1. The FATF and its work with less compliant jurisdictions

To this end, the FATF is doing much work to establish a global network of countries which consistently apply recognised international standards on AML and CTF. Its members and the members of FATF-style regional bodies agreed to adopt the FATF's Recommendations and Special Recommendations and to assess each other for their levels of compliance. The FATF has also developed a process for identifying, examining and engaging with vulnerable jurisdictions, so that special outreach and attention can be extended to address key concerns. It is important that relevant institutions and organisations be brought into the process to help expedite the capacity building effort in developing countries.

2. The FATF's work with the private sector

It is also noteworthy that the FATF is stepping up its effort to work more closely with the private sector in devising preventive measures. It organised a forum in December 2007 to provide opportunities for representatives from the public and private sectors to exchange ideas and develop AML/CTF typologies. It has also issued guidance for a risk-based approach to AML/CTF, to assist with the delivery of outcomes. In addition, the FATF established a Private Sector Consultative Forum to provide a formal structure for the exchange of information.

3.   Ongoing needs for global cooperative efforts

To be effective, international organisations, national governments and private sector organisations must work together to deny terrorists and criminals the opportunity to raise and transmit funds. Special assistance must be given to developing countries, many of which are struggling to implement and enforce the AML/CTF legislation due to weak criminal laws, capacity constraints and competition from the informal sector.

VII. Conclusion

Terrorist attacks since 11 September 2001 have shown that terrorism is a real threat. It is important that relevant stakeholders remain willing to work closely together to detect and disrupt terrorist financing and terrorism activities.

Targeting the financing structures of terrorist networks has proven challenging for financial institutions. They are rarely able to recognise terrorist transactions as such. More often, they contribute by identifying suspicious transactions for further investigation by counter-terrorism agencies. In addition, their ability to access financial information on suspected terrorists has become one of the most powerful investigative tools for assisting authorities to uncover the operational infrastructure of terrorism.

Global efforts to dismantle terrorist financial infrastructures will succeed only if the public and private sectors work together. If the financial sector is to detect terrorist-related transactions, it needs to know and understand the interests and activities of terrorist groups. There should be appropriate and effective processes for sharing intelligence between law enforcement agencies and the financial sector. This will help in cases where terrorist finance is particularly difficult to discern and detect, such as when transfers involve small amounts or funding is received from legitimate sources.

Also, legislators and regulators must ensure that the full brunt of CTF compliance does not fall on the financial sector, especially on banks, alone. Terrorist funds are also moved by cash couriers, money value transfer service providers and non-profit organisations and through developing countries. A number of developing countries struggle to put in place the pre-conditions to an effective CTF strategy, such as appropriate laws, capacities and resources. International organisations and states must pool their capacities and resources to close the loopholes exploited by terrorist financiers and other financial criminals.

In all, countering the financing of terrorism is a multi-dimensional challenge. Collaboration between law enforcement, intelligence agencies and financial institutions is critical in identifying and tracking the flow of terrorist and extremist money. Each jurisdiction and sector of the economy and society has a role to play in sharing information on terrorist financing cases, typologies, detection techniques and best practices. They should collectively aim to contribute to a better understanding of terrorist financing and to disrupt and prevent terrorist financing and terrorism activities.

BOB UPTON*

The financing of terror: a private sector perspective

Nothing great is easy.
Captain Matthew Webb (1848–1883)[1]

I. Introduction

Combating international terrorism requires the development and deployment of a range of tools targeting those who promote, sponsor, facilitate and execute acts of terror. States, as well as public and private sector actors within states, must work together if law enforcement is to effectively deter and detect cross-border terrorist activity.

Recognising this, states agreed to a range of new measures to combat terrorism and terrorist financing following the terrorist attacks on New York and Washington (DC) on 11 September 2001 (9/11). Amongst other things, the United Nations Security Council (UNSC) passed resolutions imposing sanctions on terrorists and their assets and the Financial Action Task Force (FATF) made nine 'Special Recommendations' on terrorist financing and began reporting on financing typologies. At the national level, governments gave law enforce-

---

* The comments and opinions expressed in this chapter are entirely that of the author. They are based on his long experience within a large retailing banking environment and his role as the Deputy Group Money Laundering Reporting Officer. They also embrace his wider international experience as an AML consultant. This article therefore provides a personal perspective which may not necessary be representative of his former employer or all firms within the reporting sector.

1 British endurance swimmer and the first man to swim the English Channel.

ment agencies increased powers for investigating and responding to suspected acts of terrorism. They also required private sector firms, already reporting under anti-money laundering (AML) regulations, to put in place additional arrangements to identify and disclose any suspicions of terrorist financing. At its own initiative, the private sector also sought ways to help law enforcement identify potential terrorists or terrorist financiers, the Wolfsberg Group producing a statement on the 'Suppression of the Financing of Terror'.[2]

This chapter contributes to the debate on the role of the private sector in counter-terrorist financing (CTF). It provides a broad description of the obligations on the sector, as well as the ability of the sector to meet those obligations within the constraint of limited available intelligence. It focuses on financial institutions in the UK and recommends a greater level of cooperation between law enforcement and the reporting sector to enrich the overall intelligence pool. Since 2001, we have learnt more about the funding and financing of terror. However, there are limits to the ability of reporting institutions to utilise this body of knowledge and translate it into practical action. Amongst other things, the nature and level of meaningful cooperation between law enforcement and the private sector varies considerably between and within jurisdictions, especially in the sensitive area of intelligence sharing. Law enforcement and reporting agencies bring different expectations to their roles and misconceptions are often fostered by poor understanding of their respective capabilities in the fight against terrorist finance and the constraints they face.

1. International counter-terrorist financing measures after 9/11

International terrorists require funds for a range of activities. Organised and coordinated terrorist groups or structures need to finance the preparation and planning of attacks, generate propaganda, recruit and

---

2   The Wolfsberg Group is an association of eleven global banks, which aims to develop financial services industry standards and related products for 'know your customer', anti-money laundering and counter-terrorist financing policies.

train operatives as well as fund associated agencies or welfare programmes. After 9/11, it was recognised that stemming the flow of
funds to terrorist groups could impede their activities and that following the money trail may help identify those involved in the process of
planning and carrying out an attack. Nonetheless, there is debate about
how much money terrorists actually need given that attackers may
utilise technically unsophisticated weapons or explosives made from
everyday materials. Moreover, terrorists increasingly prefer to self-
finance as this helps them limit the paper trail and avoid detection
through the nature of their financial transactions or their association
with known terrorist groups.

International measures against terrorist financing and associated
money laundering consists of a multi-faceted approach. This approach
includes the work of the UNSC's 1267 Committee[3] as well as the
1373 Counter-Terrorism Committee established in 2001,[4] together
with measures articulated in FATF's 9 Special Recommendations. In
implementing UNSC Resolution 1373 and criminalising the financing
of terrorism and associated money laundering, states have introduced
national laws containing measures broadly impacting on financial
institutions:

– Measures freezing and confiscating terrorist the of individuals
and entities named in terrorist sanctions lists issued under UNSC
Resolutions and regional and national lists as incorporated into
local law (Special Recommendation III)
– Measures requiring the reporting of suspected terrorist financing
to the national Financial Intelligence Unit (FIU) (Special Recommendation IV)

3   Prior to 9/11, the UNSC had established a counter-terrorism tool in the form of
the 1267 Committee. The role of this Committee, which was established in 1999
under Resolution 1267, was to monitor sanctions against the Taliban and subsequently al-Qaida (as of 2000).
4   Following the 9/11 attacks, the UNSC established the Counter-Terrorism Committee under UNSC Resolution 1373. This resolution obliges member states to
take a number of measures to prevent terrorist activities and to criminalise various forms of terrorist action, as well as measures which assist and promote cooperation amongst countries, including adherence to international counter-terrorism instruments.

- Measures designed to improve the transparency of wire payment systems to better track payments and 'follow the money trail' (Special Recommendation VII)
- Measures requiring the use of 'enhanced due diligence' when dealing with transactions and clients in so-called 'vulnerable sectors', such as alternative remittance services and non-profit organisations (NPOs) (Special Recommendations VI and VIII)

The majority of the legal obligations on financial institutions are essentially reactive: they involve responding to sanctions lists, reporting suspicions of terrorist financing and reviewing the outputs of wire payment transactions. Other measures are preventative in nature (e.g., the application of enhanced due diligence when commencing a business relationship involving vulnerable sectors or monitoring transactions for indications of uncharacteristic behaviour). However, such monitoring may also assist in identifying any linkages with listed entities and individuals associated with terrorism and may therefore have a 'detective' element. The ability of the reporting sector to comply with CTF legislation also depends on the information held on record, the extent to which data can be analysed and the intelligence sources at an institution's disposal.

II. Meeting the reporting obligation: how financial institutions fulfil their obligation to detect and report on terrorist finance

To meet their CTF obligations, financial institutions must identify and report any reasonable grounds for knowing or suspecting terrorist financing. To effectively do this, they require intelligence on terrorist financing which is timely, current, relevant and actionable. This information needs to be sufficiently targeted so that the financial institution can isolate the targeted customer from those undertaking legitimate business transactions. A range of compliance tools and sources of information are at their disposal.

1. Intelligence sources

Intelligence about the names of suspected terrorist and terrorist financiers and about the processes of terrorist financing may be obtained from the following sources:

– Official lists – Official lists are lists that have the force of law in a particular jurisdiction. They may include the UNSC's al-Qaida and Taliban list, as it has been incorporated into local law, as well as national and legally binding regional lists. Official lists are often referred to as 'block lists' because institutions are required to block or freeze the customer's funds or resources once identified. In other jurisdictions, those same lists may be 'unofficial'
– Unofficial lists – Unofficial lists are lists that do not have the force of law in a particular jurisdiction. They are also known as 'watch lists' because they may contain more names than the local official lists and so institutions choose to monitor (or 'watch') them. An example is the Terrorist Sanctions List distributed by the US Office of Foreign Assets Control (OFAC). For institutions which fall outside the jurisdiction of the USA, the OFAC list is considered to be a watch list where it does not duplicate the UN list. Although they are not required to monitor it, they may choose to do so because it helps them identify more potential terrorist financing transactions
– Terrorist financing typology reports from the FATF and local agencies
– Intelligence from local FIUs and branches of law enforcement involved with counter-terrorism and public reports from these agencies, e.g., reports on the cost of terror, the 9/11 attacks or the 2005 bombings in London
– Press releases, media comment and articles
– National terrorist threat assessments or risk assessments
– 'War-stories' and the views of law enforcement officers

2. *Transaction monitoring and information technology systems*

Electronic information held by a firm can be analysed by running programmes designed to search for matches against names or other criteria. In addition, data-mining techniques can be employed to further analyse the information held and search for other connectivities. However, the extent to which financial institutions can exploit the information at their disposal varies with the nature of the business, the extent to which information is held in a searchable format, the information technology (IT) systems employed and the institutions' IT capabilities. At one extreme, firms may employ the latest computer search techniques and, at the other, they may manually search for name matches by comparing lists against a printout of customer information.

Financial institutions will have a range of information on record as part of their customer due diligence enquiries and their credit and fraud risk routines. The extent of the information held and the checks completed will depend upon whether the customer is a natural or legal person. It will range from information required to identify the customer and beneficial owners to information on the structure and ownership of a business and the source of wealth or funds employed. More extensive checks and further information will be obtained for those customers, sectors and situations requiring enhanced due diligence. In addition, institutions will hold transactional data on the credits, debits and payment activities across an account relationship or in connection with a service. These compliance and other tools are additional to the human intelligence provided by aware and alert staff.

Most financial institutions use transaction monitoring tools to monitor account or relationship activity. These vary in sophistication: some may use the very latest in artificial intelligence and neural net technology to identify uncharacteristic account behavior, others may simply report based on volume or value parameters. All transaction monitoring tools encounter problems in attempting to identify patterns of behaviour linked to the funding or financing of terror due to the absence of effective identifiers.

In any case, once provided with meaningful intelligence in the form of names, firms may be able to enrich the intelligence value of any matches by searching for, and reporting on, potential links to other information. This may include information about:

- The use of the same mobile telephone number by multiple customers
- Matches with passport and identification data belonging to missing/stolen passports or deceased persons
- Any previous production orders on the customer from other agencies or arms of law enforcement, their nature and origin
- The use of the same memorable data[5] by others, unless this is extremely common data (e.g., the name of a football club)
- The previous addresses of the customer
- Disbursements and payments with common linkages (e.g., the use of vulnerable sectors or suspect payment vehicles to move funds)
- Suspect relationships apparent from transactional, business or other associations (e.g., beneficial ownership information and other relationships)
- The nature and extent of previous Suspicious Activity Reports (SARs) submitted by the firm on the same customer

These potential linkages need to be viewed in context and it may only be within the capacity of larger firms to identify them in the first place. Nonetheless, where relevant and suspicious, these linkages should be included in the report submitted to the FIU as this helps ensure that the SAR contains the full range of information in relation to the customer and is as rich with intelligence as possible.

---

5   Memorable data is information used to confirm the identity of a customer who is not face-to-face (physically present) with an employee, such as it occurs in internet banking, telephone banking, credit card business etc.

III. Challenges to the implementation of counter-terrorist financing measures by the private sector

At first glance, these intelligence sources and technology systems give reporting institutions a reasonable chance of detecting terrorist money. However, a number of practical challenges impede the reporting sector's ability to provide intelligence to law enforcement. The main issues are described below.

1. *Applicability of AML techniques*

Firms' obligations with respect to CTF are usually contained in AML legislation, the additional obligations being incorporated with the words 'and terrorist financing'. However, applying techniques designed to detect money laundering is likely to be counterproductive, even if the terrorist funds are raised through crime.

First, there are essential differences between money laundering and terrorist financing. Terrorists raise funds by legal and criminal means and they move their funds using cash couriers, money services businesses (MSBs), NPOs, charities and informal remittance systems as well as banks. It is often the sheer diversity of the methods employed to acquire, transfer and deploy funds intended for terrorism, which makes detecting terrorist financing so difficult.

Second, terrorists and organised criminals have different reasons for acquiring and moving funds. In the case of serious organised crime, the motive is personal gain or wealth. Terrorists, on the other hand, employ the funds to support their cause. The fact that terrorists may be involved in serious organised crime does not help financial institutions to distinguish between 'normal' criminal activity and terrorist financing.

Third, it is particularly difficult to apply risk-based principles to CTF. The adoption of a 'risk-based approach' is a prominent feature of the Third European Union (EU) Money Laundering Directive and FATF standards. However, firms struggle with this requirement in an area such as terrorist financing where the risks to the domestic and global community are too great to countenance. As a result, many firms decline to adopt such an approach or only seek to employ it when reviewing the output of account screening against official and unofficial lists.

2. Inadequate information in terrorist lists

Terrorist sanction lists are particularly important tools in CTF. They have a dual function. On the one hand, terrorist lists name people and entities to whom sanctions apply. A confirmed match with an official list may lead an institution to freeze a customer's assets or funds. On the other, lists are a source of intelligence on suspected terrorists, meaning that a match may lead the institution to officially report suspicions of terrorist financing to the FIU. Following an internal investigation of any name matches, the financial institution may also undertake a wider assessment of the account relationship with the customer.

Initially, the lists produced by the UNSC in relation to al-Qaida, Usama Bin Laden and the Taliban, failed to contain adequate identifiers of associated individuals and entities. Some of the names were incomplete, others were nicknames. This made it extremely difficult to identify the target or isolate him/her from other people with similar or identical names. The position has improved over time, with adequate identifying information being required as part of the listing process. However, the original problem highlights challenges in applying and using sanctions lists as a source of intelligence, problems which arise most frequently in conjunction with name match technologies, payment screening and the unofficial lists.

3. Name match criteria

Arabic names present an ongoing challenge for financial institutions and their compliance systems. Some Arabic cultures follow different naming protocols and some Arabic names, when transliterated into

European languages, may be spelt in different ways. A common example is the name Mohammed.

One scenario is that, in following the payment trail of a listed individual or entity, a competent authority discovers that a reporting institution did not identify a customer through its internal processes. A rapid investigation by the firm concerned highlights differences in the spelling of the customer's name, which its systems did not identify. It may also highlight differences in the search parameters being employed by different firms undertaking the same task. An external observer may well question why a person can be identified by one firm but not another. The expectations of competent authorities on name match criteria have yet to be articulated and readers will look in vain for a consistent approach or guidance from institutions such as the UN, EU and OFAC.

For firms, this increases the risk that they are inadvertently holding an account or other assets of a sanctioned person. To reduce this risk, many financial institutions run programmes which check their customer account base and new relationships for direct name matches to lists, partial or near matches, alternative spellings, reversed (first and last) names and other permutations. These systems occasionally employ 'fuzzy logic' to widen the search parameters. The very comprehensiveness of this process can be a hurdle, however. It tends to generate thousands of false-positive matches, each of which has to be reviewed and investigated in order to assess whether it relates to the intended target. To assist in the elimination process, some firms employ so-called 'white lists' to discount names already investigated during earlier searches.

4.   Payment screening

In addition to account screening, some of the larger retail banks apply 'real time' payment screening. This involves the interception and screening of payments in transit and the investigation of any name matches before the payment is made. This approach meets the requirement of ensuring that funds are not made available to the listed party and caps a firm's exposure. However, relatively few institutions currently have the capability, IT infrastructure, expertise or resources to undertake this task. Where a full or partial match is identified, it needs to be promptly investigated and any enquiries resolved in order to meet the clearing cycle timescales, an increasing challenge given the increasing speed of banking transactions.

There are also doubts about the utility of payment screening methods when compared to the time, effort and resources needed to establish and review their outputs. One large European institution reviewed more than 85,000 alerts from payment screenings during 2006; of these only 15 transactions were confirmed as involving someone on a list. The conversion rate of 0.02% may indicate that terrorists are employing other, less transparent, methods of moving funds, such as cash couriers.

5. Multiplicity and consistency of lists

Irrespective of the legal status of each list, a consistent approach to the use of unofficial lists as a source of intelligence has yet to be considered. For example, the OFAC's 'specially designated nationals' (SDN) list is not directly binding outside the US but is used in many other countries as an intelligence source to screen accounts and payments. Guidance on the use of such lists by international and regional bodies will help to ensure a common approach and set consistent expectations of financial institutions. It will also provide a further source of intelligence, although not all jurisdictions may wish to participate or endorse the use of such lists.

6. Typology reports and background intelligence sources

Terrorist financing typologies form part of an intelligence cycle. Historic methods, techniques, mechanisms and instruments are analysed in order to assist in the identification of potential indictors and vulnerable sectors. Case studies provide a method of illustrating the acquisition, movement and deployment of funds informed by research or the financial analysis of an attack or thwarted attack. Where consistent trends or patterns are identified, they may be capable of predicting future trends from which further indicators may be developed.

Typology reports and case studies have evolved over the years into an important body of knowledge on terrorist financing. The latest FATF Report on Terrorist Financing published in February 2008, contains almost 40 case studies from member states. It is an informative document using the most recent intelligence. Yet few, if any, of the case studies contain actionable indicators that firms could use to align their transaction monitoring systems or discriminate between terrorists or terrorist financiers and those undertaking legitimate business activity. Other typologies have similar weaknesses, even if they help to identify the exploitation of new sectors and techniques or confirm the continued use of existing ones. Therefore, typologies inform the development and focus of enhanced due diligence measures and supervision strategies, though they do not help with specific clients or transactions.

7. *Intelligence provided by local FIUs or law enforcement*

The extent to which FIUs and law enforcement agencies may be able to share intelligence with reporting institutions is constrained by a number of legal and administrative factors, including the absence of formal intelligence sharing gateways, legal and security constraints and privacy issues. As a result, the extent of useful actionable intelligence is limited and often confined to case studies or a sensitised analysis of a recent investigation into terrorist financing.

IV. The need for greater cooperation between law enforcement and the private sector

The introduction of domestic legislation and international measures on counter-terrorist financing since 9/11, has given law enforcement and the private sector a range of tools to deter, investigate and disclose suspicions of terrorist financing. They have separate but complimentary roles to play and are most successful when they are mutually supportive and coordinated. Sadly, leveraging the combined knowledge, expertise and capabilities of law enforcement and the private sector requires a greater degree of understanding, commitment and organisation than is currently apparent in most jurisdictions. Government agencies in some jurisdictions adopt a 'command and control' style approach to the private sector. This approach is characterised by the expectation that firms will simply respond to requests and instructions from law enforcement and the guidance from FIUs and banking supervisors.

In other jurisdictions, law enforcement seems keen to engage in mutually supportive dialogue with the private sector and other concerned parties. Its goal is to build capacity and share current experience, intelligence and information about techniques being used to finance terror. However, building an effective partnership between law enforcement and the private sector remains a challenge, due to legal and administrative constraints, interdepartmental issues and concerns about the extent to which the private sector can and should be trusted with sensitive material.

To improve the quality of the relationship and the flow of information between the public and private sectors, some FIUs have established contact groups with trade bodies or representatives from reporting agencies. The aim of these groups is to highlight recent trends or terrorist typologies, including through the discussion of local case studies. For law enforcement, this approach consolidates relationships and encourages engagement by key reporters. For private sector agencies, it is an opportunity for constructive dialogue on terrorist financing and the sharing of actionable intelligence.

Such an approach is already well established in the UK. The FIU, in conjunction with anti-terrorism branches of law enforcement, may release declassified results of investigations into the financing of a particular attack or thwarted attack. This provides reporters with an early indication of the techniques adopted and assists in the identification of actionable indictors. In addition, the UK FIU chairs a 'Vetted Group' of law enforcement professionals and representatives from the private sector who have been security cleared. The Group receives sensitive material and discusses the most effective method of utilising and distributing the non-classified elements in the form of an alert product. Both sides work as a team, adding their experience and knowledge to support their common objectives. The private sector representatives may not discuss or utilise any of the intelligence obtained during these meetings. Although the Vetted Group currently considers issues involving serious organised crime, its remit can be extended to embrace terrorist financing.

In some countries, such as the Russian Federation, the financial sanctions process has been extended to embrace a national list. The list includes persons who have been convicted of, are on trial for or are being investigated in connection with, terrorist offences. The UK has also employed the sanctions process by exception, to list and rapidly identify those involved in an impending terrorist attack. As the names of those listed are often supported by adequate identifiers, they provide one of the most effective methods of rapidly identifying the assets and account relationships of customers, as well as blocking access to funds.

V. Conclusions

From this, it is apparent that the financing of a deadly and determined terrorist attack cannot be identified by financial transactions or account behaviour alone. It requires a 'nugget' of meaningful intelligence in order to focus the efforts of financial intuitions and help identify the customer. Based on the experience of a large British bank, most of suspicious activity reports related to terrorism post 9/11 are reactive, responding to official and unofficial lists as well as external intelligence. Few, if any, are based on typology reports or case studies. When analysing its account relationships with some of those involved in the bombing of the London transport system, the bank concerned commented that,

> [T]hey had the outward appearance of normality in their financial dealings and lifestyle. They had cheque books, loans, credit cards, life insurance policies and were indistinguishable in their spending habits from others.

Although this is a UK perspective, it is likely to be representative of the experience of many others and to amply illustrate the reality of attempting to identify terrorist financing, particularly before an attack occurs.

Nonetheless, identifying and disrupting the flow of funds to those financing terror, remains an essential part of the global approach to combating international terrorism. Financial institutions remain committed to playing their part in the process, even if their overall contribution is inhibited by the factors described above. It would be naïve to conclude that financial products and services are not currently being used or abused for this purpose. However, the extensive use of cash couriers and other alternative remittance systems may indicate that the private sector has already created a hostile environment for those financing terror.

The way forward includes a more informed and enlightened approach to cooperation between the public and the private sectors. The benefits of such cooperation have yet to be fully recognised. The overall impression is that law enforcement and the private sector have not yet fully coordinated their strengths or optimised their contributions to the cause, despite the fact that they both have greatly increased their awareness of international terrorism and the methods employed to finance acts of terror. Unless addressed, this gap may render the execution of the global counter-terrorist financing strategy suboptimal.

Yehuda Shaffer*

Detecting terrorist financing through financial intelligence: the role of FIUs

I. Introduction

After the attacks of 11 September 2001 (9/11) the international community reached a consensus on the need to enhance global cooperation on counter-terrorist financing (CTF).[1] A common definition of 'terrorist financing' had already been agreed upon in Article 2 of the International Convention for the Suppression of the Financing of Terrorism.[2] The existence of this definition made it possible to avoid the usual debates about the relevance of 'legitimate' motives and the difference between 'terrorists' and 'freedom fighters'. Quite simply, it stigmatises any terrorist activity against civilians, without exceptions.

Consequently, the Financial Action Task Force (FATF) declared its existing 40 Recommendations on anti-money laundering (AML) to be effective tools against terrorist financing and made nine further Special Recommendations (Special Recommendations).[3] Following the FATF's lead, in 2003, the Egmont Group of Financial Intelligence

---

*   Yehuda Shaffer is the founder and director of Israel's Financial Intelligence Unit, the Israel Money Laundering and Terror Financing Prohibition Authority (IMPA), located in the Ministry of Justice. A lawyer with a Masters in Public Administration (MPA) from the Kennedy School of Government at Harvard University, he was previously a senior official in the High Court of Justice Department of the Israeli government.

1   UN Security Council Resolution 1373.

2   United Nations, International Convention for the Suppression of the Financing of Terrorism, UN 9 December 1999, available at http://www.un.org/law/cod/finterr.htm.

3   FATF, *Special Recommendations on Terrorist Financing*, FATF/OECD 24 October 2004, available at http://www.fatf-gafi.org.

Units (FIUs) amended its Statement of Purpose to affirm the commitment of its members to assist in the fight against the financing of terrorism.[4] Governments around the world changed their laws on the reporting obligations of private sector organisations. As a result, the AML regime and the information reported by the financial sector to FIUs on money laundering are now being used to combat the financing of terror as well.

In this chapter, I shall attempt to highlight some of the lessons learned with regard to the detection of terrorist financing through financial intelligence. I look at the obligations on financial institutions to detect and report suspicious financial activity, the role of FIUs in processing this information and the challenges they face in utilising this financial intelligence in the fight against terrorism. As we shall see, a detailed legal framework is necessary but not sufficient: a technological effort is also needed as is coordination and cooperation between governments and government agencies at the national and international levels.

II. The purpose of imposing the CTF rules on financial institutions

In implementing rules against terrorist financing, FIUs and government agencies primarily aim to uncover the financial trail used by terrorist organisations in raising and moving funds. This overall goal includes several separate goals:

–   To prevent terrorist attacks by freezing assets for planned terrorist operations
–   To accumulate operational intelligence about the identity of terrorist organisations and their supporters through the analysis of financial intelligence

---

4   The Egmont Group of Financial Intelligence Units, *Statement of Purpose*, Guernsey 23 June 2004, available at http://www.egmontgroup.org.

– To uncover and remove the sources of terrorist financing

In sum, the goal is to use information from the private sector to alienate terrorist groups from the global economy, to deter those who might be inclined to support terrorist organisations and – ultimately – to push terrorist groups to take higher risks in raising and moving money.

III. CTF-related reporting obligations of financial institutions

Under Special Recommendation IV,[5] financial institutions, and other businesses or entities with AML obligations, must report suspicious transactions to the FIU:

> If financial institutions, or other businesses or entities subject to anti-money laundering obligations, suspect or have reasonable grounds to suspect that funds are linked or related to, or are to be used for terrorism, terrorist acts, or by terrorist organisations, they should be required to report promptly their suspicions to the competent authorities.

Special Recommendation IV therefore requires states to impose two additional duties on entities already subject to AML reporting obligations. First, reporting entities must obtain new information as part of their due diligence procedures and, second, they must report transactions to the FIU at a lower level of suspicion: not only when the financial information is suspicious, but also when there is a reasonable suspicion of a relationship to terrorism. This lower threshold requires reporting entities to focus their attention and resources on monitoring activities considered 'high risk' from a CTF perspective.

---

5   FATF, n 3.

IV. The application of AML strategies to CTF

The application of AML strategies to CTF was understandable given the similarities between criminal and terrorist groups. Terrorist organisations are also 'ongoing criminal enterprises' that use crime to raise funds and achieve their criminal objectives. They use methods of money laundering pioneered by organised criminal groups to disguise the source and purpose of their funds and distance themselves from their financiers. Furthermore, both organised crime and terrorist groups may be active internationally and may use international financial tools. In many ways, a successful terrorist group will be like any other criminal organisation in that it will have been able to build and maintain an effective financial infrastructure. Hence, it is only logical that the regulations and institutions put in place to combat organised crime and money laundering were utilised to fight terrorism and the financing of terrorism.

However, the decision to use anti-organised crime and money laundering strategies was also based on the assumption that reports from financial institutions and other entities would contain useful financial intelligence on terrorism, i.e., that intelligence from the private sector would help FIUs and other competent authorities to detect terrorist funding. This is not self evident; there are important differences between organised criminal and terrorist groups. In contrast to traditional organised criminal groups, the objectives of terrorist organisations are usually not acquisitive. That is, the groups are not so much interested in making a profit as in achieving political or ideological goals. Their funding, moreover, is in many cases 'clean' as it often comes in the form of legitimate donations and contributions; at the very least, the purpose of the funds may be unclear. Above all, terrorist groups, in contrast to 'normal' criminals, seek to operate outside the formal financial and banking systems.

V. Familiarity with terrorist financing typologies

The usefulness of financial intelligence in combating terrorist financing depends, first and foremost, on the quality of the information reported by reporting institutions to the FIUs. To detect suspicious transactions and report useful information, financial institutions must be familiar with terrorist financing typologies,[6] especially with those on alternative remittances, non-profit organisations (NPOs) and wire transfers.[7] They must also collect relevant crucial information, e.g., meaningful originator information on wire transfers (including cover payments), clients suspected of operating unregistered money services businesses (MSBs) and beneficiaries of NPOs. In addition, financial institutions must check beneficiary information against national and international lists of suspected terrorists, e.g., the United Nations (UN) list under UN Security Council (UNSC) Resolution 1267,[8] official regional and country lists established pursuant to UNSC Resolution 1373, the Office of Foreign Assets Control (OFAC, US Treasury) list,[9] the European Community (EC) list[10] and other lists of relevant government agencies in relevant jurisdictions.

---

6   See, for example, FATF, *Terrorist Financing* (FATF/OECD, 2008) available at http://www.fatf-gafi.org/dataoecd/28/43/40285899.pdf.
7   See the FATF Special Recommendations VI to VIII.
8   List of UN Nations Security Council Committee established pursuant to resolution 1267 (1999) concerning Al-Qaida and the Taliban and Associated Individuals and Entities, available at http://www.un.org/sc/committees/1267/consolist.shtml.
9   List of the Office of Foreign Assets Control (OFAC, US Treasury), available at http://www.treas.gov/offices/enforcement/ofac/.
10 Council of the European Union, *Regulation (EC) No. 2580/2001 on specific restrictive measures directed against certain persons and entities with a view to combating terrorism*, 27 December 2001, available at http://eur-lex.europa.eu/smartapi/cgi/sga_doc?smartapi!celexapi!prod!CELEXnumdoc&lg=EN&numdoc=32001R2580&model=guichett.

1. Alternative remittance systems

At high risk of abuse by terrorists are funds transfers through non-bank financial institutions, alternative remittance services and informal money or value transfer systems, such as money remitters and *bureaux de change*. These businesses often provide wire transfer functions directly with counterpart businesses or through conventional financial institutions. They are used by terrorist groups to avoid the monitoring systems of mainstream financial institutions or investigative authorities. This makes it particularly important that reporting institutions involved with alternative remittance services familiarise themselves with 'red flags' of potential terrorist financing, as discussed below.

2. Dealings with charities

Another activity which calls for enhanced due diligence is the transfer of funds by charities into areas of conflict. NPOs have been identified as vulnerable to possible abuse by terror financiers in that their funds can be diverted to terrorist organisations or activities.

Charities and their financial institutions should be in a position to know and to verify that funds have been actually spent as advertised and planned. The FATF therefore considers it best practice for NPOs that handle funds to maintain registered bank accounts, to keep their funds in those accounts and to utilise formal or registered financial channels for transferring funds, especially overseas. The Middle East and North-Africa (MENA) FATF has additionally issued best practice guidelines, which are a good example of how banks can enhance measures to manage CTF risks when dealing with charities (especially when operating in areas of conflict). The MENA FATF[11] recommends the implementation of several new measures, including the:

---

11   Middle East and North Africa Financial Action Task Force, *Best practices issued by the Middle East and North Africa Financial Action Task Force Concerning the Charities*, September 2005, available at: http://www.menafatf.org/images/UploadFiles/CharitiesEng.pdf.

–   Approval of all international transfers from charitable accounts by supervisory bodies
–   Identification of donors and beneficiaries of charities when deposits and withdrawals are made into and from charitable accounts
–   Complete abandonment of disbursements of aid in cash
–   Restriction of cheque payments to those which are made exclusively to the order of the first beneficiaries and deposited in their bank account through correspondent accounts

The importance of monitoring charity transactions relates to a common misunderstanding about the potential effectiveness of CTF efforts, namely, that financial institutions cannot track down the relatively small amounts of money needed by individual terrorists to execute attacks. Terror organisations actually need large sums of money to maintain their organisational infrastructure and carry out specific operations. For instance, the Middle East terror group, Hamas, maintains a network of 'social welfare' (*da'awa*) agencies which it uses as a basis for its terrorist activity. Hamas utilises this network to facilitate attacks and to build grassroots support among the Palestinian population. Frequently, Hamas *da'awa* operatives ferry the suicide bombers and the explosives to the point of departure for missions. Numerous Hamas members with terrorist records are officials of Hamas charity committees.[12] To conclude this point, efforts should focus not (only) on the financial trail of the individual terrorist but (also) on the financial infrastructure of terror groups and their criminal enterprise.

3.   Wire transfers

Finally, to meet their CTF obligations, reporting institutions must apply enhanced due diligence to wire transfers. Wire transfers are a rapid and secure method for transferring value from one location to another and do not involve the physical movement of currency. It is

---

12   Levitt Matthew, *Charitable Organisations and Terrorist Financing: A War on Terror Status-Check* (Washington Institute for Near East Policy, 19 March 2004).

particularly difficult for investigators to trace individual transactions given the increased rapidity and volume of wire transfers and the lack of international standards on recording, maintaining and transmitting key information. The continued development of worldwide networks, such as the network of the Society for Worldwide Interbank Financial Telecommunications (SWIFT),[13] has enhanced the reliability and efficiency of interbank payment systems. When combined with telephone and internet banking services, this has increased the potential for abuse by terrorist financiers and money launderers.

It is therefore not surprising that wire transfers were a key means by which the 9/11 hijackers obtained the means to plan and carry out their attacks.[14] Terror groups use false identities, 'straw men' or front companies to disguise their connection to wire transfers. They also structure the flow of funds through several different financial institutions to make the transfer appear as if it comes from different and seemingly unrelated sources. Cover payments conducted by correspondent banks and lacking essential details are another particular concern.[15]

---

13   A network facilitating the exchange of payments and other financial transactions world-wide.

14   See John Roth, Douglas Greenburg and Serena Wille, *Monograph on Terrorist Financing: Staff Report to the Commission* (US National Commission on the 9/11 Terrorist Attacks Upon the United States, Washington 2004) 134, available at http://govinfo.library.unt.edu/911/staff_statements/911_TerrFin_Monograph.pdf.

15   See further, Basel Committee on Banking Supervision, *Consultative Document: Due diligence and transparency regarding cover payment messages related to crossborder wire transfers*, (Bank of International Settlements, Basel 2008), available at http://www.bis.org/publ/bcbs139.pdf?noframes=1.

VI. The role of FIUs in CTF

1. FIUs and their core functions

If a reporting institution suspects that a transaction is linked to terrorism, it makes a suspicious transaction report (STR) to the local FIU. The Statement of Purpose of the Egmont Group defines an FIU as:

> A central, national agency responsible for receiving, (and as permitted, requesting), analysing and disseminating to the competent authorities, disclosures of financial information (i) concerning suspected proceeds of crime and potential financing of terrorism or (ii) required by national legislation or regulation, in order to combat money laundering and terrorism financing.[16]

Hence, an FIU may be independent or part of a law enforcement agency. Its main roles are to process and analyse financial data and intelligence, on the one hand, and to detect transactions related to terrorism, on the other. In addition, FIUs have traditionally played a significant role in researching terrorist financing typologies, educating the financial sector about possible 'red flags' for suspicious transactions and fostering international cooperation on CTF and AML.

2. FIUs and CTF

In 2004, the Egmont Group clarified that CTF belongs to the core functions of an FIU.[17] Consequently, the Group will only consider an agency an FIU if, at a minimum,

- a system of mandatory reporting of suspicious transactions related to [terrorist financing] [is] established in the jurisdiction
- the FIU [is] the central reception point of such disclosures

---

16 Egmont Group of Financial Intelligence Units, n 4.
17 See the *Egmont Group Heads of FIU Decision in Guernsey 2004* as incorporated into the *Egmont Group Statement of Purpose*, to reflect the countering of terrorism financing (CTF) as a core function of the FIU and its interpretative note, available at http://www.egmontgroup.org/files/library_egmont_docs/fiu_def_tf_compl_int_note.pdf.

- the [terrorist financing] reporting obligation to the FIU [is] formally imbedded in the law, irrespective of all de facto or goodwill motivated situations […]
- the FIU [has] full authority and ability to exchange [terrorist financing] related information with its counterparts

The Egmont Group went on to emphasise that an FIU's CTF obligations are not simply an extension of its AML obligations because the phenomena themselves are different:

> Terrorism financing encompasses the use of legitimate, or clean funds. Terrorism financing as [a] predicate offence to money laundering is insufficient under Egmont criteria where it covers only proceeds of crime. A reporting obligation based solely upon lists of designated or suspected terrorists is also insufficient. Moreover, both national and international terrorism should be covered.[18]

3.   The FIU and information technology tools

Today a typical investigation into terrorist financing will include financial intelligence, some of which was reported from the financial sector to the local FIU. For example, a financial institution may report that standing orders of monthly charity donations have been shifted to a newly established shell company or NPO shortly after administrative measures were taken against another NPO to which the donations were previously paid. The FIU may then performs a link analysis to determine whether there are mutual shareholders and controllers of companies and other entities linked to terror organisations.

As this example shows, investigating terrorist financing depends very much on the ability of FIUs to process and analyse large quantities of financial information, perform link analysis with information from other government agencies and transform all this information into knowledge useful in a criminal investigation. This can be achieved only by combining the professional expertise of the financial analyst with sophisticated information technology (IT) tools. For this

---

18   Egmont Group of Financial Intelligence Units, *FIU Definition 'Countering of Terrorism Financing Complementary' Interpretative Note*, available at http://www.egmontgroup.org/files/library_egmont_docs/fiu_def_tf_compl_int_note.pdf.

reason, FIUs have developed extensive IT tools to enable the efficient processing and analysis of suspicious transactions. These are then sold to financial institutions to assist them in detecting reportable suspicious activity. They are often also useful for the operation of the FIU itself.

One type of IT tool is the alert generator. Alerts are generated through analysis of the information on the client, on certain predefined events and on profile analysis. Customer analysis involves the study of customers, their behaviour patterns, their connections to other customers and entities and their potential risk factors based on information gained through 'know your customer' (KYC) procedures. Analysis of predefined events means that an alert is produced when a set of events is identified or certain rules are met. A common example of such an event is the structuring of cash or cash equivalents or circulation of funds between several accounts, including by wire transfer in and out of the jurisdiction. In profile analysis, the customer's recorded behaviour is compared to other dynamic predefined profiles maintained by the system. The system detects deviations from the customer's historical behaviour, deviations from peer group behaviour and/or similarities to known suspicious behaviour patterns. A further tool, enterprise business intelligence, analyses intelligence information, performs link analysis and data mining and provides basic information retrieval capabilities. All these features are combined and transformed into sophisticated visualisation tools that allow analysts to:

– Access data
– Search and extract information from a wide variety of data sources simultaneously
– Visualise large quantities of financial transactions
– Identify and display relationships between individuals and entities involved in terrorism
– Discover connections between bank accounts and people, organisations and other accounts
– Discover indirect relationships that show addresses, phone numbers, accounts or identification numbers used by numerous individuals

–   Uncover different types of transactions used by terrorist groups
     using chronological and geographic data

Analysis performed at the FIU must include careful examination of
the financial documentation. For example, the wording used by the
donors to describe a charitable purpose in a SWIFT payment order
may link the transaction to a terrorist group.

4.   'Red flags' of terrorist financing

However, an FIU's IT systems are only as good as the information
they analyse. It is therefore essential that reporting institutions are
alert to the 'red flags' of CTF and AML, i.e., facts about the customer,
the transaction or the external circumstances of the transaction, that
have been found to correlate with terrorist financing transactions.
These red flags are relevant not only to banks but also to other financial intermediaries and institutions, such as MSBs.

The nature or activity of the customer

Examples of red flags related to the nature or activity of the customer
include:

–   The use of false or multiple identifications
–   The use of the same or similar identifications by two or more
     customers
–   Apparent collaboration between customers
–   The location of customer in a different place to the financial insti-
     tution
–   The payment of repetitive cheques to the same person from the
     same people or repetitive cheques from other people into the
     same or different accounts
–   The involvement of companies with multiple addresses or bank
     accounts, and/or with insufficient address information (e.g., a post
     office box rather than a street address)
–   An unusual volume of activity

–   The use of money orders and cheques, which are discounted by a money changer, deposited by them as a lump sum into a bank account as part of the money changing business and withdrawn with a bank cheque and deposited in the account of a different charity Links between transactions and suspicious entities on watch lists or with organisations known to be involved in terrorism or in raising money for charities suspected of supporting terrorism

–   Links with entities which appear on a 'national' terrorist list of another country

The nature of the transaction

Other red flags relate to the nature of the transaction. These include:

–   Structuring or 'smurfing', i.e., apportioning transactions into smaller transactions which do not meet the reporting threshold

–   Large or even sum transactions

–   Atypical currency transactions

–   Frequent transactions

–   Transactions to or from a foreign country with missing details

–   Transactions to or from Non-Cooperative Countries and Territories (NCCTs) or other non-regulated territories

–   The use of multiple bearer instruments

–   The use of intermediaries, such as public figures or attorneys, to make deposits or withdraw cash

–   The use of charities for international transactions to areas of conflict, especially when the transaction is to an individual

–   Unusually high cash deposits

–   Withdrawals of assets shortly after they are credited to the account

The external circumstances of the transaction

Finally, the circumstances of the transaction may raise 'red flags' for institutions. These could include:

–   Notations or initials on the back of cheques or money orders

–   Improper endorsements

–   Missing endorsements

- Repetitive endorsements
- Small dollar value transaction which require the payment of a large fee
- Cheques dated months before or after the date of deposit
- Cheques suspected of being forged or stolen
- Client requests to exchange cash or cheques with a cheque from a financial institution or with other cheques presented previously for discount
- The use of unique cheques (e.g., from government agencies or insurance companies)
- High levels of activity on dormant accounts
- Unusually fast money movements or unusually high volumes of money moving through accounts
- Multiple payments from different persons to one account
- Repeated credits just under the reporting limit

VII. Challenges and lessons learned

FIUs have a distinct and crucial role in CTF. However, in executing their core functions of 'receiving, [...] analysing and disseminating [...] disclosures of financial information concerning [...] potential financing of terrorism'[19] they face several challenges. These are considered in this final section, drawing on the Giessbach Declaration of the International Seminar on Combating the Financing of Terrorism of October 2007 (Giessbach I), proposing 'lessons learned' in enhancing the effectiveness of financial intelligence in combating terrorist financing.[20]

19 Egmont Group of Financial Intelligence Units, n 16.
20 See International Seminar on Combating the Financing of Terrorism (CFT), *Giessbach Declaration*, Giessbach, Switzerland, 15–17 October 2007. Available at: http://www.amlcft-seminar.org/Giessbach%20Declaration.pdf.

1. Quality information

Information quality determines the effectiveness of the FIU. As noted above, the FIU does not gather intelligence itself but receives information in the form of STRs from the private sector, which it analyses and sends to competent national authorities or FIUs abroad. Therefore, it is imperative that FIUs work with other stakeholders to improve the quality of information they receive and distribute. According to the participants at Giessbach I:

- FIUs should improve the feedback they provide to financial institutions regarding typologies, red flags and indicators in dealing with MSBs, NPOs and wire transfers. Where appropriate, they should be able to provide *ad hoc* feedback to financial institutions
- FIUs should seek, and state secret service agencies should give, more guidance on terrorist *modus operandi*
- Together with other stakeholders, FIUs should build trust between government agencies and financial institutions and between the FIUs and the secret services, developing mechanisms, such as a system of contact points in different key institutions
- FIUs should train their personnel to analyse financial intelligence for the hallmarks of terrorist financing

2. Quality information exchange

Next to information quality, information exchange is crucial. Experience from several jurisdictions shows that there is often a lack of guidance for FIUs on how to deal with other national administrative agencies involved in CTF (e.g., prosecutors, FIUs, police, tax agencies, secret service, supervisors etc.). As a result, coordination and consistency are often lacking. To address these difficulties the participants at Giessbach I called on national governments to:

- Allow FIUs, tax authorities, secret services and regulatory agencies to exchange sensitive information between themselves, particularly when they are undertaking intelligence-led regulatory inspections

−   Improve rules for international cooperation between FIUs on ex-
    pedited information exchange ('fast tracks'), classified informa-
    tion and information sharing with all FIUs
−   Encourage the (spontaneous) exchange of open source informa-
    tion between FIUs, e.g., by implementing central databases or
    standardising data regarding criminal records, national lists
−   Consider whether to create a platform, such as a permanent inter-
    agency committee, which would allow CTF stakeholders to ex-
    change operational information and intelligence with each other
−   Work together to develop legal safeguards for fundamental indi-
    vidual rights in CTF cases

3.   Clear and universal definitions of intelligence and evidence

Finally, even if quality information is gathered and exchanged, prosecutors may be unable to use it in criminal proceedings due to national
rules on the admissibility information gathered by intelligence agencies. The Giessbach Declaration therefore notes that national governments, FIUs and intergovernmental agencies should decide on 'clear
boundaries' between intelligence and evidence, as well as procedures
for declassifying information so that it can be used in criminal prosecutions.

VIII. Conclusion

The shocking events of 11 September 2001 fuelled the development of
an international regime to counter the financing of terrorism and the
expansion of the role of FIUs to include CTF. This was role was formally recognised at the international level by the Egmont Group in
2004. Since then, national FIUs have made significant advances in
developing technologies and procedures which can detect red flags of
potential terrorist finance. Though they also identified common chal-

lenges, they have been able to formulate practical strategies for enhancing their effectiveness, as the Declaration from Giessbach I shows. Moreover, there is anecdotal evidence that the global CTF campaign is raising the cost of finance for terrorism. Though measuring success is difficult in this area,[21] intelligence from several countries indicates that terrorist groups have been discouraged from using the formal financial system and are favouring increasingly risky transmission methods, such as cash couriers and alternative remittance systems. The higher risk is reflected in higher exchange rates and fees for terrorist transactions.

In conclusion, the eight years since 9/11 have shown just how difficult it can be to detect terrorist funds and bring terrorist financiers to justice. Reporting institutions, FIUs, secret services agencies and other national authorities face many challenges in utilising financial intelligence to combat the financing of terrorism. But if effectively managed, the financial 'War on Terror' can help reduce the threat of terrorist attacks not only by gathering valuable intelligence on terrorists but also by making it more difficult and costly for them and their supporters to move their funds.

---

21 For several CTF 'success stories' see, Matthew Levitt and Michael Jacobson, *The Money Trail: Finding, Following, and Freezing Terrorist Finances* (The Washington Institute for Near East Policy, 2008) available at http://www. washingtoninstitute.org/templateC04.php?CID=302.

Henriette Haas[*]

Systematic Observation as a tool in combating terrorism

I. Profiling and case analysis in counter-terrorism

Preventing and responding to the financing of terrorism often seems like the proverbial search for a needle in a haystack: how to distinguish terrorists from other banking customers and prevent terrorist money from being used to fund an attack? Time and again people put their hopes in psychological profiles of terrorists and the possibility of thus identifying leads and suspects. Yet, psychological research on known terrorists has established no distinct personality profile for the future terrorist (AIVD 2002). While some terrorists were criminals before they found a political excuse for their behaviour, others were misguided young people, searching for individual identity and meaning. Their vulnerability to manipulation and exploitation was related to their personal histories and cannot be generalised. At the wrong moment, they fell prey to indoctrination by a militant group (AIVD 2002, Manningham-Buller 2006). The same holds true for sympathisers and extremists who support terrorist activities ideologically, financially or logistically. Other terrorist cells, usually very small ones, are started by self-motivated violent extremists, who find information on *modus operandi* on the Internet. For those radicalised individuals, propaganda on thousands and thousands of extremist webpages creates a sense of belonging to a 'global Jihad movement', independent of personal background and social environment (Deutsches Bundesministerium des Inneren 2008: 204).

[*]   Senior Lecturer in Forensic Psychology, University of Zurich, Psychological Institute, Methodology Division, Switzerland (henriette.haas@access.uzh.ch).

Hence, 'offender profiling', as portrayed in film and television, is unhelpful in counter-terrorism. It is equally unhelpful in other areas of criminal justice. The idea that delinquents have a distinct personality, which accords with their specific type of crime, cannot withstand comparison with the scientific data (Haas & Killias 2003). There is still room for psychologists in criminal investigations. However, instead of speculating on the criminal mind, criminal psychologists conduct an extremely meticulous analysis of the available material in a case, taking even the smallest 'signs' of evidence into account. Together with the rest of the investigative team (detectives, supervisors, forensic scientists and pathologists), they then brainstorm, generating a range of hypotheses that can be checked for consistency with the evidence. Thus, so-called 'profiling' is not about personalities, it is about gathering the maximum amount of intelligence from the available data.

To improve our capacity for scientific observation, the author has been developing the method known as 'Systematic Observation' since 2003. The procedure takes universally accepted scientific principles from epistemology and cognitive science and develops them into a set of guidelines, which logically structure the process of observation. This system has proven successful in the investigation of terrorist acts and there is potential for its integration into compliance systems used to identify terrorist finance before it enters the financial system.

II. Deduction of the five rules from principles of epistemology and cognitive science

Which influences guide human perception? One of the earliest theories about perception in psychology is *Gestalt* theory, also called *Theory of Forms* (not to be confused with *Gestalt* therapy). Its premise is that a form to be recognised is always composed by a shape that is suspended on a ground (Koffka 1935: 184). Using this approach, we can consider a criminal case as a form. The shape of a criminal case consists of all human behaviours that led to it and to its concealment. The ground consists of all other incidents and behaviours, which happened coincidentally at the same time and place. Identifying the shape and the ground in a given criminal form is a complex process of interpretation, in which the due diligence procedure or the police investigation is only the first stage.

The process which leads to the correct recognition of a form can be disturbed in various ways. In a series of experiments, *Gestalt* psychologists have found that perception follows various intuitive paths, which tend to lead to false assumptions. Cognitive psychologists and economists have established the negative influence that those common perceptual biases generally have on decision-making (e.g., Tversky & Kahneman, 1981). The first influence is the influence of proximity, meaning that physically or temporally close objects are often interpreted as causally belonging together. The second influence concerns a resemblance between, or similarity of, objects: similar objects (or events) tend to be identified as belonging to the same class of objects or as being attributable to the same cause. The third influence reveals a human tendency to complete partial shapes by imputing substitutes prematurely. The fourth influence, sometimes called 'the law of the good form', says that we prefer the obvious, the simple and the symmetric shape over coincidental, complex or messy forms. So, there is an overall human tendency to jump to conclusions, to simplify and to make superficial interpretations. This may have been useful at the beginning of evolution but it is less helpful in this complex world of crime and finance. Human nature being what it is, we need a new, more scientific approach to train and handle perception.

III. The five rules of Systematic Observation

Essentially, the method of Systematic Observation consists of a logically ordered set of principles that guide perception in a systematic way. They are:

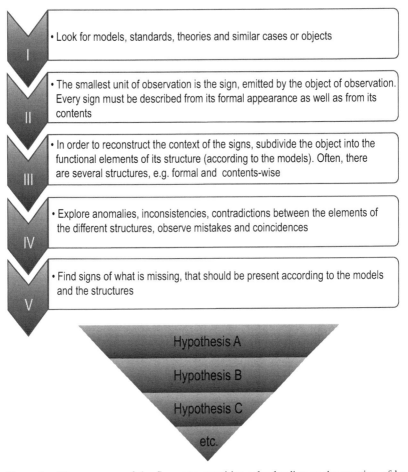

I • Look for models, standards, theories and similar cases or objects

II • The smallest unit of observation is the sign, emitted by the object of observation. Every sign must be described from its formal appearance as well as from its contents

III • In order to reconstruct the context of the signs, subdivide the object into the functional elements of its structure (according to the models). Often, there are several structures, e.g. formal and contents-wise

IV • Explore anomalies, inconsistencies, contradictions between the elements of the different structures, observe mistakes and coincidences

V • Find signs of what is missing, that should be present according to the models and the structures

Hypothesis A
Hypothesis B
Hypothesis C
etc.

Figure 1 – The sequence of the five meta-cognitive rules leading to the creation of hypotheses

The sequence of the rules ensures that the activity of observing is pursued systematically and not selectively. The first rule opens the observers' mind (his/her perception and reasoning) and provides hints as to what he/she must look out for. The second rule tells the observer how to treat the smallest units of perception, called 'signs'. The third rule ensures that the observer has a complete picture of all formal and material aspects of the object of observation. The fourth rule helps the observer distinguish between relevant signs and accidental signs and between natural and artificial signs; this enables him/her to establish a deterministic sequence of signs. The last rule completes the process, in so far as missing elements, if they exist, are also taken into account.

In following this five-step process, the observer will come up with hypotheses, which can then be discussed in the light of the picture which emerges from the available evidence. This is a separate task for which there is another systematic procedure instead of the everyday heuristic approach.

I. Rule I: comparison with models, standards and similar cases

Modern notions of perception take into account the contribution of the perceiving subject. In cognitive psychology, perception is understood as a cyclic activity (Neisser 1976: 20). We perceiving subjects, we explore our environment. From this environment, we receive stimuli, which we compare to our previous knowledge (mental schemata or models). The schemata contain the collected knowledge derived from past experience and assist us in recognising what we are perceiving; they also (re)direct our exploration to the relevant environmental stimuli. The comparison between mental models and stimuli from the environment can also lead to a modification of the existing knowledge as some clues from the environment may not match our schemata. In that case, the memorised information must be adapted and the arsenal of schemata must be enlarged.

Usually, people begin by exploring the environment and 'stay there for a while'. But – and this is the first rule – we can also enter the perceptual cycle by consulting models for a given object, case or situation immediately, in order to increase our personal supply of schemata (standards, theories, etc.) right from the start. When it comes to a crime scene, we can order the back-office to start collecting theoretical information and files from similar cases quickly. The comparison with different models can attract our attention to details that we neglected before. But it can do even more, by helping us realise certain differences between our object of observation and the consulted models. Thus, we may be led to new, unknown or atypical aspects of the case.

Our own professional experience provides another useful set of mental schemata, though it does have the disadvantage of being subjective and influenced by random factors. The search for models, standards and similar cases will enlarge our individual horizon by introducing us to more objective knowledge and different perspectives. It is critical to start the process of opening our consciousness as soon as possible in any observation, as our goal is to avoid the permanent loss of relevant information.

II. Rule II: separate formal aspects from the contents and observe them both

Having found the relevant models, we return to exploration. Semiotics tells us that the smallest unit of perception is a 'sign'. All science begins with a description of signs that were left from signals emitted from material as well as from immaterial phenomena. The Swiss linguist de Saussure (1916, 1995: 99) defined the sign as an entity with two 'faces': it has an (outer) appearance and an (inner) meaning. The double nature of the sign (appearance and signification) allows us to state the second rule of Systematic Observation: consider separately those aspects that refer to the formal structure of the object and those that refer to its contents (or signification) and always look at models for both aspects. The appearance of a sign can have no relation at all to its signification. For instance, the appearance of the linguistic sign composed by the four letters f-r-o-g has nothing to do with any animal but by pure convention the word 'frog' bears a meaning, which refers to the animal.

The rule that the sign is the basic unit of perception also determines the admissibility of a given interpretation with respect to its meaning. Umberto Eco (1973: chap. 5, 5.19) has said that we must interpret a sign as a coded communication within a given social, cultural and individual context. As a result, the sign receives its signification only by, and within, its context. This is easily illustrated by the sentence 'my dog ran out of the house when it was raining cats and dogs.' 'To rain cats and dogs' is an English colloquialism meaning 'to rain heavily'. In this sentence, the meaning of the word 'dog' – as a sign – is not unique and depends entirely on the context of the words around it: my pet dog did not run out of the house to play with some stray dogs that had fallen from the sky in a rain shower. Rather, it ran outside during heavy rain. Thus, a neutral description of the form of a sign is much easier to accomplish than a neutral description of its content. So, when in doubt, we need to indicate multiple interpretations of a sign's potential meaning.

In forensic science, signs of evidence have highly individual meanings, in contrast to linguistic signs that have a more or less common signification. What then is the relationship between the appearance and signification of a sign of evidence? Some signs of evidence can be parts or bits of a whole. For example, traces of blood are simply part of the blood of an injured person or animal. Other signs of evidence, such as the date of a specific transaction, are purely abstract. There are other facts again that consist of intentionally deceptive signs, whose form indicates exactly the opposite of their appearance (think, for instance, of a gift which is really a bribe).

Semiotics, the scientific study of signs, differentiates between natural and artificial signs (Eco 1977: chapter 2.8, paragraph 2.8.7). Natural signs are signs that occur even when there is no intention to send a message (e.g., psychiatric symptoms, mistakes, chemical processes in a dead body, signature aspects in violent crime), while artificial signs are wilful communications (e.g., threat letters, the staging of crime scenes to manipulate the police or the bait presented to potential victims in a confidence operation).

III. Rule III: dissect the structure of an entity into its functional elements (using models)

As the meaning of a sign is only apparent when it is viewed in its context, the third rule requires us to reconstruct the entire context of the signs. This is an important and difficult step since, having collected ample material, we may no longer know where to begin: we may have lost the overview of the case. To develop principles of Systematic Observation, we need to know more about structuralism and linguistics, the science of the structure of language.

Linguists were the first to deal with the challenge of dissecting symbolic objects of human communication into their functional elements. According to Grawitz (2001: 318):

> [...] Structuralism has a very peculiar conception of the linguistic system: it is essentially considered as a system of signs. [...] The system appears like a net of differences between signs [...] Linguistic research appears from then on mostly as a definition of minimal units, separated by an operation of commutation: whatever changes the meaning when it is substituted by another element can be considered a minimal unit.

Grawitz (2001: 431) later described the position of the French anthropologist Lévi-Strauss (1958), who applied this method to social science and to human behaviour:

> [...], the structure implies limited characteristics. Combinations and transformations of them permit to pass from one system to another and to understand their relationships. The idea of a structure involves an element of transformation and of prevision.

Minsky (1985: chap. 12, paras. 12.4 - 12.5) in *Society of Mind* then added a new recurrent aspect to the definition of structures. He underlined the fact that within any structure there is an inherent function and the components represent its sub-functions. Structures, in this sense, can be perpetually refined into smaller sub-structures and imbedded in larger super-structures.

Establishing underlying structures is, in fact, the most challenging task of Systematic Observation. While the second rule deals with the smallest unit of perception, the third rule deals with the smallest units of the material or immaterial objects we are observing. Using the models to structure the object of observation into its functional elements, helps ensure that we are comprehensive and that we can break down an object which is too large to be grasped at once. We treat each object as a mathematical set of j elements and n corresponding functions: $M=\{e1, e2, e3, ..., ej, f1, f2, f3, ..., fn\}$. Having defined these sets for every model ($M1$, $M2$, etc.), we can describe all elements and functions, one after the other. To give an example: the elements of a social interaction could be classified by the so-called W-questions: 'Who has done what to whom, what instruments or methods have been used, where and when did it happen, why and under which circumstances did it happen?' or as $M=\{$who, done what, to whom, with what, where, when, why, which circumstances$\}$.

The procedure can be tedious since several models generally fit one object and the procedure has to be completed with all those structures.

IV. Rule IV: exploring inconsistencies, errors, contradictions and strange coincidences

By observing every one of the structural elements, we build a fairly comprehensive picture of the object. However, these facts do not always produce a coherent picture. It is important to observe and to register objectively all signs of evidence even if they do not fit the scheme, neither levelling out inconsistencies, nor exaggerating them. Sometimes, we may hit upon facts that make no sense at all. Should we leave these facts aside to avoid giving an impression of incompetence? Most certainly not! It is a sign of professionalism to admit that something is not (yet) understood. The very essence of scientific thinking and professional integrity is to register everything, including the incomprehensible and the contradictory.

Let us remember unknown phenomena occur embedded within of chance events (Kind 1987: 43). At the beginning of the process, we cannot know the difference between accidental elements and the determined structure of an individual's or a group's actions. Only certain inconsistencies may point to what is relevant and what is not. In Systematic Observation, we search for anomalies in the signs within a previously established structure (e.g., contradictions between the contents of different statements) and between different structures (e.g., contradictions between the contents of a text and its grammatical characteristics). Investigators pay a lot of attention to inconsistencies, because they suspect them of being artificial signs, i.e., communications from a subject who wants to blur the facts or deceive others. Nevertheless, such behaviour is not always linked to the subject matter of the investigation. People lie for many different reasons and they may hide things that have nothing to do whatsoever with the present case.

So, contrary to the logic used in detective novels, the fourth rule is not the only principle of Systematic Observation and neither is it the first step in the process of analysing criminal cases or problems in general. Exploring inconsistencies, contradictions and bizarre coincidences comes only after the analysis of the objects in terms of models and functional elements, for only then can they be interpreted on the basis of the entire case, by comparing different elements with each other. A spelling mistake has one meaning, if the text is written by a well-educated person and another, if the text is written by a semi-literate person and contains dozens of other spelling mistakes.

Contradictions that appear at the beginning of a case, in witness statements or a suspect's deposition, are obviously useful for investigators. However, subtle inconsistencies may emerge later, disturbing a seemingly neat and obvious case or (in the finance industry) a valuable project that is well under way. Such inconsistencies are likely to pass unnoticed or to be shoved aside by investigators or compliance officers. They are annoying. Giddens (1984: 167) describes this phenomenon in more abstract terms:

> The work of Kuhn and other authors show that researchers ignore or want to make disappear with far-fetched explanations all those results of their experiments or observations which are incompatible with their theories or which would even prove them false.

Therefore, obeying the fourth rule also means submitting to tedious supplementary examinations, instead of defending older hypotheses against new insights. Thomas Henry Huxley (1870/2001: 229) described the attendant emotional challenge: 'The great tragedy of Science is the slaying of a beautiful hypothesis by an ugly fact'.

V. Rule V: discovering negative signs (concerning missing elements)

The fifth and last rule refers to tracing signs of missing elements that should be present. The basic sets of functional elements $M1 = \{e1, e2, e3, [...] ej, f1, f2, f3, [...], fn \}$, $M2 = [...]$, $M3 = [...]\}$ provide clues on what is missing. This activity terminates the Systematic Observation and guarantees that the entire situation has been taken into account. Nordby (2000: 63) commented on the difference between a sign of evidence and proof: 'Absence of proof is not proof of absence but the absence of a sign can itself be a sign'.

VI. Checking a hypothesis for plausibility

In working on a criminal case, we are reconstructing a unique historical event between several actors by taking into account and interpreting different signs. Nordby (2000: 206) explained why observers can come to very different conclusions on the same case:

> Part of seeing a sign involves recognising its significance and building it into an inference. Dismissing signs and what follows deductively from them as irrelevant along one path and including them as relevant along another, may result in contradictory conclusions drawn from the same observations.

So, we can say that the processes of observation and interpretation are composed by two inverse ways of reasoning: inclusion and exclusion. On the one hand, we need to include all relevant aspects of the case and, on the other hand, we need to exclude everything that is not important. Then again, at the beginning we do not know which is which – even if we think we do. Given that signs of evidence do not necessarily speak for themselves, we are obliged to complete our knowledge about a case (i.e., the shape and the ground) in the most exhaustive way possible. This task was accomplished by the applying the five rules of observation.

In a second step, we brainstorm and list all the ideas and hypotheses that have come to mind in the process of collecting signs of evidence. Then, in the third step, we can start to interpret the picture of the signs that has emerged from the evidence. At this point, we want to be very critical and we want to create total transparency about the situation for our current work and for later stages of the investigation. We can leave nothing to chance. We need to undertake this process in a rational way and account for all the information we have gathered in the previous phases.

To achieve this level of thoroughness, it can help to prepare a three-way table of all signs supporting a particular hypothesis, all signs militating against that hypothesis and all inconclusive signs. This helps us sort the signs and make a preliminary evaluation of each hypothesis with respect to its plausibility.

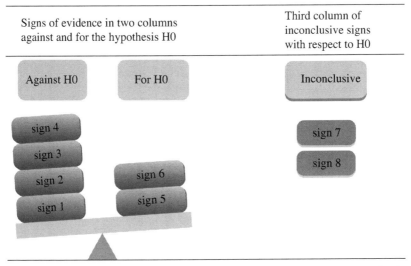

Figure 2 – Weighing the signs for and against a hypothesis H0 and accounting for the rest

The third column, which contains all inconclusive signs with respect to a given hypothesis H0, is also very important since some of those signs may assume a new meaning and be useful at a later stage of an investigation. Condensing the information in this way helps the observer to decide which leads should be pursued and which ones should be abandoned.

IV. Systematic Observation in the criminal investigation – the case of the 'anthrax letter'

1.　The facts of the case

To demonstrate the application of the method in a more complex case, let us take one of the anthrax letters of 2001. Two weeks after the attacks on the World Trade Centre and the Pentagon of 11 September 2001 (9/11), an editor's assistant at the New York Post discovered a strange blister on her finger. Her doctor diagnosed skin anthrax, a disease almost impossible to contract living and working in a big city. In the course of the following weeks, there was an unusual incidence of this disease throughout the USA. In total, five people were killed and another 17 fell ill from a strain of anthrax later connected to the 'anthrax letters' (Federal Bureau of Investigation (FBI) 2008). Even though there is a heavy metal band by the name of 'Anthrax', the general public knew very little about this bacterium, let alone that it could be used as a biological weapon.

A month later, in October 2001, the FBI discovered a wet envelope in the offices of the New York Post. Inside was a letter and something looking like wet dog food. The substance was later identified as a new strand of technically refined anthrax spores. This material only exists inside high-security laboratories; it cannot be bought on any black market and it cannot be fabricated by an amateur. The letter paper and the pre-stamped envelope were produced in batches of millions per year and sold in the United States (US). The stamp (unreadable in the photo) showed that the letter was sent on 18 September 2001 from Trenton, New Jersey. Unfortunately, no one had seen the person who deposited the envelope.

Let us assume, for the sake of the exercise, that no traces of human DNA, fibres or fingerprints could be found on the envelope or on the letter, except those from postal employees. Let us also assume that experts on handwriting declared that they could not determine whether the letter was written by someone intentionally altering his/her handwriting or by someone with little practice in the Latin alphabet. Under these circumstances, how would you proceed if it were up to you to decide which leads were to be taken in this investigation? According to *Gestalt* psychology, one might first suspect another attack by al-Qaida, given that the attacks on the World Trade Centre and the Pentagon had occurred only a few days earlier. Both crimes occurred within a short time of each other and are similar in many ways: they targeted innocent civilians, they were technically sophisticated and 'innovative' in terms of their *modus operandi*, they were committed against public services and they were both likely to create mass panic. Whoever committed these crimes wanted the broadest media attention possible. Knowing that the propensities of spontaneous perception are often misleading, in the following we will proceed systematically.

Figure 3 – The letter to the New York Post containing technically refined spores of anthrax[3]

II. Applying the Rules I–V

Applying Rule I: conducing a comparison with models

In investigating crimes, there is often little evidence from which to draw inferences. Let us look first at the envelope containing the anthrax letter: can anything be derived from that? The answer is yes, by using a comparison of models. For this purpose, we take the address of the New York Post as it appears in the phonebook and on the company website and place it side-by-side with the envelope:

Corpus delicti (envelope)   Standard

New York Post
1211 Avenue of the Americas
New York, NY 10036-8790

Figure 4 – Comparing the *corpus delicti,* as it appears on the FBI website[4], with the NY Post's standard address, as listed on its website.[5]

Comparing the address on the *corpus delicti* with the model addresses, we indeed find a difference between the postal (zip) codes: the code on the envelope contains six digits whereas the code on the standard address contains ten. This detail might easily have escaped our attention had we not consulted the model address. The extra four digits (known as the 'ZIP+4' code) are mainly intended for business mailers and are not mandatory in the US. This would not be at all obvious to a foreigner operating from abroad. Thus, this piece of information, gained by comparison with a model, leads us to a hypothesis concerning the perpetrator's familiarity with US Postal Services. In conclud-

---

4   Available at www.fbi.gov/page2/august08/anthrax_gallery7.html.
5   Available at www.nypost.com.

ing our examination, we also notice that the handwriting has a downward slant; we register this sign, even if there is no explanation at hand.

Then, we look at the threat letter itself. Here, we want to consider several models. On the one hand, we have different norms for letter-writing and different models for letters in different social contexts and cultures. In this case, we would look at the standard elements for business letters in the US and the way in which religious Muslims quote the Qu'ran in their letters. For example, in business correspondence, Americans generally use the following format:

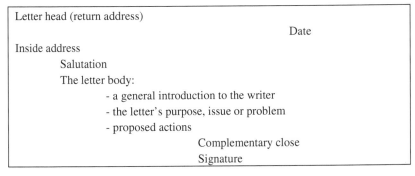

Letter head (return address)

                                                       Date

Inside address
      Salutation
      The letter body:
            - a general introduction to the writer
            - the letter's purpose, issue or problem
            - proposed actions
                  Complementary close
                  Signature

Figure 5 – Model of a standard business letter (Zahorsky 2008)

Letters by religious Muslims customarily include some standard features, which are missing in this case. For example, one would expect such a letter to begin with the 'Basmala', the religious commitment that introduces the chapters of Qu'ran, as well as other texts with a religious connotation (see Renfer in Renfer & Haas 2008: 322).

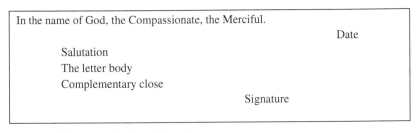

In the name of God, the Compassionate, the Merciful.

                                                       Date

      Salutation
      The letter body
      Complementary close
                    Signature

Figure 6 – Model for religious Islamic letters

We also wonder why the exclamation 'Allah is great' was written in English and not in Arabic. The phrase is an incorrect but very common translation of the so-called *Takbeer* 'Allahu akbar' (comparable to the Halleluiah in the Judeo-Christian Bible). According to Marc Renfer, it is recited in its original language by religious Muslims in numerous contexts, e.g., in prayer, in praise or in times of distress or in war.[6] The *Takbeer* actually means 'God is greater' (than man).

الله اكبر

Figure 7 – The *Takbeer* 'Allahu akbar'

Dr. Thomas Hansjakob[7] rightly cautioned, in a personal communication to the author, that criminal behaviour, deviant per definition, cannot be analysed in the light of norms only. The choice of models must account for our perception of the norm and of the deviance as well. We work like doctors, who compare their patients' symptoms with the statistics of average healthy individuals and also of typical pathologies. Thus, we usually take case samples and statistics from the same type of crime and compare them to the facts of our case. This is adequate for 'standard' crimes. However, where a crime is highly innovative, we have to content ourselves with models from similar crimes. Thus, for the sake of the exercise, our model in examining the anthrax letter was a manifesto referring to bombings.

The following threat letter was sent after the Atlanta Bombings at Centennial Olympic Park on 27 July 1996, Sandy Springs Professional Building on 16 January 1997 and the Otherside Lounge on 21 February 1997:

---

6   Marc Renfer, MA, personal communication 2008, first author of another joint paper on the application of Systematic Observation in counter-terrorism is specialist in Arabic, Persian and Turkish linguistics.

7   Thomas Hansjakob is Chief Prosecutor in the Canton of St Gallen and Editor of the well known German textbook on reasoning in criminal cases (Walder-Hansjakob 2006).

THE BOMBING'S IN SANDY SPRING'S AND MIDTOWN WERE CARRIED-OUT BY UNITS OF THE ARMY OF GOD. THE ABORTION WAS THE TARGET OF THE FIRST DEVICE. THE MURDER OF 3.5 MILLION CHILDREN EVERY YEAR WILL NOT BE "TOLERATED". THOSE WHO PARTICIPATE IN ANYWAY IN THE MURDER OF CHILDREN MAY BE TARGETED FOR ATTACK. THE ATTACK THEREFORE SERVES AS A WARNING: ANYONE IN OR AROUND FACILITIES THAT MURDER CHILDREN MAY BECOME VICTIMS OF RETRIBUTION. THE NEXT FACILITY TARGETED MAY NOT BE EMPTY.

THE SECOND DEVICE WAS AIMED AT AGENT OF THE SO-CALLED FEDERAL GOVERNMENT I.E. A.T.F. F.B.I. MARSHALL'S E.T.C. WE DECLARE AND WILL WAGE TOTAL WAR ON THE UNGODLY COMMUNIST REGIME IN NEW YORK AND YOOUR LEGALSTIVE – BUREAUCRATIC LACKEY'S IN WASHINGTON. IT IS YOU WHO ARE RESPONSIBLE AND PRESIDE OVER THE MURDER OF CHILDREN AND ISSUE THE POLICY OF UNGODLY PERVERSION THAT'S DESTROYING OUR ARE PEOPLE. WE WILL TARGET ALL FACITLITIES AND PERSONNELL OF THE FEDERAL GOVERNMENT.

THE ATTACK IN MIDTOWN WAS AIMED AT THE SODOMITE BAR (THE OTHERSIDE). WE WILL TARGET SODOMITES, THERE ORGANIZATIONS, AND ALL THOSE WHO PUSH THERE AGENDA.

" DEATH TO THE NEW WORLD ORDER"

Figure 8 – A manifesto sent after the Atlanta bombings (ATF 1997).

The 'Army of God' letters were sent to a local newspaper and to Reuters press agency in Atlanta. All three bombings were later found to be the work of anti-abortion extremist, Eric Robert Rudolph. Arrested in 2003, Rudolph was charged with bombing attacks that killed two people and injured and maimed more than 150 others. He pleaded guilty and was sentenced to life in prison in 2005 (ATF Pressroom: 2003, 2005). Although it seems that he did have supporters (especially his brother), Rudolph essentially acted alone and the 'Army of God' was a fiction.

Looking briefly at his criminal manifesto, we see that it is full of spelling mistakes and some formal requirements are missing. Nonetheless, it meets the requirements of a business letter as the writer presents himself in the main body of text, names the issue and threatens action.

Applying Rule II: considering the formal aspects and
the contents of each sign and describing them

Having observed the formal features of the documents, such as the
address, we now turn to their contents. What, then, are the contents of
an address? As this next step is about victimology,[8] we ask, 'Is the
letter addressed to an organisation or a person?' and 'Why was this
particular organisation targeted?' After all, the New York Post, unlike
the World Trade Centre or the Pentagon, is not a national symbol that
represents the US in the eyes of the world. Rather it is a local tabloid,
which is quite unknown abroad. It does not seem to be the most meaningful target for an international terrorist group. Surely, if the perpe-
trator(s) of the anthrax attacks was/were linked to al-Qaida, he, she or
they would have sent the deadly letters to the New York Times, the
Washington Post or CNN. These major news companies could have
been chosen just as easily and would have been capable of attracting
even more international media attention.

Applying Rule III: observing complex objects by structural analysis

If, in observing the envelope, we addressed the lack of material by
using a comparison with models, with the letter itself we face the opposite problem: so much material that we have difficulty knowing
where to start. Nevertheless, it is again the comparison with models,
which helps us to subdivide the object into its structural components
and thus to observe it. We have already seen the two models of the
American business letter and letters by religious Muslims. Within a
letter, several sub-structures are possible. Here we ordered them on a
scale ranging from the most formal aspects to the contents properly
speaking.

---

8   In real life, one would have to investigate and interview the victim thoroughly.

The letter[9]	Different structures
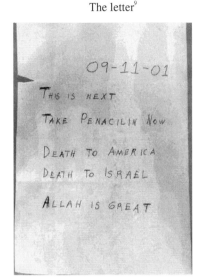	a. Physical evidence: paper, ink, human DNA, fingerprints, fibres, spores, etc. b. Graphics and typography: format, stains, letters of the alphabet, numbers. c. Linguistics: words, sentences, punctuation, paragraphs, language (vernacular, foreign, feigned foreign, etc.), spelling, grammar, style (rhythm, rhyme, etc.). d. Elements of a typical business letter: return address, city, date, inside address, salutation, main body, closing, signature. e. Contents of the drama: actors, how the actors are named, the sequence of themes.

Figure 9 – Different structures of a letter and their elements

There is not the space here to conduct a complete analysis of the letter, so we will have to make do with some examples. Starting with graphics and typography, we observe that the writer has used a typographic function called 'small capitals'. Next, we see that the figure '1' resembles European handwriting style. The American way of writing the number one is like the capital letter 'I'. However, the perpetrator used a typographic feature called 'serifs' (little decorative lines, such as in the '1'), instead of *sans* serif, which is more common in Europe. Furthermore, the number nine is written in the American style as a '9', whereas Europeans mostly draw a curve at the bottom of the number, e.g., '9'. The date, by the way, is again written in the American style ('09-11-01') and not in the European style, in which the day is com-

9   Available at www.fbi.gov/page2/august08/anthrax_gallery7.html.

monly placed before the month (e.g., '11 September 2001' abbreviated as '11.09.01').

Considering linguistics, we notice that the manifesto is in English not in Arabic, that each line has exactly three words and that the writer of this text used very short sentences without full stops. Most readers will also recognise the misspelling of penicillin as 'penacilin'. There is a kind of hacked rhythm in this text, which is similar to military commands. The impression that the whole letter was quite carefully composed is also sustained by the well-respected margins in the layout. Altogether, it seems that this letter was not written in a hurry. On the contrary, our perpetrator(s) seem(s) to have paid considerable attention to detail in order to communicate exactly what he, she or they wanted to say and nothing else. The comparison with a business letter can be useful to determine the level of professional functioning of an anonymous author. Some authors write in such a confused style and layout that it is obvious that they could not function in a 'white collar' job.

Finally, to examine the contents under the microscope, we put up the list of actors (including the pronouns, if there are any) and a list of themes (naming the list of actors is actually an idea that was developed by Sapir (1999)). Within the list of actors, we often find the anonymous author himself because it is difficult for people to transmit an issue that is important to them without leaving any psychological 'footprints'. Following this assumption, we might want to look for an Israeli author or, more likely, an American.

List of the actors	List of the themes
a. America b. Israel c. Allah	a. What comes after the crimes of 9/11 b. Protect yourself with penicillin c. America and Israel should feel threatened d. A poor translation of the *Takbeer*

Figure 10 – Actors and themes of the drama

Incidentally, in letters which announce a future attack, the list of themes sometimes leaves clues about the seriousness of a threat, in that the degree of aggressiveness may increase or decrease within the sequence of themes. After structuring the object in different ways, we may also realise that a clear distinction between form and contents can only be made in theory but not in practice. Form and contents cannot be classified into absolute categories as they are relative with respect to one another.

Applying Rule IV: exploring anomalies, inconsistencies, errors, contradictions and coincidences

Given that the author of the anthrax letter has written his message quite carefully and that refined anthrax spores are accessible only to a small circle of highly trained specialists, there is a bizarre contradiction. How can a person who is apparently familiar with the safety procedures necessary when handling anthrax, not be able to spell the word 'penicillin'? Penicillin not only a much more common *substance* than anthrax but it is also a much more common *word*. Penicillin is, moreover, essential for protecting against infection in case of accidental exposure to the anthrax bacterium. Thus, anybody familiar with the first substance is also familiar with the second. For us, the essential question is whether the misspelling of penicillin is a natural sign (i.e., a symptom, such as dyslexia) or whether is it an artificial sign (i.e., a message conceived to manipulate). Why is the word 'penicillin' spelt with an 'a' instead of an 'i'? It may be possible to confuse these sounds in American pronunciation but in many other languages, such as German, French or Italian, one would never make this mistake.

Another anomaly can be observed with respect to the religious Muslim's model letter: a religious Muslim would refer first to Allah because his/her faith is the single most important issue. By contrast, the author of the anthrax letter mentions Allah only at the end. It is also curious that somebody would want to poison so many people and warn them at the same time. No warnings were issued before 9/11 and thus we could have assumed that the terrorists were aiming for the highest possible death toll. So why does *this* perpetrator want to endanger the life of his victims but not necessarily kill them? Is the goal to scare or is there yet another motive behind this crime?

Applying Rule V: discovering negative signs

The real difference between the excellent and the ordinary observer is a capacity to identify what is missing. What can be said about the anthrax letter using the rule on the absence of signs? Comparing our letter with the letter that was sent after the Atlanta bombings in Sandy Springs (ATF 1997), we notice that anthrax perpetrator mentions no group name and remains hazy with respect to the issue. In statement analysis, one would interpret this as a lack of commitment in the confession (Sapir 1999). What is the purpose of sending these letters if no political or personal demands are specified? Why not send the deadly spores alone? We wonder what the real issue is here. Could it be that the perpetrator cannot reveal his/her goal because it could lead to identification?

III. From observation to interpretation: checking hypotheses for plausibility

After applying the five rules to the facts of the case it is time for us to formulate hypotheses and check them for their plausibility. This is the second stage of the method. Kind tells us what it means to identify the pattern of a crime in an investigation (1987: 43):

> [...] the identification of pattern in crime investigation may perhaps be defined simply as the identification of a deterministic sequence in a series of apparently chance events.

The method of systematic exploration of all potentially meaningful details does bring with it a certain danger: how can we know that we have not been misled into too much speculation? How can we avoid losing ourselves in far-fetched hypotheses? What is to be done when a controversy over different conflicting hypotheses arises? We use a plausibility check in the form of the three-way table discussed above.

Signs pointing against the hypothesis H0	Signs in favour of hypothesis H0	Inconclusive signs
	A very sophisticated *modus operandi* was used in both attacks.	
The anthrax letter purports to be written on 11 September 2001 but was sent one week later.	Both attacks were committed within one week of each other.	
	Both attacks were hideous crimes against many innocent civilians.	
		The address is written with a downward slant.
		The author's knowledge of how to write the zip code implies that he has been living in the US for some time.
Perhaps: the spelling mistake in 'penacilin'.		The perpetrator could be dyslectic
There is no group named, the issue remains rather vague.	A manifesto with allusions to Islamist terrorism.	
The authors of the (real) 9/11 attacks did not write a manifesto.		
The author offers no proof that he/she knows the Arabic language, that he/she has inside knowledge of Al-Qaida or that he/she is a Muslim.		

| The victim is not a symbol for the US. It is not primarily a target of international interest. | |
| The perpetrator seems to simulate a non-American way of writing the figure '1', however, he/she does so incorrectly. | |

Figure 11 – Plausibility Check for Hypothesis H0: the perpetrator of the anthrax attacks belongs to Al-Qaida (Obviously in a real investigation all four letters would be analysed, many more of these signs would be investigated and other hypotheses would be checked more thoroughly than it was possible in this exercise.)

The plausibility check (Figure 10) shows that four signs point to a Jihadist terror group (as it would be called today) as potential senders of the anthrax letter. Two of those signs could be interpreted either way. On the other hand, we have five clear signs in favour of an American perpetrator with either personal or political motives focused on internal US politics. This is also sustained by the overall nebulous quality of the manifesto, which is quite typical for staged crime scenes and copycat crimes. The hypothesis of a copycat crime is therefore more plausible than the one of 'proper' terrorist attack.

IV. *Applying Systematic Observation to the anthrax letter: results*

The preceding analysis of the anthrax letter was first published when the case was still unresolved (Haas 2003). In August 2008, the FBI closed its investigation into the anthrax attacks, ending one of the most complex and expensive investigations in its history. In documents available to the public on the Internet, it revealed a compelling chain of evidence implicating the renowned microbiologist, Dr. Bruce Ivins, as the sole perpetrator of these crimes. In 2005, the origin of the spores was traced to the US laboratory in Fort Detrick. The only specialist having access and links to the crimes was Dr. Ivins. In the course of the investigation, he had demonstrated both bizarre and deceptive behaviour. His presumed motive for the attacks was to promote and finance his research on a vaccination against anthrax. As we can see, not even this highly intelligent and scientifically trained individual was able to hide his ignorance of Islam and cover his own psychological 'footprint' as an American copycat of the 9/11 attacks.

V. Empirical testing of the Systematic Observation method

As Systematic Observation takes some time, the consequent application of its rules is only justified in cases of some importance. However, the method can be learned and once it is known and practiced
regularly, investigators detect suspicious signs with much more ease.
With some routine, they grasp many more signs of evidence right
from the beginning and save themselves the unnecessary work of pursuing false assumptions. After initial pilot studies, the author and colleagues conducted an experiment in 2006 using 41 graduate students
in psychology as volunteers (Haas, Tönz, Gubser-Ernst, Pisarzewska,
in preparation). We found that participants who applied the method
after six hours of training were able to observe more signs and draw
more correct inferences from the evidence than untrained observers. In
2007 we conducted another study with 174 criminal investigators in
eight different Swiss Cantons. Their mean age was 42 years and on
average participants had 17 years of professional experience as investigators. At the end of the training, 67 percent of investigators found
the method to be useful or very useful for their work and 80 percent
considered the method to be a good or very good instruction and training in critical thinking.

VI. Systematic Observation in customer due diligence
   for financial intermediaries

*I.   Systematic Observation as a tool for prevention in
     counter-terrorist financing*

Systematic Observation can also be employed to prevent terrorist
funds from entering the global financial system. Legal standards relating to due diligence in the banking sector require client identification
and verification. In Switzerland, para. 3 of the Federal Act on the Pre-

vention of Money Laundering requires financial intermediaries, 'prior to commencing business relationships [to], identify the contracting party on the basis of a conclusive document'. When the potential customer is a natural person, the financial intermediary must establish his/her identity by examining and photocopying an official document, such as a passport or identity card. Employees must record the person's first name, surname, date of birth, nationality and home address. At the same time, the intermediary must identify the beneficial owner of the funds.

This is not a trivial task considering that customers of Swiss banks come from all over the world and there is no internationally accepted legal definition of the main elements of a name. Westenburger (2008) illustrates of how the elements of proper names can be defined in different countries. The Western model of 'first name plus surname' (e.g., 'Hans Müller from Germany') is not standard. Other countries may register elements like the father's (first) name instead of surname, the grandfather's first name, the mother's name or middle names. Alternatively, they may provides other definitions 'proper name', 'given name' or 'supplement to name' in their national laws. According Westenburger (2008) more challenges in the identification of proper names arise from the translation of foreign alphabets into the Latin alphabet and from the adaptation of names to reflect the bearer's sex in some languages. In addition, some names are extremely widespread within a community and may indicate a title or membership of a large family clan rather than a surname. Finally, there are the difficulties of identifying a person who has legally changed his/her named due to marriage, naturalisation or for other reasons. In Spain, for example, a name consists of the first name, the mother's name as a middle name and the last name, e.g., 'Felipe Dias Gonzales'. By contrast, a Russian woman whose father's name is 'Aleksandrovič' may appear in her passport with the surname of 'Asimova' and the given names of 'Svetlana Aleksandrovna'. An Egyptian man's passport could contain a first name (e.g., 'Tarek'), the father's name (e.g., 'Mohammed Abdel Aziz'), and the family name (e.g., 'Ahmed'). A Libyan passport, by contrast, would only give a full name ('Mohammed Musa ben Yussuf') and would not distinguish between first names and surnames.

Thus, the transmission of the name from parents to children is also variable across the world.

II. Customer identification with Systematic Observation

Can Systematic Observation be applied to prevent terrorist financing, as well as to investigate terrorist acts after they occur? Applying the Rule I, we need to compare all relevant official identification models with information about terrorists. It is essential to consult the embassies' models and standards for establishing the authenticity of identification papers. It may also be useful to check databases, such as the Council of Europe's Public Register of Authentic Identity and Travel Documents Online (PRADO). From this data a comparison is made with information available about individuals, groups and nations involved in terrorist activities, the observer consulting the respective lists and databases on terrorism.[10]

Using the second rule, we note that a person's name is a sign in the semiotic sense in that it has a formal (outer) appearance and an inner meaning. As we have seen, names are defined quite differently from one culture and nation to another. As a person can be a naturalised citizen, e.g., he could be a certain 'Mr Felipe Gonzales from Switzerland'. A financial intermediary observing formal signs according to Rule II, would then ask if this client is also in possession of another passport, e.g., a Spanish or Latin American passport, and if the client once used his/her mothers' name as the middle name.

Having discussed the formal appearance of a name, in the third step we ask, 'What is its content?' Here the content is obviously the human being described and identified in the passport. To verify if the passport matches the person, the employee of the financial intermediary must compare the photograph and the description (age, sex, height, eye colour, etc.) in the client's identification papers with the real person standing in front him/her.

---

10 For Switzerland these are available at www.gwg.admin.ch/d/aktuell/angebot/ index.php).

Rule III tells us that a sign, such as a passport, consists of a set of different elements each of which must be observed individually. These elements are: the cover, the different pages with information about the bearer and about countries that he/she has visited recently, as well as the stamps and the sophisticated printing techniques, holograms, marks and perforations used to make passports forgery-proof (Schneider & Höpfner 2008). Each element of this structure must be looked at and compared with the model identification document. This means, for one thing, checking all pages of the document. Only if all pages are controlled, can the banker know whether clients have recently travelled to 'failed states' or if they happen to figure on a list of terrorist suspects.

On the basis of such an inventory of signs, the next step (Rule IV) is to look for any anomalies and inconsistencies. Note that this 'Sherlock Holmes' rule only makes sense on the basis of the previous steps. If one were to jump directly to this rule, much of the relevant information would be missed and anomalies might not be noticed at all. We remember too at this point that anomalies can arise for different reasons and are not only caused by criminal intent. One source of inconsistencies in the spelling of names is differing translations of names from one alphabet into another, e.g., 'Kader' may also be spelt as 'Kadir' depending on the transliteration.

The fifth and last rule (Rule V) – recording what is missing – rounds up the procedure and is based on our analysis of all models and their inherent structures. In the case of customer identification, the knowledge of foreign names and passport models is crucial to identifying missing information in a suspicious document. Then again, we also need to look out for missing pages, stamps, holograms, perforations, etc. (Schneider & Höpfner 2008).

*III. Challenges and opportunities in applying
Systematic Observation to counter-terrorist financing*

The same procedure can be applied to unusual customer demands or transactions, e.g., a lack of interest in otherwise attractive investment opportunities. However, there are particular practical obstacles to using the method as a preventative tool, such as data processing practices which blur or destroy potentially suspicious details. When information is entered into a computerised database, paper records containing the original information may not be kept or scanned. This effectively blinds the financial intermediary to important details. To avoid this situation, all employees should be properly instructed in the relevance of seemingly 'small errors' and told how they can prevent their loss. In particular, workers need to be instructed to introduce data into their computerised system *exactly in the way the information was presented by the client* and to *refrain from correcting* any mistakes and mishaps that came from the client. Another solution, suggested by Dr. Hans-Peter Bauer at the 2008 Giessbach II counter-terrorist financing seminar, would see clients filling out the computerised forms themselves. In this way, all intentional manipulations and blanks could be automatically recorded.

VII.   Conclusion

Systematic Observation is a meta-cognitive tool to establish an inventory of all signs of evidence from documents, photographs and other case material. The procedure was first developed for criminal investigations (Haas 2003) and consists in the application of five easily memorised formulas which help professionals, analysts and investigators to be more proficient observers. The rules are:

I.   Compare the object of observation to models, standards, theories or similar cases
II.   Separate formal aspects from the contents and analyse them both separately
III. Structure the object into functional elements and explore each of them
IV.   Explore anomalies, inconsistencies, contradictions, mistakes or coincidences
V.   Discover the absence of signs (with models and after structuring the object)

After going through the process of systematically registering every important detail, we are able to draw first hypotheses. Every hypothesis should then be checked for its plausibility by listing systematically every sign speaking for it in one column, every indeterminate sign in a middle column and every sign against it in a third column. This procedure creates more transparency for the situation and prevents us from paying selective attention to some isolated parts of the evidence. This, in turn, provides good grounds for constructive discussions about the decisions to be taken.

The present chapter has shown how this method can be applied in the area of counter-terrorism. First, we have seen that Systematic Observation can be used to analyse threats (written or electronically recorded) and to distinguish 'terrorist' from other general criminal activity. Second, we have considered how Systematic Observation can serve as a preventative tool to help private sector institutions to identify suspicious transactions and improve the effectiveness of their compliance systems.

Bibliography

AIVD Dutch General Intelligence and Security Service (2002). *Recruitment for the Jihad in the Netherlands – from Incident to Trend.* Leidschendam, NL. Retrieved October 2008 from: www. aivd.nl/actueel-publicaties/aivd-publicaties.

Bureau of Alcohol, Tobacco, Firearms and Explosives (ATF): Atlanta Bomb Task Force (1997). *Atlanta Bombing Case Consolidation – Centennial Olympic Park Case, Sandy Springs Professional Building, and The Otherside Lounge.* Retrieved October 2008 from http://www.atf.gov/explarson/atlanpr1.htm.

Bureau of Alcohol, Tobacco, Firearms and Explosives (ATF) (2003–2005). *ATF Pressroom news releases,* Retrieved October 2008 from www.atf.gov/press/index.htm.

Bundesministerium des Inneren Deutschland (2008). *Verfassungsschutzbericht 2007.* Berlin, Germany. [Report by the German Office for Protection of the Constitution (Homeland Security)]. Retrieved October 2008 from www.verfassungsschutz.de.

Council of Europe (2008). *PRADO – Public Register of Authentic Identity and Travel Documents.* Available at www.consilium. europa.eu/prado/EN/homeIndex.html.

de Saussure, F. (1995) *Cours de linguistique générale.* [Course in General Linguistics]. Paris, France: Grande Bibliothèque Payot. (Original work published 1916).

Eco, U. (1973). *Segno.* [The Sign]. Milano, Italy: Istituto Editoriale Internazionale.

Federal Bureau of Investigation (FBI) (9 November 2001). *Amerithrax: Linguistic/Behavioral Analysis.* Retrieved October 2008 from www.fbi.gov/page2/august08/amerithrax080608a.html.

Federal Bureau of Investigation (FBI) (6 August 2008). *Headline Archives ANTHRAX INVESTIGATION – Closing a Chapter.* Retrieved October 2008 from www.fbi.gov/page2/august08/ amerithrax080608a.html.

Giddens, A (1984). *Interpretative Soziologie.* [Interpretative Sociology]. Campus Verlag Frankfurt.

Grawitz, M. (2001). *Méthodes des sciences sociales*. [Methods in Social Science]. Paris, France: Editions Dalloz.

Haas, H., P. Tönz, J. Gubser-Ernst & M. Pisarzewska (work in progress). *The Basics of Observation – A Method to Improve Perception in Case-Work*.

Haas, H. (2005). 'Vom Nichtwissen zum Wissen'. [From Ignorance to Knowledge]. *Ungewußt – Zeitschrift für angewandtes Nichtwissen*, 12: 64-85. Available at www.uni-siegen.de/~ifan/ungewu/heft12/index.htm.

Haas, H. (2003). 'Kriminalistischer Erkenntnisgewinn durch systematisches Beobachten'. [The Gaining of Knowledge by Systematic Observation in the Criminal Investigation]. *Kriminalistik* 57: 93-100.

Haas, H. (2003). Observer et rédiger des documents en psychologie légale. *Actualités psychologiques*. Institut de psychologie, University of Lausanne.

Haas, H. & M. Killias (2003). 'The Versatility vs. Specialization Debate: Different Theories of Crime in the Light of a Swiss Birth Cohort.' In: C Britt & M Gottfredson (2003). *Control Theories of Crime and Delinquency (Advances in Criminological Theory*, Vol 12, New Brunswick: Transaction Publishers.

Huxley, T. (2001). Biogenisis and Abiogenisis. Collected Essays. Vol. 8, *Discourses Biological & Geological*. Chestnut Hill, MA: Adamant Media Corporation. (Original work published in 1870).

Kind, St. (1987). *The Scientific Investigation of Crime*. Manchester, UK: Forensic Science Services.

Koffka, K. (1935). *Principles of Gestalt Psychology*. New York, NY: Harcourt Brace.

Kuhn, T. (1996). *The Structure of Scientific Revolutions*. 3rd Ed, Chicago, IL: University of Chicago Press. (Original work published 1962).

Lévi-Strauss, C. (1958). *Anthropologie structurale*. [Structural Anthropology]. Paris, France: Editions Plon.

Manningham-Buller, E. (10. Nov. 2006). *Terrorist threat to UK – MI5 chief's full speech*. The Times. Available at www.timesonline.co.uk/.

Minsky, M. (1985). *The Society of Mind*, New York, NY: Simon & Schuster.

Neisser, U. (1976). *Cognition and Reality*, San Francisco, CA: Freeman.

Nordhy, I (2000). *Dead Reckoning: The Art of Forensic Detection*, Washington DC: CRC Press.

Renfer M. & H. Haas (2008). 'Systematic Analysis in Counterterrorism: Messages on an Islamist Internet-Forum'. *International Journal of Intelligence and Counter Intelligence*. 21:2: 314–336.

Sapir, A. (1999). *Workbook: The LSI Course on Scientific Content Analysis SCAN & Workbook: The LSI Advanced Workshop on Scientific Content Analysis SCAN*. Phoenix, Arizona. Available at www.lsiscan.com.

Schneider, K. & J. Höpfner (2008). *Anzeichen für gefälschte Legitimationspapiere*. [Red Flags with Respect to Counterfeited Identification Documents]. Presentation 6. Jahreskongress zur Geldwäschebekämpfung Ostdeutsche Sparkassenakademie, *Bankerscampus 2008*. Lecturer at the Akademie für Personenstandswesen in Bad Salzschlirf. Available at www.bildungscampus.de/content/de/bankerscampus/veranstaltungen/index.php?content=kurs&kurs=s1821470301_bc.

Tversky, A. & D. Kahneman, (1981). *The framing of decisions and the psychology of choice*. Science, Vol 211 (4481): 453–458.

Walder, H, continued by Hansjakob, Th (2006). *Kriminalistisches Denken*. [Reasoning in Criminalistics]. Kriminalistik Verlag 7th Ed, Heidelberg.

Westenburger, H. (2008). *Namensrecht ausländischer Staaten*. [Legal Definitions of Names in Foreign States]. Presentation 6. Jahreskongress zur Geldwäschebekämpfung Ostdeutsche Sparkassenakademie, Bankerscampus 2008. Lecturer at the Akademie für Personenstandswesen in Bad Salzschlirf. Available at www.bildungscampus.de/content/de/bankerscampus/veranstaltungen/index.php?content=kurs&kurs=s1821470301_bc.

Zahorsky, D. (2008). *The Proper Business Letter Format. About.com Small Business Information*. Retrieved on 28 October 2008 from http://sbinformation.about.com/od/bizlettersamples/a/letterformat.htm.

GIUSEPPE LOMBARDO[*]

Terrorist financing and cash couriers: legal and practical issues related to the implementation of FATF Special Recommendation IX

I. The rationale for measures aimed at countering illegal cross-border transportations of currency

When money can cross borders electronically in a matter of seconds via wire transfers, the idea of criminals or terrorists crossing borders with bundles of cash may seem implausible. But, while it is true that electronic fund transfers may be quicker and easier, they leave a paper trail that can be detected: how safe are these transfers from the perspective of criminal organisations and terrorist groups?

In an interview with an American newspaper, Stuart Levey, Under-Secretary of Treasury for Terrorism and Financial Intelligence, said that intelligence gathered from captured terrorist suspects and other sources indicates 'a trend toward bulk cash smuggling and [the] use of cash couriers'.[1] As the banking and financial systems have become more and more regulated, and charities have been subjected to more scrutiny, terrorist groups have turned to couriers to avoid the anti-money laundering/counter-terrorist financing (AML/CTF) restrictions introduced by many states in response to recommendations of the Financial Action Task Force (FATF). As a result, the cross-border

---

[*] Consulting Counsel, International Monetary Fund. The chapter is based on a presentation delivered on 2 October 2008 at the conference, 'Combating the Financing of Terrorism' (Giessbach II) in Davos, Switzerland. The opinion expressed are solely of the author and do not represent the view of the International Monetary Fund.

1   'Terror funding shifts to cash', USA Today online, 18 June 2006.

transportation of cash money is one of the major methods for terrorists (and money launderers) to move funds from one country to another. Physical transportation of cash money, be it the proceeds of crime or funds intended to be used to finance terrorist activities or organisations, decreases the traceability of the funds – a risk which is associated with the performance of a transaction in a financial market subject to AML/CTF requirements – and, therefore, ensures anonymity.

Recognising that the borders of many countries are vulnerable to illicit transportations of currency (or other bearer negotiable instruments that serve the same purpose) and that there is a high risk that these funds will go undetected, the FATF in October 2004 issued a 'Special Recommendation' to guide states in tackling this phenomenon. In Special Recommendation IX, the FATF has sought to ensure that terrorists and other criminals cannot finance their activities or launder the proceeds of their crimes through the physical cross-border transportation of currency and bearer negotiable instruments. However, the effective implementation of Special Recommendation IX has proved to be challenging.

My contribution examines the legal and practical challenges in four parts. In the first part, by way of introduction to the problem, it presents some cash smuggling techniques and 'red flag' indicators for identifying illegal cash couriers. In the second part, it reviews the requirements of Special Recommendation IX and, in the third, it discusses some of the major legal and practical issues in the implementation of this Special Recommendation. Finally, in the fourth part, it briefly notes some of the key considerations in moving the implementation of Special Recommendation IX forward.

II. Examples of techniques to smuggle currency and 'red flag' indicators for the detection of suspicious behaviour

The al-Qaida operation, which culminated in the attacks of 11 September 2001 (9/11), is an effective example of cash smuggling by terrorists. Although the bulk of the funds had been wired to the United States (US), money (in the form of currency and travellers' cheques) was physically transported several times as the members of the Hamburg cell and the 'muscle hijackers' arrived in the US.[2] These funds were partly used to open new bank accounts and, partly, to replenish accounts already used by preceding operatives.

How other terrorists and criminals smuggle their money will depend on a variety of factors. In general, cash smugglers are likely to favour busy border crossings, where they can easily 'lose themselves' in the volume of travellers and transactions. However, if they are making a land crossing, they may prefer remote border areas, especially those manned by corrupt border-crossing officials or areas where the smuggling network enjoys tribal or clan support. Air travel is more tightly scrutinised but it allows the courier to reach many foreign destinations quickly and with little pre-planning.

In terms of smuggling techniques, criminals and terrorists smuggling currency borrow from the long-standing tradition of goods smuggling. The money belt is a more 'classical' method for smuggling, as is the concealment of currency in shoes, vehicles or other machinery. More 'ingenious' techniques include the concealment of currency in Scuba tanks, stuffed toy animals, mint candies, bicycle tyres and even in felt-tipped pens.

---

2   For further details, see T. Parkman and G. Peeling, *Countering Terrorist Finance – a Training Handbook for Financial Services*, Gower, Farnham (UK) 2007: 45–46; National Commission on Terrorist Attacks upon the United States, *Final Report of the National Commission on Terrorist Attacks upon the United States*, Government Printing Office, Washington (DC) 2004, Chap. VII, available at http://govinfo. library.unt.edu/911/report/index.htm (accessed January 2008).

In many cases, however, law enforcers will not detect the cash-courier *per se* but will suspect some form of smuggling on the basis of unusual circumstances or the behaviour of persons at the border. The following objective circumstances are examples of red flags identified in the case of cash couriers:

–   Passport pages that appear to have been intentionally torn or destroyed, concealing frequency of travel to source countries
–   Passport holders with a history of lost or stolen passports
–   Travellers whose appearance does not conform to their claimed employment or whose alleged purpose for travelling is inconsistent with their alleged employment
–   One-way tickets
–   Routes that include unnecessary stops or are overly long
–   Tickets that were purchased on the same day as the person applied for a passport or the day of departure
–   Tickets that have been exchanged numerous times
–   Tickets that have been purchased from a travel agency or broker with a known or alleged connection with illegal activities
–   Identification documents that were recently issued
–   Documentation that is counterfeit

Along with these objective red flags, the behavioural factors may also indicate cash smuggling. Border-crossing officials may suspect cash smuggling if a traveller, e.g.:

–   Gives vague reasons for his/her trip
–   Answers to questions too slowly or too elaborately (as if rehearsed)
–   Is unable to answer questions about his/her trip arrangements (i.e., how, when and where the ticket was purchased)
–   Appears nervous when delayed by questioning
–   Is vague or evasive when answering questions
–   Makes little or no eye contact with the interviewer, is awkward or moves stiffly

III. FATF Special Recommendation IX

To deal with the physical transportation of cash for terrorist financing and money laundering, the FATF introduced Special Recommendation IX, which states:

> Countries should have measures in place to detect the physical cross-border transportation of currency and bearer negotiable instruments, including a declaration system or other disclosure obligation.
>
> Countries should ensure that their competent authorities have the legal authority to stop or restrain currency or bearer negotiable instruments that are suspected to be related to terrorist financing or money laundering, or that are falsely declared or disclosed.
>
> Countries should ensure that effective, proportionate and dissuasive sanctions are available to deal with persons who make false declaration(s) or disclosure(s). In cases where the currency or bearer negotiable instruments are related to terrorist financing or money laundering, countries should also adopt measures, including legislative ones consistent with Recommendation 3 and Special Recommendation III, which would enable the confiscation of such currency or instruments.[3]

Together with its Interpretative Note, Special Recommendation IX establishes a set of principles on preventing and responding to the physical transportations of proceeds of crime or terrorist finance across borders. It is aimed not only at the detection and repression of illegal cash couriers, but also – and more importantly – at the prevention of illegal transportations of cash. As discussed later, a central component for the effective implementation of Special Recommendation IX, albeit only implicit in the language of the Recommendation, is the use of tactical intelligence and pro-active and strategic analysis for targeting illegal cash couriers.

---

3   After the completion of this paper the FATF agreed to revise the text of the Methodology criteria on Special Recommendation IX to address issues relating to the application of Special Recommendation IX to supranational jurisdictions. The FATF also agreed to developing further best practices on Special Recommendation IX, applicable to both national and supranational approaches, to further elaborate on how information is acquired, obtained and shared.

1. Key concepts and scope

The Interpretative Note to Special Recommendation IX[4] defines its key concepts and, with them, its scope. 'Currency',[5] 'bearer negotiable instruments'[6] and 'physical cross-border transportation'[7] are all given special meanings. The definitions of 'false declaration' and 'false disclosure' are worth special note, for they refer to one of the key obligation embodied in Special Recommendation IX, discussed later on:

> (6) The term false declaration refers to a misrepresentation of the value of currency or bearer negotiable instruments being transported, or a misrepresentation of other relevant data which is asked for in the declaration or otherwise requested by the authorities. This includes failing to make a declaration as required.

4   FATF, *Interpretative Note to Special Recommendation IX: Cash Couriers*, FATF/OECD, 24 October 2004, available at http://www.fatfgafi.org/dataoecd/5/48/34291218.pdf.
5   'Currency' is said to '[refer] to banknotes and coins that are in circulation as a medium of exchange': FATF, n 4, para. 4.
6   These are defined to include, '[...] monetary instruments in bearer form such as: travellers cheques; negotiable instruments (including cheques, promissory notes and money orders) that are either in bearer form, endorsed without restriction, made out to a fictitious payee, or otherwise in such form that title thereto passes upon delivery; incomplete instruments (including cheques, promissory notes and money orders) signed, but with the payee's name omitted': FATF, n 4, para. 3. In a footnote to para. 3, the Note indicates how states adopting the Special Recommendation should respond to discoveries of alternatives stores of value stones. The footnote states, '[...] If a country discovers an unusual cross-border movement of gold, precious metals or precious stones, it should consider notifying, as appropriate, the Customs Service or other competent authorities of the countries from which these items originated and/or to which they are destined, and should cooperate with a view toward establishing the source, destination, and purpose of the movement of such items and toward the taking of appropriate action'.
7   In the context of Special Recommendation IX, 'physical cross-border transportation' encompasses '(1) physical transportation by a natural person, or in that person's accompanying luggage or vehicle; (2) shipment of currency through containerised cargo or (3) the mailing of currency or bearer negotiable instruments by a natural or legal person': FATF, n 4, para. 5.

(7) The term false disclosure refers to a misrepresentation of the value of currency or bearer negotiable instruments being transported, or a misrepresentation of other relevant data which is asked for in the disclosure or otherwise requested by the authorities. This includes failing to make a disclosure as required.[8]

2. Core obligations under Special Recommendations IX

Introduction of a 'declaration' or a 'disclosure' system

According to Special Recommendation IX, countries should have measures in place to detect the physical cross-border transportation of currency and bearer negotiable instruments. To this end, they may opt for either a 'declaration' or a 'disclosure' system. The declaration system is based on the obligation of all persons 'to submit a truthful declaration to the designated competent authorities' when physically transporting currency, or bearer negotiable instruments worth more than a pre-set amount, across borders. The maximum threshold for that pre-set amount is currently EUR/USD 15,000. The disclosure system is based on the obligation of all persons making a physical cross-border transportation of currency or bearer negotiable instruments 'to make a truthful disclosure to the designated competent authorities' upon request. According to the Interpretative Note,

> [...] Countries that implement a disclosure system should ensure that the designated competent authorities can make their inquiries on a targeted basis, based on intelligence or suspicion, or on a random basis.[9]

Mandatory features of declaration/disclosure systems

The FATF specifies minimum requirements for both systems. These are set out in para. 10 of Special Recommendation IX.[10] The following are among the most significant:

---

8   FATF, n 5, para. 6 and 7.
9   FATF, n 4, para. 9(b).
10   FATF, n 4, para. 10.

[…] (b) Upon discovery of a false declaration/disclosure of currency or bearer negotiable instruments or a failure to declare/disclose them, designated competent authorities should have the authority to request and obtain further information from the carrier with regard to the origin of the currency or bearer negotiable instruments and their intended use.

[…] (c) Information obtained through the declaration/disclosure process should be available to the financial intelligence unit (FIU) either through a system whereby the FIU is notified about suspicious cross-border transportation incidents or by making the declaration/disclosure information directly available to the FIU in some other way.

[…] (e) In the following two cases, competent authorities should be able to stop or restrain cash or bearer negotiable instruments for a reasonable time in order to ascertain whether evidence of money laundering or terrorist financing may be found: (i) where there is a suspicion of money laundering or terrorist financing; or (ii) where there is a false declaration or false disclosure.

A key requirement is that the designated authority be able to stop or restrain currency and bearer negotiable instruments that are suspected of being related to terrorist financing or money laundering or when there is a false declaration/disclosure.[11] This is intended to allow the authorities to ascertain whether evidence of money laundering or terrorist financing can be found so that the currency or instruments may be subject to a provisional measure and secured for confiscation. The standard looks somehow 'vague' when, in the above-mentioned instances, it says that competent authorities should be able to stop or restrain cash or bearer negotiable instruments for 'a reasonable time'.

Information from suspects – 'requesting and obtaining',
'recording and retaining'

The Interpretative Note also stipulates how competent authorities should react if they detect irregularities or falsehoods in declarations or disclosures. Para. 10(b) states:

Upon discovering a false declaration/disclosure or a failure to declare/disclose, designated competent authorities should have the authority to request and obtain

---

11   FATF, n 4, para. 10(e).

further information from the carrier with regard to the origin of the currency or bearer negotiable instruments and their intended use.

It also recommends that states record and retain certain information, at the very least, 'the amount of currency or the value of the bearer negotiable instruments declared/disclosed or otherwise detected and the identification data of the bearer(s)'.[12] The obligation applies when a person declares that he/she is carrying more than the prescribed threshold and where authorities discover a false declaration/disclosure or suspect money laundering or terrorist financing.

Sharing information between agencies nationally and internationally

The information obtained through the declaration/disclosure system should be made available to the Financial Intelligence Unit (FIU). Either the FIU may be notified about suspicious cross-border transportation incidents or the declaration/disclosure information will be made directly available to the FIU in some other way. An extension of this requirement is para. 10(d) of the Interpretative Note which requires states to 'ensure that adequate cooperation exists at domestic and international levels among customs immigration and other related authorities'.

The language used to express this requirement could be clearer. The FATF Methodology only refers to the 'information obtained through the processes implemented in Criterion IX.1 of the Methodology'. It seems to imply that only the information contained in the declarations or obtained through the disclosures is covered by the obligation to report to the FIU. However, as a practical matter, the obligation makes more sense if it is interpreted more broadly, to refer to the information gathered through the entire process of implementing Special Recommendation IX. Also, the language of Special Recommendation IX is rather vague when referring to cross-border transportation 'incidents'. If interpreted restrictively, it would refer only to cases where no declaration/disclosure was made or the declaration/disclosure was false. It would not capture cases in which the declaration/disclosure is

---

12   FATF, n 4, para. 10(f).

truthful but some other factors (such as the red flags mentioned above) generate a suspicion of money laundering or terrorist financing.

Applying provisional and repressive measures

Finally, Special Recommendation IX requires that countries take provisional measures in relation to persons who physically transport currency or bearer negotiable instruments across borders in connection with terrorist financing or money laundering. Competent national authorities should also confiscate such smuggled items and apply 'effective, proportionate and dissuasive' sanctions to persons who make a false declaration/disclosure contrary to Special Recommendation IX.

IV. Effectiveness, legal shortcomings and issues in implementation

As I mentioned earlier, Special Recommendation IX is a very complex recommendation. Among the 80 jurisdictions which were assessed by the FATF, the FATF-style regional bodies (FSRBs), the International Monetary Fund (IMF) and the World Bank (WB) since the introduction of Special Recommendation IX, only five were rated as 'compliant'. 36 countries were rated 'non-compliant' and 25 as only 'partially compliant'.

Aside from the situation in which countries had no declaration/disclosures systems in place at all, the most significant legal shortcomings are:

–   The lack of restraining powers related to the cross-border transportations of cash or equivalents
–   The lack of enforcement powers or responsibilities for customs authorities with regard to money laundering or terrorist financing
–   The lack of provisions requiring competent authorities to make information gathered through the implementation of Special Recommendation IX available or accessible to FIUs

– The lack of effective systems for collecting, storing and analysing information

1. The lack of restraining powers

The requirement that competent authorities be able to request and obtain further information from the carrier with regard to the origin of the cash has not been a particular issue. By contrast, the requirement that authorities be able to stop or restrain the currency on the basis of 'suspicions' of money laundering or financing of terrorism so that they can look for evidence of money laundering or terrorist financing has proved problematic, particularly when the person has made a truthful declaration/disclosure. On the one hand, the Special Recommendation requires that competent authorities be able to stop and restrain currency when there are 'suspicions' of money laundering or terrorist financing and not only when they establish a person has failed to declare/disclose or has made a false declaration. On the other hand, in most jurisdictions, a mere suspicion of a crime does not *per se* justify the type of restraining measures referred to in Special Recommendation IX, let alone the adoption of provisional measures, such as seizure or sequestration.

2. The lack of enforcement powers or responsibilities for customs authorities with regard to money laundering and terrorist financing

Another significant legal shortcoming in the implementation of Special Recommendation IX is that customs services are not considered law enforcement authorities in some countries and so do not have enforcement powers or the authority to seize or confiscate currency. When they do have such powers, they can usually only be used for the enforcement of customs-related obligations and not in relation to possible money laundering or terrorist financing.

*3.   The lack of provisions requiring that the Special Recommendation
     IX information be made available or accessible to the FIU*

The requirement that information obtained through the Special Recommendation IX process be available to the FIU has also been implemented unevenly. As noted above, states are supposed to provide a
system for notifying the FIU about suspicious cross-border transportation incidents or for making declaration/disclosure information directly available to the FIU in some other way. Interestingly, some
states oblige their customs services to report suspicious operations or
activities to the FIU. But – strictly speaking – this does not fully cover
'cross-border transportation incidents' when such 'incidents' do not
amount to a suspicious operation or activity.

The difficulties for FIUs in accessing information of a legal or
practical nature couple with the failure of competent authorities to
appreciate the value of this information as a means of building up
intelligence and tracing illegal cash couriers and routes which can be
used for countering money laundering and the financing of terrorism.
Together, these failings form a dangerous *trait d'union* between the
legal and practical shortcomings in the implementation of Special
Recommendation IX.

*4.   Non-existent or weak systems for collecting, storing and
     analysing information*

If countries do have a declaration/disclosure system in place, the most
significant shortcomings arise from the way the Special Recommendation IX information is collected, stored and analysed. This is indicative of a lack of intelligence and risk-based strategies, which is a serious deficiency in the effective implementation of the 'preventive'
component of Special Recommendation IX.

When jurisdictions do have a declaration/disclosure system, in
most cases, the declarations or the records on disclosures are only
stored in hard copy. This makes it virtually impossible to build up
intelligence for detecting suspicious behaviour, identifying cash couriers and routes or even querying past records in real time. For example,

without a computerised system that can process information gathered through the Special Recommendation IX process, it will be very difficult to spot a person who has crossed the border of a given country ten times and declared the currency that he/she was carrying each time.

But even if the information is transformed into an electronic format and loaded into a database, very few countries have risk-based strategies to process this information into AML/CTF intelligence. This is perhaps the most problematic issue related to the effective implementation of Special Recommendation IX: given the volume of cross-border movements, if the information is not utilised as part of a risk and intelligence-based approach to produce pro-active and strategic analysis, it will be of very little help in efforts to counter illegal cash couriers.

The last (though not the least) legal and practical shortcoming of most declaration/disclosure systems is poor cooperation between FIUs and authorities responsible for the implementation of Special Recommendation IX. Typically, these authorities share very little information and intelligence with their colleagues, domestic and international. This then compounds difficulties in acting on information gathered through Special Recommendation IX processes.

V. Moving forward

We end with some brief suggestions on ways to make the implementation of Special Recommendation IX more effective. How can states and international organisations address the shortcomings identified above? What are the core considerations in charting the 'way forward' for Special Recommendation IX?

A necessary (though not sufficient) step is to address the legal gaps which prevent the proper implementation of Special Recommendation IX. Competent national authorities must be able to stop or restrain cash which they suspect of being smuggled as part of a money laundering or terrorist financing operation. Likewise, customs authorities must be able to use their enforcement powers for AML/CTF, as well as for other types of crime. Information gathered through the Special Recommendation IX process – this means all the information, not just the information related to 'incidents' – should be made available to the FIU.

But legal changes will be frustrated if they are not accompanied by the appropriate policy changes. If we want to increase the likelihood that Special Recommendation IX will disrupt terrorist groups and help us prevent and detect illegal cash couriers we must do two things. First, we need to develop an intelligence-based approach to detecting cash couriers and routes. This presupposes the computerisation of the information gathered and its processing according to a risk-based approach. Second, we then need to enhance domestic and international cooperation, the sharing of information between customs authorities and FIUs within and between states. Other changes may be necessary. But until states take these basic steps, it is unlikely that they will discourage terrorists from physically moving their money across borders.

KILIAN STRAUSS[*]

Combating terrorist financing: are transition countries the weak link?

I. Introduction

Terrorist operations are like other operations involving complex logistics in that they depend on financial flows for their realisation. Recognising this, states and international organisations have developed a number of initiatives aimed at removing terrorists' access to funds and financial services. These initiatives encounter a series of problems. It is well known that the funds needed to commit a terrorist act can be relatively insignificant and may remain legal for a long period of time (until an attack is carried out) making their detection extremely difficult. In addition, given the strengthened international effort to combat terrorist financing, terrorists are increasingly looking for jurisdictions where the barriers to detection are high due to insufficient legislation, poor financial intelligence or weak law enforcement.

According to the United States' (US) Country Reports on Terrorism,[1] Afghanistan, Iraq, Lebanon, Pakistan and Sudan are currently among the most important terrorist havens in the world[2] and the

---

*   Kilian Strauss is Senior Programme Officer at the Secretariat of the Organisation for Security and Cooperation in Europe (OSCE) in Vienna. This contribution was written in his private capacity and does not represent or engage the opinion of the OSCE or its participating states.

1   US Department of State Office of the Coordinator for Counter-Terrorism, *Country Reports on Terrorism,* 2007, available at http://www.state.gov/s/ct/rls/crt/2007/index.htm.

2   'Terrorist safe havens are defined [...] as ungoverned, under-governed or ill-governed areas of a country and non-physical areas where terrorists that constitute a threat [...] and are able to organise, plan, raise funds, communicate, recruit, train and operate in relative security because of inadequate governance capacity, JJK

Philippines and Somalia constitute an important threat to international security due to confirmed or presumed terrorist activity. What all of these countries have in common are weak legal, political and economic systems. Among their key weaknesses are fragile financial sectors and limited capacities for financial oversight. These systemic weaknesses place them at an increased risk of being targeted by terrorists, who are searching for alternative channels to transfer their funds in the face of increased international regulation.

As a result, although terrorism has become a global phenomenon over the last few decades and leaves virtually no country untouched, weak states and countries in transition are particularly vulnerable to infiltration by terrorists and terrorist financiers. As terrorists generally look for legal and regulatory loopholes to hide their fund movements, we ask in this chapter whether transition countries are the 'weak link' in international efforts to combat terrorist financing.

II. International instruments on combating terrorist financing

Since the 1970s, the international community has made efforts to prevent and combat the financing of terrorism.

1. Initiatives in the United Nations General Assembly

The United Nations General Assembly (UNGA) took an early lead on counter-terrorism, establishing the Ad Hoc Committee on Internation-

political will or both. Physical safe havens provide security for terrorist leaders, allowing them to plan acts of terrorism around the world': US Department of State Office of the Coordinator for Counter-Terrorism n 1, 184. See also Liana Sun Wyler, *CRS Report for Congress: Weak and Failing States: Evolving Security Threats and US Policy*, Congressional Research Service, updated 28 August 2008, available at http://www.fas.org/sgp/crs/row/RL34253.pdf.

al Terrorism in 1972.[3] This was followed by the adoption of the Declaration on International Terrorism in 1994[4] and the creation of a new committee to draft international conventions on terrorism in 1996.[5] The Committee drafted the Convention on the Suppression of the Financing of Terrorism,[6] which was adopted by the UNGA on 9 December 1999 and entered into force in April 2002. As of September 2008, it had 160 parties. Work has also been undertaken to develop a comprehensive convention on international terrorism, though it is not yet complete.

An important feature of the 1999 UN Convention on Combating Terrorist Financing is its definition of the 'financing of terrorism'. It is defined as an offence by which a person,

> [...] by any means, directly or indirectly, unlawfully and wilfully, provides or collects funds with the intention that they should be used or in the knowledge that they will be used in full or in part, in order to carry out a [terrorist act].[7]

2. Initiatives of the United Nations Security Council

The UN Security Council (UNSC) also has a long history of dealing with counter-terrorism, its most prominent actions of recent years being the targeted sanctions regime of the late 1990s and early 21st Century. In Resolutions 1267 (1999) and 1333 (2000), it decided that UN members would seize the assets of named terrorists and terrorist organisations and, following the terrorist attacks on the US in 2001, it adopted Resolution 1373 (2001), which established the Counter-Terrorism Committee to report on counter-terrorism efforts around the world, amongst other things.[8]

---

3   Established on 18 December 1972 by UNGA Resolution 3034 (XXVII).

4   Measures to Eliminate International Terrorism A/RES/49/60, adopted at the 84th UNGA Plenary Meeting on 9 December 1994.

5   Established by UNGA Resolution 51/210 of 17 December 1996.

6   Full text available at http://untreaty.un.org/english/Terrorism/Conv12.pdf.

7   Art. 2.

8   Key UNSC Resolutions on terrorist financing include: UNSC Resolution 1267 (1999) of 15 October 1999 on the Freezing of the Funds and Other Financial Resources of the Taliban; UNSC Resolution 1333 (2000) of 19 December 2000

3. *Initiatives of the Financial Action Task Force*

Also in 2001, the Financial Action Task Force (FATF) adopted eight Special Recommendations on Terrorist Financing, later adding a ninth. The FATF issued Guidance Notes[9] to clarify certain aspects of the Special Recommendations and asked its members to assess their own success in implementing the measures by 1 May 2002.[10] Though the Recommendations are technically only addressed at FAFT member states, the same invitation was later issued to all countries of the world. Moreover, UNSC Resolution 1617 (2005), has made all FATF Recommendations virtually binding for UN member states under Chapter VII of the UN Charter, whether they are members of the FATF or not.

on the Freezing of the Funds and Other Resources of Usama Bin Laden and the Al-Qaida Organisation; UNSC Resolution 1363 (2001) of 30 July 2001 on the Establishment of a Mechanism to Monitor the Implementation of Measures Imposed by UNSC Resolutions 1267 (1999) and 1333 (2000); UNSC Resolution 1373 (2001) of 28 September 2001 on Threats to International Peace and Security Caused by Terrorist Acts and Mandating the Formation of the Counter-Terrorism Committee; UNSC Resolution 1377 (2001) of 12 November 2001 Calling Upon States to Implement Fully Resolution 1373 (2001); UNSC Resolution 1390 (2002) of 16 January 2002 Effectively Merging the Freezing Measures of Resolutions 1267 (1999) and 1333 (2000); UNSC Resolution 1452 (2002) of 20 December 2002 Allowing for Some Exclusions to the Freezing Requirements of Resolutions 1267 (1999) and 1333 (2000) to Cover Expenses for Basic Expenses, including Food, Rent, Legal Services and Charges for Routine Maintenance of Assets and for Extraordinary Expenses after Approval of the '1267 Committee'; UNSC Resolutions 1455 (2003) of 17 January 2003 on Measures to Improve the Implementation of the Freezing Measures of Resolutions 1267 (1999), 1333 (2000) and 1390 (2002); UNSC Resolution 1617 (2005) of 29 July 2005. A more complete list is available at http://www.un.org/terrorism/securitycouncil.shtml.

9   Available at www.fatf-gafi.org.

10   The FATF's 9 Special Recommendations on combating terrorist financing cover: 1) ratification and implementation of UN instruments, 2) criminalisation of the financing of terrorism and associated money laundering, 3) the freezing and confiscating terrorist assets, 4) suspicious transactions reporting, 5) international cooperation, 6) alternative remittance systems, 7) wire transfers, 8) non-profit organizations (NPOs) and 9) cash couriers.

4. Initiatives in regional organisations

A number of initiatives on terrorist financing have been adopted at the regional level. For example, the Council of Europe (CoE),[11] the European Union (EU)[12] and the Organisation for Security and Cooperation in Europe (OSCE) have all taken steps to improve the detection of terrorist funds in Europe. Since 2001, the OSCE has been working very closely with the Global Programme against Money Laundering (GPML) of the United Nations Office for Drugs and Crime (UNODC) to directly implement the Programme of Action endorsed at the Bishkek International Conference, 'Enhancing Security and Stability in Central Asia: Strengthening Comprehensive Efforts to Counter Terrorism'.

Moreover, in July 2002, OSCE participating states decided by Permanent Council Decision No. 487[13] to complete the FATF's self-assessment questionnaire. In 2004, the Permanent Council adopted Decision No. 617[14] on Further Measures to Suppress Terrorist Financing. As a result, the OSCE, in cooperation with UNODC, the North Atlantic Treaty Organisation (NATO) and the US State Department, organised a high level conference on combating terrorist financing in November 2005, which included a session on the role played by charities in the financing of terrorism.

11 Council of Europe Conventions, available at http://conventions.coe.int/Treaty/Commun/ListeTraites.asp?CM=8&CL=ENG.
12 Framework Decision of 13 June 2002 on Combating Terrorism (2002/475/JHA); Commission Communication on the Prevention of and Fight against Terrorist Financing of October 2004 (20.10.2004 COM(2004) 700); Commission Communication of November 2005 (COM (2005) 620); The Third Money Laundering Directive of September 2005 (Directive 2005/60/EC); Regulation on the Disclosure of Cash or Equivalent in excess of € 10,000 Entering or Leaving EU of 26 October 2005, Regulation on Information on the Payer Accompanying Transfers of Funds (EC) No. 1781/2006 Implementing FATF Recommendation VII, all available at http://eur-lex.europa.eu/.
13 OSCE Permanent Council Decision 487 of 11 July 2002 on Financial Action Task Force (FATF) Self Assessments on Terrorist Financing, www.osce.org/documents/pc/2002/07/938_en.pdf.
14 OSCE Permanent Council Decision 617 of 1 July 2004 on Further Measures to Suppress Terrorist Financing, www.osce.org/documents/pc/2004/07/3300_en.pdf.

5. National initiatives with international scope

Some national legislation may have a wide reaching international impact. An example is the US PATRIOT Act which strengthens, *inter alia*, the oversight of the banking sector.[15]

III. Key policy issues on terrorist financing

Since 2001, the international community has been extremely active in its efforts to adopt, amend and improve international standards aimed at combating terrorist financing. Despite the flurry of activity, however, the number of actual convictions for the financing of terrorism has so far been limited and the overall sums involved remain relatively small[16] when compared to most cases of money laundering. Some general challenges are worth noting here.

1. Diversified origins of terrorist financing

It is well known that terrorists derive funds from a variety of sources, legitimate and illegitimate. Terrorists may receive donations, e.g., through charitable organisations, NGOs, religious institutions or religious schools as well as from wealthy individuals. A number of terrorist groups derive revenues from legitimate businesses. Some groups

---

15   The Uniting and Strengthening America by Providing Appropriate Tools Required to Intercept and Obstruct Terrorism Act of 24 October 2001 (Public Law 107-56), available at http://epic.org/privacy/terrorism/hr3162.html.

16   Estimates of the cost of the 11 September 2001 attacks range from USD 250,000 to 500,000. The Madrid bombings of 2004 are thought to have cost as little as USD 15,000, while the 2005 attacks on London may have cost only some USD 2,000. Other simpler attacks may only involve a few bags, some train tickets and a handful of phone calls: Mark Rice-Oxley, 'Why terror financing is so tough to track down', *Christian Science Monitor*, 8 March 2006, available at http://www.csmonitor.com/2006/0308/p04s01-woeu.html.

may even enjoy the financial support of sympathetic governments. Income from these 'legitimate' sources is the most difficult to detect.

Terrorists also increasingly resort to 'profitable' criminal activities (e.g., trafficking of human beings, drugs or weapons) to generate funds. As a result, they are also using money laundering techniques to recycle the proceeds of their illegal activities. This shows clearly that terrorist groups have adapted to the new conditions and are using flexible, decentralised and innovative methods to generate fresh funds.

2. *Alternative transfer mechanisms*

Another particularly vulnerable part of the international financial architecture are alternative remittance systems, commonly known as *hawala* or *hundi*. Used mainly in South Asia and the Middle East, *hawala* or *hundi* are cash-based money transfer systems. Although many *hawala* operations work within legal regulations and only a small proportion of remittances are terrorist funds, they generate virtually no written or electronic records[17] and are largely unregulated, even in developed countries, such as the US. Therefore, they are a particular thorn in the side of the international financial and law enforcement community.

Furthermore, if alternative remittance systems are unavailable or inappropriate, terrorists may smuggle items of value, such as precious metals, gems or cash, as a means of moving their funds.

3. *Complex and international cases*

The relatively small number of criminal convictions can be put down to the fact that terrorist financing may be highly complex and may span several countries and continents. As a result, it may be that no

---

17 The estimated global turnover of funds channeled through *hawala* is between USD 100 billion and 300 billion, according to UN Department of Economic and Social Affairs: Leonides Buencamino and Sergei Gorbunov, *Informal Money Transfer Systems: Opportunities and Challenges for Development Finance*, DESA Discussion Paper Series, November 2002, available at www.un.org/esa/desa/papers/2002/esa02dp26.pdf.

single country or institution holds all the information needed to obtain a conviction or take action against terrorist assets. Poor coordination between the financial sector, financial intelligence units and law enforcement agencies nationally and international is an additional hurdle.

4.   *Free movement of people and capital*

Tracking terrorist funds becomes even more complicated when the increasingly free movement of people and capital across the world is taken into account. Controlling the flows of terrorist funds is especially difficult in common areas, such as have been established between members of the EU and the Commonwealth of Independent States and the parties to the North American Free Trade Agreement. The tendency to deregulate, while freeing up economic potential and creating wealth, makes it more difficult to track terrorist funds, in particular when legitimate businesses are involved in supporting terrorist networks.

5.   *'Following the money trail' versus freezing funds*

Even when national law enforcement authorities identify and trace suspected terrorist financial flows, they often prefer to 'follow the money trail' in order to learn more about the larger terrorist network than to arrest or freeze the assets of an individual terrorist. According to Bill Tupman of Exeter University, 'intelligence services face a difficult choice of whether to confiscate the money and bring a criminal case or follow the cash and see where it ends up'.[18]

---

18   See above, Rice-Oxley, n 16.

6. Successful legal challenges to counter-terrorist financing regimes

Conflicts between international counter-terrorist financing (CTF) measures and fundamental rights have led to successful legal challenges to asset freezing laws in national and regional courts.

7. International standards inconsistently implemented

The most important policy issue is the inconsistent implementation of international standards. Since terrorist funds often cross borders, laws and regulations means little if some countries are unable or unwilling to implement them. The international fight against terrorism can therefore only be as effective as the weakest link in the chain and often this means transition countries.

IV. Transition countries: the problem and the threat

The main aim of international efforts to combat global criminal phenomena, such as terrorist financing, money laundering and organised crime, is the development of effective cooperative frameworks between countries and international organisations. As in all systems composed of different elements and players, the chain of defence is only as strong as its weakest link. Weak states and countries in transition are one weak link in international defence mechanisms against terrorist financing, as highlighted by the above-mentioned US list of terrorist havens and a recent statement by the FATF about countries and territories, such as Iran, Uzbekistan and Turkmenistan.[19]

In this chapter, countries in transition are defined as countries transforming their economy and institutions, usually from a centrally planned, 'socialist' economy to a market-based economy. These

---

19   FATF Statement of 25 February 2009, available at http://www.oecd.org/dataoecd/18/28/42242615.pdf.

countries include the former Soviet Republics in Central, South-Eastern and Eastern Europe, as well as China, Mongolia and Vietnam. In a wider sense, the term also encompasses colonies and dependencies in the process of becoming independent states. The transition process implies major changes to a state's structure, above all to its legal and economic system, governmental institutions and overall political framework. As far as the issue of terrorist financing is concerned, changes in the financial system, especially the banking sector, financial supervision and financial investigation, are particularly important.

V. The susceptibility of transition countries to abuse by terrorist financiers

If terrorism was mostly a local or regional phenomenon in the 1960s and 1970s, recent developments have shown that it is now a global scourge. This is particularly true for the financial flows underpinning international terrorism.

Following the terrorist attacks on the US in 2001 and other high profile terrorist acts over the last decade, developed states adopted increasingly stringent legal and regulatory frameworks, which aim to make it more difficult for terrorists to channel funds through the international financial system. In developed economies, increased supervision and growing vigilance have improved detection of terrorist funds. Terrorist networks, such as al-Qaida, are now frequently working in and through transition countries, exploiting their weak regulatory capacities and vulnerability to corruption. Inadequate bank supervision, weak anti-money laundering (AML) legislation, ineffective law enforcement and a culture of 'no-questions-asked' bank secrecy,[20] combine with informal networks of corrupt officials and

---

20 Maurice Greenberg, William Wechsler and Lee Wolosky, *Terrorist Financing, Report of an Independent Task Force*, Council on Foreign Relations, Washington (DC), 2002: 9.

criminal organisations to help terrorists – and terrorist financiers – avoid detection.

1. Weak legal frameworks and poor regulation of the financial sector

Often, the main point of weakness in a transition country is its legal framework. As a result of the transition and more general deficiencies in the rule of law, these states may lack comprehensive laws and law enforcement capacities. This includes insufficient regulation in the financial sector and related sectors, such as insurance, real estate and casinos. Adding to the problems, the financial sector may itself be underdeveloped, with weak mechanisms for identifying, reporting and detecting terrorist money or other laundered funds.

2. Poor implementation of existing laws

But even if the appropriate laws exist, their implementation is often inconsistent. Government agencies responsible for implementation may lack sufficient staff or funding or existing staff may lack experience in combating terrorism and terrorist financing. Terrorists and other criminals also benefit from weak coordination among government agencies. And, if cases cross borders, international cooperation is often very slow, if it is not refused altogether.

3. Corruption undermines law enforcement

Substantial corruption in almost all transition countries also undermines the effective implementation of laws and efforts to address terrorism, organised crime and money laundering. Corrupt officials, especially in the areas of border security and law enforcement, con-

stitute a major threat to national and international security and may
seriously impede the fight against terrorism and terrorist financing.[21]

VI. Policy options and possible countermeasures

Combating terrorist financing is a highly complex activity, bedevilled
by numerous challenges. Given the weaknesses mentioned above, the
sheer number of terrorist cells and the increasing decentralisation of
terrorist networks, it is unlikely that the problem of terrorist financing
can ever be fully solved. But small steps are important in undermining
the ability of terrorists to carry out attacks and operations. This means
that the issue *can* be addressed but it will require many joint and long-
term efforts. For governments of transition states, the most important
tasks in improving their legislative and regulatory frameworks with
regard to terrorist financing are as follows:

*1. Reinforce regulatory and legislative efforts to
    introduce international standards*

The starting point is for transition states to acknowledge the international standards on counter-terrorism. Within the OSCE area, most
participating states have ratified the key international counter-terrorism treaties and conventions, including the 1999 Convention on the
Suppression of the Financing of Terrorism. The most important measure to be taken is, therefore, to adjust national legislation to the
standards of the Convention. This includes, above all, the criminalisation of terrorist financing and the introduction of laws which allow
for the freezing and confiscation of terrorist assets, as required by the

---

21   Kamala Sarup, 'Corruption Increases Terrorism', *Scoop*, 18 July 2005, available
     at http://www.scoop.co.nz/stories/HL0507/S00246.htm.

UNSC, regional bodies and national governments and as recommended by the FATF.[22]

2. *Strengthen the supervision of the financial sector*

Supervision of the financial sector, including underground banking businesses and alternative remittance systems, must be strengthened. This should include bringing banking supervision and AML laws, regulations and institutions completely up to international standards.

3. *Regulate charities*

Particular focus must be placed on the regulation of charities, which are sometimes abused for funding illegal activities, including those of terrorists. They should be encouraged (even required) to operate transparently, especially in areas of conflict.

4. *Regulate alternative stores of value*

States should adopt or strengthen regulations on the trade in gems, precious metals and other stores of value, which can be used to transfer terrorist wealth.

5. *Implement legislation*

The implementation of legislation is crucial, not just its adoption. In many countries, the adoption of new legislation is cited as proof that international standards are being met. However, the adoption of a law makes little difference if it is not implemented, i.e., enforced.

22   See above, n 10.

6. Improve customer identification

Financial institutions should seek to prevent terrorist organisations from accessing their services by stringently applying customer identification requirements using the latest 'know your customer' (KYC) techniques and enhanced due diligence. When verifying customer identities, financial institutions must consult the latest lists of known or suspected terrorists, as published, *inter alia*, by the UNSC's Taliban and al-Qaida Sanctions Committee.[23] Customer information must be maintained and regularly updated. Banks should also be encouraged to build specific CTF components into their compliance and due diligence processes and to recognise typical terrorist financing patterns and trends. Suspicious individuals and activities must be reported to the relevant authorities, while keeping a balance between the number of reports and their relevance. Banks should also respond promptly to governmental enquiries about suspicious transactions and individuals.

7. Limit contacts with unregulated financial operators

Banks should seek to restrict their business relationships with unregulated financial operators, such as informal remittance businesses. Often, however, banks enter in direct competition with these outfits, which are usually cheaper – a particular attraction to many migrant workers. In order to compete better with alternative remittance systems, such as *hawalas*, banks should consider lowering the fees for international bank transfers, amongst other things.

8. Conduct capacity building and training

An important component in strengthening the fight against terrorist financing is capacity building and training, especially for staff of financial intelligence units (FIUs), law enforcement agencies, prosecu-

---

23   Available at http://www.un.org/sc/committees/1267.

tors and judges, to allow them to acquire the skills to successfully investigate and prosecute financial crimes.

9 *Improve interagency cooperation*

Better interagency cooperation and coordination within countries is crucial, with the relationships between the financial sector, FIUs, law enforcement, prosecution and the judiciary being particularly important.

10. *Improve international cooperation*

Countries must strengthen international cooperation in combating terrorist financing by improving information exchange and developing and implementing mutual legal assistance and extradition regimes. As speed is of the essence in financial intelligence, cooperation between FIUs should be optimised and the time needed to block terrorist assets shortened.

VII. Operating beyond the state – virtual havens

For all these reasons, transition countries constitute a huge challenge to international efforts to combat the financing of terrorism, as well as money laundering and organised crime. At the same time, the weakest states are not always the most attractive locations for international terrorists. More complex terrorist operations may require access to global financial services, modern telecommunications and functioning transportation systems that do not always exist in transition countries.[24] Terrorists also make increasing use of modern technology, including the Internet, to raise, launder or transfer funds. These oper-

24   See above, n 8.

ations do not require physical safe havens. Such 'virtual' havens are highly mobile and difficult to follow and control as they are not based in any particular state. Combating terrorist financing over the Internet constitutes a particular challenge that many law enforcement agencies are only now starting to tackle.[25]

VIII. Conclusion

It is often said that, in the global war on terror, the man with the money is as dangerous as the man with the gun. What may be added is that the 'man with the money' is increasingly active transnationally, including in jurisdictions with weak financial and regulatory capacities. In the face of more stringent controls and CTF measures in developed economies, terrorists look for alternative channels for their funds. Many have become highly skilled at playing on the weaknesses of countries in transition. With legislative loopholes, high levels of corruption and ineffective law enforcement mechanisms, transition states are properly described as the 'weak link' in the international CTF regime. This combines with poor cooperation at the international level to create a danger to the countries through which funds are channelled and the rest of the international community.

Hence, international efforts to combat the flow of terrorist funds into transition states are crucial to combating terrorism globally. As emerges from the recommendations made above, among the most important steps for transition states are the adoption of international standards, such as the FATF's Special Recommendations and the improvement of cooperation between government agencies and with other states. This is not simply a matter of adopting the 'right laws'. In addition, we must address the lack of capacity and political will in a number of transition states. Here, international organisations, such as the OSCE or UNODC, have an important role to play by applying

---

25   See Wyler, above n 2 and Marco Gercke, 'Cyberterrorism: How terrorists use the Internet', in this volume.

political pressure and providing legislative and technical assistance. In so doing, however, they will have to strike a balance between combating terrorism and protecting civil liberties.

Beyond this, the international community should aim to reduce the pool of potential financial contributors and sources of income. This includes (but is not limited to) taking action with regard to charities and alternative remittance services. Increasingly, terrorists work with and through organised crime networks in generating funds for their activities and subsequently laundering them. For law enforcers this is both an opportunity and threat: if terrorist attacks generally require relatively small amounts that are difficult to detect, the growing use of money laundering represents a chance for financial intelligence and law enforcement to identify funds early and so to 'nip' terrorist activities 'in the bud'.

CTF is a vital tool in the global fight against terrorism, not just an additional measure. While we should be aware that the problem of terrorist financing cannot be solved easily, it should be addressed with as much determination and creativity as possible. Our goals as an international community should be to make financial transfers as difficult as possible for terrorists, recognising that our efforts will most likely only have an impact in the long-term. Finally, given the ingenuity of terrorists and their supporters, especially when resorting to new tools, such as the Internet, we will need both creative thinking and courage in taking new approaches to combat the threat of international terrorism.

MARCO GERCKE*

Cyberterrorism: how terrorists use the Internet

I. Introduction

Over the past decades, more and more societies have turned into information societies, accessing the great opportunities made possible by the evolution of a Worldwide Web. This trend is generally characterised by an emerging use of information technology to access and share information.[1] The availability of online services has influenced the means of communication for many Internet users. Other examples of popular Internet services are online banking and telephone communications using 'voice over internet' protocol (VoIP).[2] But it is not

* Dr. Marco Gercke teaches criminal law with a focus on cybercrime at the University of Cologne, Germany. Thanks go to Denise Berger and Radha Ivory of the Basel Institute on Governance for their valuable feedback on this chapter. For more information, please contact: gercke@cybercrime.de.

1 For more information on the information society, see Masuda, *The Information Society as Post-Industrial Society*; Dutta/De Meyer/Jain/Richter, *The Information Society in an Enlarged Europe*; Maldoom/Marsden/Sidak/Singer, *Broadband in Europe: How Brussels can wire the Information Society*; Salzburg Center for International Legal Studies, *Legal Issues in the Global Information Society*; Hornby/Clarke, *Challenge and Change in the Information Society.*

2 Regarding the new opportunities, see, e.g.: *Communication from the Commission to the Council, the European Parliament, the European Economic and Social Committee and the Committee of the Regions*, 3, available at http://ec. europa.eu/information_society/eeurope/i2010/docs/communications/new_chall_ en_adopted.pdf. Regarding the extent of the integration of Information Communication Technologies (ICTs) into the daily lives and the related threats, see Goodman, 'The Civil Aviation Analogy – International Cooperation to Protect Civil Aviation Against Cyber Crime and Terrorism' in Sofaer/Goodman, *The Transnational Dimension of Cyber Crime and Terrorism*, 2001: 69, available at http://media.hoover.org/documents/0817999825_69.pdf.

only the communication sector that has shifted services to the Internet: information technology and Internet services are today used to control and manage many functions in buildings, transportation systems, waterways and energy grids.[3] Both the new means of communication and the use of information technology to control critical infrastructure have influenced the ability of terrorist organisations to use the Internet for their purposes.

II. Internet-related activities of terrorist organisations

Back in the 1990s, discussions about the use of the Internet by terrorist organisations focused on network-based attacks against critical infrastructure, such as transportation systems and energy supplies (cyberterrorism) and the use of information technology in armed conflicts (cyberwarfare).[4] However, at the time, very few such incidents had been reported. Apart from states' general interest in keeping successful attacks confidential, one of the main reasons for the lack of reports could be the low levels of interconnection compared to the current situation. At least, if we believe the figures, falling trees posed a greater threat to energy supplies in the past than successful hacking attacks.[5]

After the attacks on the United States of 11 September 2001 (9/11), the use of Internet Communication Technologies (ICTs) by

---

3   Bohn/Coroama/Langheinrich/Mattern/Rohs, 'Living in a World of Smart Everyday Objects – Social, Economic & Ethical Implications' in *Journal of Human and Ecological Risk Assessment*, Vol. 10, 2004: 763 et seq., available at http://www.vs.inf.ethz.ch/res/papers/hera.pdf.

4   Gercke, 'Cyberterrorism, How Terrorists Use the Internet' in *Computer und Recht*, 2007: 62 et seq.

5   See Report of the National Security Telecommunications Advisory Committee – Information Assurance Task Force, *Electric Power Risk Assessment*, available at http://www.aci.net/kalliste/electric.htm.

terrorists was discussed intensively.[6] Reports[7] revealed that the offenders had used the Internet during the preparation of the attack.[8] The group that plotted 9/11 did not carry out an Internet-based attack but used the Internet as a communication tool.[9] Within this context, investigators discovered the various ways in which terrorists use the Internet,[10] among them, communication, recruitment and the collection of information about potential targets. Discussions of cyberterrorism

---

6   See Lewis, *The Internet and Terrorism*, available at http://www.csis.org/media/csis/pubs/050401_internetandterrorism.pdf; Lewis, *Cyberterrorism and* Cybersecurity, available at http://www.csis.org/media/csis/pubs/020106_cyberterror_cybersecurity.pdf; Gercke, n 4; Sieber/Brunst, *Cyberterrorism – The Use of the Internet for Terrorist Purposes*, Council of Europe Publication, 2007; Denning, 'Activism, Hacktivism, and Cyberterrorism: the Internet as a Tool for Influencing Foreign Policy' in Arquilla/Ronfeldt, *Networks & Netwars: The Future of Terror, Crime, and Militancy*, 239 et seq.,2002, RAND corporation, Embar-Seddon, 'Cyberterrorism, Are We Under Siege?', *American Behavioral Scientist*, Vol. 45: 1033 et seq.; US Department of State, 'Pattern of Global Terrorism, 2000' in Prados, *America Confronts Terrorism*, 2002: 111 et seq.; Lake, *6 Nightmares*, 2000: 33 et seq.; Gordon, *Cyberterrorism*, available at http://www.symantec.com/avcenter/reference/cyberterrorism.pdf; US-National Research Council, *Information Technology for Counterterrorism: Immediate Actions and Future Possibilities*, 2003:, 11 et seq.; OSCE/ODIHR, *Comments on legislative treatment of 'cyberterror' in domestic law of individual states*, 2007, available at www.legislationline.org/upload/lawreviews/93/60/7b15d8093cbebb505ecc3b4ef976.pdf.

7   See Rötzer in *Telepolis News,* 4 November 2001, available at http://www.heise.de/tp/r4/artikel/9/9717/1.html.

8   The text of the final message was reported to be: 'The semester begins in three more weeks. We've obtained 19 confirmations for studies in the faculty of law, the faculty of urban planning, the faculty of fine arts, and the faculty of engineering'. The names of the faculties were apparently the code for different targets. For more detail, see Weinmann, 'How Modern Terrorism Uses the Internet' in *The Journal of International Security Affairs*, Spring 2005, No. 8; Thomas, *Al Qaeda and the Internet: The danger of 'cyberplanning'*, 2003, available at http://findarticles.com/p/articles/mi_m0IBR/is_1_33/ai_99233031/pg_6; Zeller, 'On the Open Internet, a Web of Dark Alleys' in *The New York Times*, 20 December 2004, available at http://www.nytimes.com/2004/12/20/technology/20covert.html?pagewanted=print&position=;.

9   *CNN News*, 04 August 2004, available at http://www.cnn.com/2004/US/08/03/terror.threat/index.html.

10   For an overview, see Sieber/Brunst, n 6; Gercke, n 4.

shifted accordingly. The new focus had a positive effect on research related to cyberterrorism in that it highlighted areas of terrorist activities that had not been known hitherto. The importance of a comprehensive approach notwithstanding, the threat of Internet-related attacks against critical infrastructure should remain within view. The vulnerability of, and the growing reliance on,[11] information technology means that the risk of such attacks should be considered in the development of strategies to prevent and respond to cyberterrorism.

III. The challenges of scientifically analysing the threat of cyberterrorism

In recent years, the fight against terrorism has become a major undertaking around the world. A comparison of approaches reveals many similarities between the national strategies.[12] The international community has recognised that international terrorism is a global threat and asked for global solutions.[13] It is not yet certain that this global approach has been successful nor to what extent different legal systems and different cultures require different interventions.

An evaluation of this issue is difficult. To begin with, there is very little data that could be used for scientific analysis apart from reports about major incidents. The same difficulties arise in assessing the threat posed by the potential exploitation of the Internet by terrorist organisations. This information is very often classified and therefore only available to the intelligence sector.[14] In addition, the

---

11   Sofaer/Goodman, 'Cybercrime and Security – The Transnational Dimension' in
      Sofaer/Goodman, n 2, available at http://media.hoover.org/documents/0817999
      825_1.pdf (last visited: May 2008).
12   Regarding different international approaches as well as national solutions, see
      Sieber in Sieber/Brunst, n 6.
13   One example of such an approach is the amendment of the EU Framework De-
      cision on combating terrorism, COM(2007) 650.
14   Regarding attacks via the Internet: Arquilla/Ronfeldt, *The Future of Terror,
      Crime and Militancy*, 2001: 12; Vatis, *Cyber Attacks During the War on Terror-*

definition of 'terrorism' is widely debated. Although there is a great degree of consensus within the international community that a fight against terrorism is necessary, agreement on what the term 'terrorism' covers has not yet been achieved.[15] Definitions are therefore either developed at the national level or by regional organisations, such as the European Union (EU).

Further, even if a common definition of the term is developed, there needs to be further agreement about which acts in the Internet should be considered 'related to terrorism'. For example, the Congressional Research Service (CRS) reported to the United States' (US) Congress that the fact that one terrorist booked a flight to the US via the Internet is proof enough that terrorists use the Internet in preparation of their attacks.[16] The argumentation seems vague: it is not apparent why the electronic booking of a flight or the transmission of e-mails should become terrorist-related activities just because they are carried out by terrorists. It is necessary to precisely define acts that are considered to be terrorist-related. This is especially important for anti-terrorism strategies that criminalise those activities.

ism, 2001: 14 et seq.; Clark, *Computer Security Officials Discount Chances of 'Digital Pearl Harbor'*, 2003, available at http://www.crime-research.org/news/2003/06/Mess0402.html; United States Institute for Peace (USIP) Report, *Cyberterrorism, How Real is the Threat*, 2004: 2; Lewis, *Assessing the Risks of Cyber Terrorism, Cyber War and Other Cyber Threats*, Center for Strategic and International Studies, December 2002, available at http://www.csis.org/media/csis/pubs/021101_risks_of_cyberterror.pdf; Wilson in *Computer Attack and Cyber Terrorism – Vulnerabilities and Policy Issues for Congress*, Congressional Research Service Report, 2003.

15 See, e.g., Record, *Bounding the Global War on Terrorism*, 2003, available at http://strategicstudiesinstitute.army.mil/pdffiles/PUB207.pdf.

16 Wilson, n 14: 4.

IV. An overview of the use of the Internet by terrorist organisations

1. Propaganda

Phenomenon

In 1998, only 12 of the 30 foreign terrorist organisations listed by the US State Department maintained websites to inform the public about their activities.[17] In 2004, the United States Institute of Peace reported that nearly all terrorist organisations maintained websites – among them Hamas, Hizbollah, PKK and al-Qaida.[18] Terrorists have also started to use video communities (such as YouTube) to distribute video messages and propaganda.[19]

The use of websites and other forums signals a more professional public relations focus by subversive groups.[20] Websites and other media are used to disseminate propaganda,[21] to describe and publish justifications of terrorist activities[22] and to recruit[23] new, as well as contact existing, members and donors.[24] Websites have been used

17 ADL, *Terrorism Update 1998*, available at http://www.adl.org/terror/focus/16_focus_a.asp.

18 Weinmann, n 8: 3. Regarding the use of the Internet for propaganda purposes, see also: Crilley, 'Information Warfare: New Battlefields – Terrorists, Propaganda and the Internet' in *Aslib Proceedings*, Vol. 53, No. 7, 2001: 253.

19 Regarding the use of YouTube by terrorist organisations, see *Heise Online News*, 11 October 2006, available at http://www.heise.de/newsticker/meldung/79311; Staud in *Sueddeutsche Zeitung*, 5 October 2006.

20 Zanini/Edwards, 'The Networking of Terror in the Information Age' in *Networks and Netwars: The Future of Terror, Crime, and Militancy*, 2001: 42.

21 US Homeland Security Advisory Council, *Report of the Future of Terrorism*, 2007: 4.

22 Regarding the justification, see Brandon, *Virtual Caliphate: Islamic Extremists and the Internet*, 2008, available at http://www.socialcohesion.co.uk/pdf/VirtualCaliphateExecutiveSummary.pdf.

23 Brachman, 'High-Tech Terror: Al-Qaeda's Use of New Technology' in *The Fletcher Forum of World Affairs*, Vol. 30, No. 2, 2006: 149 et seq.

24 See Conway, 'Terrorist Use of the Internet and Fighting Back' in *Information and Security*, 2006: 16.

recently to distribute videos of executions.[25] There are a number of factors that support this development:

– The Internet enables terrorist organisations to reach up to 1.5 billion users worldwide.[26] Although just a small portion of the users will be interested in terrorist content, the potential number of people that can access the information provided on terrorists' websites remains high

– Compared to other media, the Internet is a rather cheap mass communication instrument. Setting up and updating a website requires neither large investments nor specialist knowledge. With the help of easy-to-use software programmes, nearly everybody can establish a website and change the content[27]

– Various legislative efforts notwithstanding, the Internet remains a rather unregulated environment. It is possible to set up websites without having to identify oneself and go through a verification process.[28] This is another difference to other instruments of mass communication

– Supervising the published content is difficult, due to the large number of providers offering services on the Internet. Even if a suspicious website is identified and the provider agrees to remove it, the person may set up a new website or maintain 'mirrors' containing copies of this very website

– The development of the Worldwide Web and its graphical interface have made it easier to update content

– The switch from Web 1.0 to Web 2.0 increased the number of Internet services that are based on user-generated content and created new means of distributing messages. Terrorist organisa-

---

25 Videos showing the execution of US citizens Berg and Pearl were made available on websites. See Weinmann, n 8: 5.

26 According to *Internet World Stats*, published by the International Telecommunications Union (ITU), available at http://www.internetworldstats.com/stats.htm. itu.int/ITU-D/, there were more than 1.58 billion people using the Internet by the end of 2008.

27 A number of Internet Services are even available for free. This is especially relevant for ad-financed services.

28 This is especially the case with regard to services that are offered free of charge.

tions are reportedly exploiting well-known portals for user-generated content, such as YouTube[29]

These developments show that terrorist organisations have increased their capacities with regard to public relations and communications. Today, terrorist organisations use their websites to publicise their aims and achievements and to solicit donations. Increasingly, they also use the Internet as a means of transmitting messages to the media and the public. Video messages, which previously would have been sent on tape to television stations, are now often made available on websites.[30] This trend is attributable to at least three factors. First, provided the organisation has used anonymous means of communication,[31] a posting on a website can be more difficult to trace than a tape delivered by messenger. Second, the ability to broadcast via the Internet means that terrorist organisations do not depend solely on media outlets to distribute their messages. Third, as postings on websites are generally available to any user, law enforcers are much less able to control the dissemination of terrorist messages through co-operation with the media sector.

Response

Potential responses to the emerging use of the Internet to disseminate terrorist propaganda are technical and legal. Both approaches face significant challenges.

The fact that terrorist organisations can easily set up webpages could be addressed by implementing registration obligations and mandatory verification procedures to ensure that the operators of such websites can be identified. Apart from the possibility of circumventing such measures by using illegally obtained identities,[32] such approaches

29   See, in this context, *Heise Online News*, n 19; Staud, n 19.
30   So Weinmann, n 8: 5.
31   Regarding the challenges related to anonymous communication, see Gercke, 'Challenges in the Fight against Cybercrime' in *Multimedia und Recht*, 2008: 294.
32   Regarding the consequence of ID-Theft for investigations, see Gercke, *Internet-Related Identity Theft*, 2007, available at http://www.coe.int/t/e/legal_affairs/legal_cooperation/combating_economic_crime/3_Technical_cooperation/CYBER/567%20port%20id-d-identity%20theft%20paper%2022%20nov%2007.pdf.

would require intensive administration from the industry or the state. The extra cost of implementing those measures would be passed on to users, eliminating those services that are offered free of charge and disadvantaging e-commerce businesses that depend on low overheads. The fact that around 250 million people use Microsoft's free e-mail service, Hotmail, shows the great popularity of those services.[33] It is therefore uncertain that this approach would find global support. The success of such a tactic would also depend on the harmonisation of the relevant obligations to prevent safe havens.[34]

Another approach would aim to criminalise the publication of information related to terrorist organisations. A number of countries already criminalise the publication of illegal content such as hate speech[35] or propaganda.[36] The challenge in implementing this approach

---

33   Regarding the number of users of free-or-charge e-mail services, see Graham, 'E-mail Carriers Deliver Gifts of Ninety Features to Lure, Keep Users' in *USA Today*, 16 April 2008, available at http://www.usatoday.com/tech/products/2008 -04-15-google-gmail-webmail_N.htm. The article mentions that the four biggest webmail providers have several hundred million users: Microsoft (256 million), Yahoo (254 million), Google (91 million) and AOL (48 million). For an overview about e-mail statistics, see also: Brownlow, *E-Mail and Web Statistics*, April 2008, available at http://www.email-marketing-reports.com/metrics/email-statistics.htm.

34   This issue was addressed by a number of international organisations. The UN General Assembly Resolution 55/63 points out: 'States should ensure that their laws and practice eliminate safe havens for those who criminally misuse information technologies'. The full text of the Resolution is available at http:// www.unodc.org/pdf/crime/a_res_55/res5563e.pdf. The G8 10 Point Action plan highlights: 'There must be no safe havens for those who abuse information technologies'.

35   In this context, see e.g., the Additional Protocol to the Council of Europe Convention on Cybercrime, concerning the criminalisation of acts of a racist and xenophobic nature committed through computer systems, ETS No. 189, available at www.conventions.coe.int.

36   An example is Sec. 86 German Penal Code (Dissemination of Means of Propaganda of Unconstitutional Organisations):
'(1) Whoever domestically disseminates or produces, stocks, imports or exports or makes publicly accessible through data storage media for dissemination domestically or abroad, means of propaganda:

is to harmonise national legal standards, some of which strongly protect the freedom on speech, whilst avoiding a ban on legitimate reports about terrorist activities. The drafting process for the Council of Europe's Convention on Cybercrime highlights the challenges that such a course of action would face. In 2001, the Convention on Cybercrime[37] and the First Additional Protocol to the Convention were opened for signature. The reason for the development of an additional protocol was the inability of the negotiating countries to agree on mandatory criminalisation of illegal content in any of these cases.[38] To enable those countries that

1. of a party which has been declared to be unconstitutional by the Federal Constitutional Court or a party or organisation, as to which it has been determined, no longer subject to appeal, that it is a substitute organisation of such a party;
2. of an organisation, which has been banned, no longer subject to appeal, because it is directed against the constitutional order or against the idea of international understanding, or as to which it has been determined, no longer subject to appeal, that it is a substitute organisation of such a banned organisation;
3. of a government, organisation or institution outside of the territorial area of application of this law which is active in pursuing the objectives of one of the parties or organisations indicated in numbers 1 and 2; or
4. means of propaganda, the contents of which are intended to further the aims of a former National Socialist organisation shall be punished with imprisonment for not more than three years or a fine'.

37   Council of Europe Convention on Cybercrime (CETS No. 185), available at conventions.coe.int. For more details about the offences covered by the Convention, see Sofaer, 'Toward an International Convention on Cyber' in Seymour/ Goodman, *The Transnational Dimension of Cyber Crime and Terror*, 2001, 225, available at http://media.hoover.org/documents/0817999825_221.pdf; Gercke, 'The Slow Awake of a Global Approach Against Cybercrime' in Computer Law Review International, 2006: 140 et seq.; Gercke, 'National, Regional and International Approaches in the Fight Against Cybercrime' in *Computer Law Review International*, 2008: 7 et seq.; Aldesco, 'The Demise of Anonymity: A Constitutional Challenge to the Convention on Cybercrime', *Entertainment Law Review*, 2002: No. 1, available at http://elr.lls.edu/issues/v23-issue1/aldesco.pdf; Jones, *The Council of Europe Convention on Cybercrime'*, *Themes and Critiques*, 2005, available at http://www.cistp.gatech.edu/snsp/cybersecurity/materials/callieCOE convention.pdf; Broadhurst, 'Development in the Global Law Enforcement of Cyber-Crime' in *Policing: An, International Journal of Police Strategies and Management*, 29(2), 2006: 408 et seq.

38   With the exception of child pornography for which we can refer to Art. 9 of the Convention on Cybercrime.

strongly protect the freedom of expression to sign the Convention, offences like hate speech and propaganda were shifted to the Additional Protocol.[39] This may be indicative of similar problems in regulating terrorist 'speech' in the Internet.

2. Collection of information

Phenomenon

Much information about possible targets is available in the Internet. For example,[40] architects involved in the construction of public buildings publish building plans on their websites. High resolution satellite pictures, previously available only to a handful of military institutions, can today be accessed for free via various Internet services.[41] Furthermore, websites on how to build bombs – even virtual training camps – provide instructions on the use of weapons using an e-learning approach.[42] In addition, sensitive or confidential information which is not adequately protected from search robots can be found via search engines.[43]

There are, moreover, signs that terrorists are exploiting this information:

---

39   Regarding the motivation to develop the First Additional Protocol, see Explanatory Report to the Convention on Cybercrime, No. 35.

40   Regarding the related challenges, see Gercke, 'The Challenge of Fighting Cybercrime' in *Multimedia und Recht*, 2008: 292.

41   Levine in *Global Security*, 27 June 2006, available at http://www.globalsecurity. org/org/news/2006/060627-google-earth.htm. Regarding the discovery of a secret submarine on a satellite picture provided by a free of charge Internet Service, see 'Google Earth: Neues chinesisches Kampf-Uboot entdeckt' in *Der Standard Online*, 11 July 2007, available at http://www.derstandard.at/?url/?id= 2952935.

42   For further reference, see Gercke, n 40: 292.

43   For more information regarding the search for secret information with the help of search engines, see Long/Skoudis/van Eijkelenborg, *Google Hacking for Penetration Testers*, Syngress Publishing, 2005.

- In 2003, the US Department of Defence was informed about a training manual linked to al-Qaida providing information on how to use public sources to find details about potential targets[44]
- In 2006, the New York Times reported that basic information related to the construction of nuclear weapons was published on a Government website that provided evidence about Iraqi attempts to develop nuclear weapons.[45] A similar incident was reported in Australia, detailed information about potential targets for terrorist attacks having been made available on government websites[46]
- In 2005, the press in Germany reported that investigators had found downloaded manuals on how to build explosives on the computer of two suspects who then attempted to attack the German public transportation system with homemade bombs[47]

Response

The discussion about a response to the phenomenon, currently focuses on criminalisation of the publication of instructions on how to commit terrorist attacks. One example is the 2008 draft amendment of the EU Framework Decision on Combating Terrorism.[48] In the introduction, the EU makes much of the fact that the existing legal framework criminalises aiding, abetting and inciting terrorism but does not criminalise the dissemination of terrorist expertise through the Internet.[49] With the amendment, the EU purports to take measures to close

---

44   'Using public sources openly and without resorting to illegal means, it is possible to gather at least eighty per cent of information about the enemy.' For further information, see Conway, n 24: 17.

45   See Broad, 'US Analysts Had Flagged Atomic Data on Web Site' in *New York Times*, 4 November 2006.

46   Conway, n 24: 18.

47   See 'BKA findet Anleitung zum Sprengsatzbau', *Sueddeutsche Zeitung Online*, 7 March 2007, available at http://www.sueddeutsche.de/deutschland/artikel/766/104662/print.html.

48   EU Framework Decision on Combating Terrorism, COM (2007) 650.

49   Art. 4 of the Framework Decision on combating terrorism states that inciting, aiding or abetting terrorist offences should be made punishable by the Member States. Art. 2 of the same instrument requires member states to hold those directing a terrorist group or participating in its activities criminally liable. How-

the gap and bring the legislation closer to the Council of Europe Convention on the Prevention of Terrorism throughout the EU. Based on Art. 3(1)(c)[50] of the Framework, the member states are obliged, e.g., to criminalise the publication of instructions on how to use explosives if the publisher knows that this information is intended to be used for terrorist-related purposes.

It is quite likely that the provision will have limited applicability to most online guides to weaponry given the need for evidence of an intention to use the information for terrorist-related purposes. As most of the weapons and explosives can be used to commit 'regular' crimes as well as terrorist-related offences (i.e., they have a dual use), the mere publication of that type of information does not prove that the publisher knew the way it would be used. Therefore, the context of the publication (e.g., the fact that it appears on a website operated by a terrorist organisation) will need to be considered.

3. Use of information technology in the preparation of 'real world' attacks

Phenomenon

There are different ways terrorists can use of information technology in preparing their attacks. Sending out e-mails or using forums to leave messages are examples that will be discussed below. Here we consider more direct ways of preparing for attacks online as it has been reported that terrorists are using online games as part of their preparation for attacks.[51] Various online games simulate the 'real world' by allowing

---

ever, these provisions do not explicitly cover the dissemination of terrorist propaganda and terrorist expertise, in particular through the Internet.

50 '[T]raining for terrorism' means to provide instruction in the making or use of explosives, firearms or other weapons or noxious or hazardous substances, or in other specific methods or techniques, for the purpose of committing one of the acts listed in Art. 1(1), knowing that the skills provided are intended to be used for this purpose.

51 See *US Commission on Security and Cooperation in Europe Briefing*, 15 May 2008, available at http://csce.gov/index.cfm?FuseAction=ContentRecords.View Transcript&ContentRecord_id=426&ContentType=H,B&ContentRecordType=B

the user to manipulate characters (avatars) in a virtual world. Theoretically, those online games could be used to simulate attacks, though it is not yet certain to what extent they have been.[52]

Response

Developing a legal response to the threat that computer and online games will be used in preparing attacks poses unique challenges. Crucially, a significant number of popular games deal with war strategies[53] or the systematic killing of others.[54] Most of the acts 'committed' in such games would be associated with criminal charges if the user committed them in the 'real world'. Criminalisation of the use of online games that might hint at activities being part of the preparation for a real attack is therefore likely to have a major impact on the computer and online gaming industry.

4.   Publication of training material

Phenomenon

The Internet can be used to spread training material such as instructions on how to use weapons and select targets. Such material is available on a large-scale online.[55] In 2008, secret service agencies

&CFID=18849146&CFTOKEN=53; O'Brian, 'Virtual Terrorists' in *The Australian*, 31 July 2007, available at http://www.theaustralian.news.com.au/story/ 0.25197,22161037-28737,00.html.

52   Regarding other terrorism-related activities in online games, see Chen/Thoms, 'Cyber Extremism in Web 2.0 – An Exploratory Study of International Jihadist Groups' in *Intelligence and Security Informatics*, 2008: 98 et seq.

53   One example is the strategy game 'Command and Conquer'. Regarding the number of users and the discussion about the need for a stricter ban on violent computer games, see Brunn/Dreier/Dreyer et al., *Das deutsche Jugendschutzsystem in Bereich der Video- und Computerspiele*, Hans-Bredow-Institut, 2007.

54   One example is the computer game 'Counter-Strike'. Regarding the use of such games by a suspect that killed several people in a German school, see Brinkelbäumer, 'Moerderischer Abgang' in *Der Spiegel*, Vol. 18, 2002: 80.

55   Brunst in Sieber/Brunst, n 6; *US Homeland Security Advisory Council, Report of the Future of Terrorism Task Force*, January 2008: 5, available at www.dhs.gov/

discovered an Internet server that allowed for the exchange of training material as well as communications.[56] Different websites were reported to be operated by terrorist organisations to coordinate activities.[57]

Response

The issue of providing training material is also addressed by the 2008 amendment of the EU Framework Decision on combating terrorism. Based on Art. 3(1)(c) of the Framework, the member states are, among other things, obliged to criminalise the 'training for terrorism'.[58] This covers acts of providing instructions with regard to the making or use of explosives, firearms or other weapons or noxious or hazardous substances or other specific methods or techniques designed for terrorist purposes.

5. Communication

Phenomenon

The use of information technology by terrorist organisations is not limited to running websites and conducting research in databases. In the context of the investigations after 9/11, it was reported that the terrorists used e-mail communication in co-ordinating their attacks.[59] The press reported that detailed instructions about the targets and the number of attackers had been exchanged via e-mail.[60]

xlibrary/assets/hsac-future-terrorism-010107.pdf; Stenersen, 'The Internet: A Virtual Training Camp?' in *Terrorism and Political Violence*, 2008: 215 et seq.

56   Musharbash, 'Bin Ladens Intranet' in *Der Spiegel*, Vol. 39, 2008: 127.

57   Weinmann, n 8: 10.

58   'Training for terrorism' means to provide instruction in the making or use of explosives, firearms or other weapons or noxious or hazardous substances, or in other specific methods or techniques, for the purpose of committing one of the acts listed in Art. 1(1), knowing that the skills provided are intended to be used for this purpose.

59   *The 9/11 Commission Report, Final Report of the National Commission on Terrorist Attacks Upon the United States*, 2004: 249, available at http://www.9-11commission.gov.

60   See n 8.

Response

Since terrorists are able to exchange encoded messages, institutions concerned with the prevention of terrorist attacks have very little hope of intercepting terrorist communications.[61] It is technically possible to intercept e-mail communication.[62] However, terrorists can use technical protection measures, such as encryption technology, to restrict access to the content of e-mail communications.[63]

Itself an older technology,[64] encryption has been transformed by the development and popularisation of computer technologies. Now, numerous software products enable home users to protect files against unauthorised access.[65] Although it is generally possible to break encryption (e.g., by a so-called 'brute force attack'),[66] this process can be extremely time-consuming. Depending on the encryption technique and key size, it may take decades.[67] For example, if an offender uses encryption software with a 20-bit encryption, the size of the key space is around one million. Using a new computer which processes one million operations per second, the encryption could be broken in less than one second. Using a 56-bit encryption, a single computer would take up to 2,285 years to break the encryption. To break a 128-bit

---

61 See Gercke, n 40: 297.
62 Branch, 'Lawful Interception of the Internet' in *Centre for Advanced Internet Architectures (CAIA) Technical Report 030606A*, 2003, available at http://caia.swin.edu.au/.
63 Regarding the impact on computer forensic and criminal investigations, see Huebner/Bem/Bem, *Computer Forensics – Past, Present And Future*, No. 6, available at http://www.scm.uws.edu.au/compsci/computerforensics/Publications/Computer_Forensics_Past_Present_Future.pdf.
64 Singh, *The Code Book: The Science of Secrecy from Ancient Egypt to Quantum Cryptography*, 2006; D'Agapeyen, *Codes and Ciphers – A History of Cryptography*, 2006; *An Overview of the History of Cryptology*', available at http://www.cse-cst.gc.ca/documents/about-cse/museum.pdf.
65 Examples include the software Pretty Good Privacy (available at www.pgp.com) or True Crypt (available at www.truecrypt.org).
66 'Brute force attack' is one method of defeating a cryptographic scheme by trying a large number of possible codes.
67 Schneier, *Applied Cryptography*, 185 and Bellare/Rogaway, *Introduction to Modern Cryptography*, 2005: 36, both available at http://www.cs.ucdavis.edu/~rogaway/classes/227/spring05/book/main.pdf.

encryption, one billion computer systems operating solely on the encryption would need thousands of billions of years.[68] Notably, the latest version of the popular encryption software, PGP, permits 1,024-bit encryption.

However, before messages can be decoded, authorities must intercept them and the interception of messages sent via VoIP communication technology constitutes another major challenge. The interception of this kind of communication can be far more difficult than the interception of phone calls.[69] In addition, terrorists can protect the communication through encryption.[70]

The legal response to these challenges is currently the subject of intensive debate.[71] Solutions under consideration include restrictions on the power of encryption software,[72] the establishment of a key-escrow system[73] and the creation of production orders.[74]

---

68 Equivalent to 10790283070806000000 years.

69 Phil Zimmermann, the developer of the encryption software PGP, developed a plug-in for VoIP software that can be used to install added encryption, in addition to the encryption provided by the operator of the communication services. The difficulty arising from the use of additional encryption methods is the fact that, even if the law enforcement agencies intercept the communications between two suspects, the additional encryption will hinder the analysis. For more information on the software, see Markoff, 'Voice Encryption May Draw US Scrutiny' in *New York Times*, 22 May 2006, available at http://www.nytimes.com/2006/05/22/ technology/22privacy.html?ex=1305950400&en=ee5ceb136748c9a1&ei=5088. Regarding the related challenges for law enforcement agencies, see Simon/Slay, *Voice over IP: Forensic Computing Implications*, 2006, available at http://scissec. scis.ecu.edu.au/wordpress/conference_proceedings/2006/forensics/Simon%20Slay %20-%20Voice%20over%20IP-%20Forensic%20Computing %20Implications.pdf.

70 Regarding the encryption technology used by Skype (www.skype.com), see Berson, *Skype Security Evaluation*, 2005, available at http://www.skype.com/ security/files/2005-031%20security%20evaluation.pdf.; for further information, see also n 69.

71 Gercke, n 40: 297.

72 The limitation of the import of such powerful software is even characterised as 'misguided and harsh to the privacy rights of all citizens'. See, e.g.: *The Walsh Report – Review of Policy Relating to Encryption Technologies*, Chap. 1.1.16, available at http://www.efa.org.au/Issues/Crypto/Walsh/walsh.htm.

73 Lewis, *Encryption Again*, available at http://www.csis.org/media/csis/pubs/011001 _encryption_again.pdf.

6. *Financing*

Phenomenon

Tracing terrorists' financial transactions became a key task in the fight against terrorism after the 9/11 attacks.[75] Most terrorist organisations depend on financial resources they receive from third parties and there are two ways in which Internet services can be used for these transactions.

First, terrorist organisations can make use of electronic payment systems to enable online donations.[76] They can use websites to publish information on how to donate money, e.g., by directing supporters to the bank account, which should be used for the transaction. The organisation Hizb al-Tahrir uses such an approach: it publishes its bank account information for potential donors online.[77] Other terrorist organisations have implemented systems for receiving online credit card donations, the IRA being one of the first to accept donations via credit card.[78] Both procedures carry the risk that the published information will be discovered and used to trace financial transactions. It is therefore likely that anonymous electronic payment systems will become more popular.

---

74   An example of this approach is Section 49 of the UK Regulation on Investigatory Powers Act. For general information on the Act, see Brown/Gladman, *The Regulation of Investigatory Powers Bill – Technically Inept: Ineffective against Criminals while Undermining the Privacy, Safety and Security of Honest Citizens and Businesses*, available at http://www.fipr.org/rip/RIPcountermeasures.htm; Ward, 'Campaigners hit by decryption law', BBC News, 20 November 2007, available at http://newsvote.bbc.co.uk/mpapps/pagetools/print/news.bbc.co.uk/2/hi/technology/7102180.stm.

75   The Commission analysing the 9/11 attacks calculated that the costs for the attack could have been between USD 400,000 and 500,000. For further information on the report, see n 59. Taking into account the duration of the preparation and the number of people involved, the cost per person would have been relatively small. Regarding the related challenges, see as well Weiss in *Terrorist Financing: The 9/11 Commission Recommendations*, Congressional Research Service Report for Congress, 4.

76   See, in this context, Crilley, n 18: 253.

77   Weinmann, n 8: 7.

78   See Conway, n 24: 4.

Second, to avoid discovery, terrorist organisations may involve, or purport to act through, less suspicious individuals or organisations, such as charities. Another (Internet-specific) ruse is the operation of fake web-shops. It is relatively simple to set up a shop in the Internet. Such businesses can be operated worldwide and they make it quite difficult to prove that financial transactions are donations rather than regular purchases. It would be necessary to investigate every transaction – which could be impossible if the online shop is operated in a different jurisdiction or employs an anonymous payment system.[79] These are great advantages for terrorist organisations.

Response

After the 9/11 attacks, a number of legal frameworks were developed to combat terrorist financing.[80] These contain effective instruments with regard to financial institutions. However, they do not provide investigative authorities with the tools necessary to trace users of Internet services and address the Internet-related aspects of terrorist financing. Not all countries have implemented procedural instruments that enable competent authorities to effectively investigate Internet-related offences. At present, the Council of Europe's Convention on Cybercrime is the only complex international legal instrument to address cybercrime.[81] Art. 16–21 contain a set of procedural instruments that are necessary for cybercrime investigations, such as the interception of content data and the preservation of traffic data.

Although it was developed under the auspices of the Council of Europe, the Convention on Cybercrime was designed as a global, rather than a regional solution.[82] Indeed, to ensure that the resulting solutions were not just regionally applicable within the Council's of Europe member states, a number of non-members[83] were invited to

---

79 Regarding virtual currencies, see Woda, 'Money Laundering Techniques with Electronic Payment Systems' in *Information and Security* 2006: 39.

80 For an overview, see Strauss, 'Combating Terrorist Financing – Are Transition Countries the Weak Link?' (published in this volume).

81 Regarding the Convention on Cybercrime, see Gercke, n 37; Aldesco, n 37; Jones, n 37; Broadhurst, n 37.

82 Explanatory Report to the Convention on Cybercrime, No. 304.

83 United States, Canada, South Africa and Japan.

participate in the negotiations and to sign the Convention. Ratification by the US[84] – a non-member with a common law system – is evidence of the success of these legal standards, which were designed without a specific legal system in mind.[85]

7. *Attacks against critical infrastructure*

Phenomenon

As mentioned, critical information infrastructure could become a target for terrorists since the growing reliance on information technology makes critical infrastructure more vulnerable to attack.[86] Interconnected systems that are linked by computer and communication networks are especially attractive targets.[87] A network-based attack would do more than cause a single system to fail. Rather, it would bring down an entire network of systems and their related infrastructures. Even short interruptions to services would cause huge

84   See McCullagh/Broach, 'Senate ratifies controversial cybercrime treaty', *CNET News*, 4 August 2006, available at http://www.news.com/Senate-ratifies-controversial-cybercrime-treaty/2100-7348_3-6102354.html.

85   Some aspects of the approach to develop a framework that is applicable not only in civil but also in common law countries, were criticised. One example is Art. 15 Convention on Cybercrime. Regarding the criticism, see Taylor, *The Council of Europe Cybercrime Convention – A civil liberties perspective*, available at http://crime-research.org/library/CoE_Cybercrime.html; 'Cybercrime: Lizenz zum Schnüffeln' in *Financial Times Germany*, 31 August 2001; *Statement of the Chaos Computer Club*, available at www.ccc.de. Due to the different approaches of ensuring the protection of the suspect in the various criminal law systems, the drafters of the Convention decided not to include specific regulations in the text of the Convention but to commit the member states to ensure that fundamental national and international standards of safeguards apply. See *Explanatory Report to the Convention on Cybercrime*, No. 145, available at http://conventions.coe.int/Treaty/EN/Reports/Html/185.htm.

86   Sofaer/Goodman, n 11.

87   Lewis, n 14.

financial damage to e-commerce businesses, government service providers and armed forces.[88]

Preventing and investigating attacks against critical infrastructure is also difficult.[89] While carrying out the attack, offenders can hide their identities by using anonymous means of communication and encryption technology.[90] Unlike a physical attack, the offenders do not need to be present at the place where the attack's effects manifest.[91] Moreover, as noted above, investigating such attacks requires special procedural instruments, investigation technology and trained personnel.[92]

Critical infrastructure is widely recognised as a potential target for terrorist attacks as it is – by definition – vital for the stability of the state.[93] Infrastructure is considered to be frail, if its incapacity or destruction would have a debilitating impact on the defence or economic security of a state.[94] This concerns, in particular, electrical power systems, telecommunication systems, gas and oil storage and transportation, banking and finance, transportation, water supply systems and emergency services. The civil disturbance caused by Hurricane Katrina highlights the dependence of developed societies on those services.[95]

The vulnerability of critical infrastructure to network-based attacks becomes apparent when we look at the air transport industry:

---

88 Shimeall/Williams/Dunlevy, 'Countering Cyber War' in *NATO Review*, Winter 2001/2002, available at http://www.cert.org/archive/pdf/counter_cyberwar.pdf.

89 Gercke, n 37.

90 CERT Research 2006 Annual Report', 7 et seq., available at http://www.cert.org/archive/pdf/cert_rsch_annual_rpt_2006.pdf.

91 Gercke, n 40: 293.

92 *Law Enforcement Tools and Technologies for Investigating Cyber Attacks*, DAP Analysis Report 2004, available at http://www.ists.dartmouth.edu/projects/archives/ISTSGapAnalysis2004.pdf.

93 Brunst in Sieber/Brunst, n 6.

94 *US Executive Order 13010 on Critical Infrastructure Protection*. Federal Register, 17 July 1996. Vol. 61, No. 138.

95 *Critical Infrastructure Protection: Sector Plans and Sector Councils Continue to Evolve*, US Government Accountability Office Communication, July 2007, available at http://www.gao.gov/new.items/d07706r.pdf.

- The check-in systems of most airports in the world are already based on interconnected computer systems.[96] In 2004, the Sasser computer worm[97] infected millions of computers around the world, among them, computer systems of major airlines, which led to cancellations of flights[98]
- A significant number of tickets today are purchased and issued online. One common technique for attacking web-based services is the Denial-of-Service (DoS) attack.[99] It was used to great effect in 2000 to render services from well-known companies, such as CNN, Ebay and Amazon,[100] unavailable, in some cases for days at a time.[101] Airlines, such as Lufthansa, have also been affected by DoS attacks on their websites[102]
- Airport control systems are another potential target for Internet-related attacks. For example, during a hacking attack against

96 Kelemen, 'Latest Information Technology Development in the Airline Industry' in *Periodicapolytechnica Ser. Transp. Eng.*, Vol. 31, No. 1–2, 2002: 45–52, available at http://www.pp.bme.hu/tr/2003_1/pdf/tr2003_1_03.pdf; Merten/Teufel, 'Technological Innovations in the Passenger Process of the Airline Industry: A Hypotheses Generating Explorative Study' in O'Conner/Hoepken/Gretzel, *Information and Communication Technologies in Tourism*, 2008.

97 *Sasser B Worm, Symantec Quick Reference Guide*, 2004, available at http://eval.symantec.com/mktginfo/enterprise/other_resources/sasser_quick_reference_guide_05-2004.en-us.pdf.

98 Schperberg, 'Cybercrime: Incident Response and Digital Forensics', 2005 and 'The Sasser Event: History and Implications', *Trend Micro*, June 2004, available at http://us.trendmicro.com/imperia/md/content/us/pdf/threats/securitylibrary/wp02 sasserevent040812us.pdf.

99 Paxson, *An Analysis of Using Reflectors for Distributed Denial-of-Service Attacks*, available at http://www.icir.org/vern/papers/reflectors.CCR.01/reflectors.html; Schuba/Krsul/Kuhn/Spafford/Sundaram/Zamboni, *Analysis of a Denial of Service Attack on TCP*, 1997; Houle/Weaver, *Trends in Denial of Service Attack Technology*, 2001, available at http://www.cert.org/archive/pdf/DoS_trends.pdf.

100 Yurcik, *Information Warfare Survivability: Is the Best Defense a Good Offence?*, available at http://www.projects.ncassr.org/hackback/ethics00.pdf.

101 Power, '2000 CSI/FBI Computer Crime and Security Survey' in *Computer Security Journal*, Vol. 16, No. 2, 2000: 33 et seq.; Lemos, 'Web Attacks: FBI Launches Probe in *ZDNet News*, 9 February 2000, available at http://news.zdnet.com/2100-9595_22-501926.html.

102 Gercke, 'The Decision of the District Court of Frankfurt in the Lufthansa Denial of Service Case', *Multimedia und Recht*, 2005: 868 et seq.

Worcester Airport in the US in 1997,[103] the offender disabled phone services to the airport tower and shut down the control system managing the runway lights[104]

Response

Most countries already criminalise network-based attacks against computer systems. But other challenges remain: how to minimise the damage potentially caused by such attacks and how to cope with the difficulties in international investigations? The Council of Europe Convention on Cybercrime[105] contains a set of provisions that seek to improve the ability of states to cooperate globally with regard to computer-facilitated offences. However, investigating such offences is still difficult due to variations in the legal standards used by different states.

V. Conclusion

Terrorist organisations are using the Internet in various ways. The confidentiality of much information about terrorism means that we lack the data to precisely determine the extent to which terrorists are using the internet, how they are doing so and what threat this poses.

---

103 *Improving our Ability to Fight Cybercrime: Oversight of the National Infrastructure Protection Center*, Hearing before the Subcommittee on Technology, Terrorism, and Government Information of the Committee on the Judiciary United States Senate One Hundred Seventh Congress First Session, July 2001, Serial No. J–107–22, available at http://cipp.gmu.edu/archive/215_S107 FightCyberCrimeNICPhearings.pdf.

104 US Government Accountability Office, *Critical Infrastructure Protection, Multiple Efforts to Secure Control Systems Are Under Way, but Challenges Remain (Communication)*, September 2007, GAO-07-1036, available at http://www.gao. gov/new.items/d071036.pdf; Berinato, *Cybersecurity – The Truth About Cyberterrorism*, March 2002, available at http://www.cio.com/article/print/30933.

105 Regarding the Convention on Cybercrime, see Gercke, n 37; Aldesco, n 37; Jones, n 37; Broadhurst, n 37.

However, it is clear from this overview, that the Internet offers considerable advantages to terrorist organisations as a means of gathering financial and moral support, preparing attacks and targeting important social institutions. It is equally apparent that states face significant challenges in preventing and investigating terrorist activities in the Internet. It would seem that they have yet to address the unique challenges of investigating cybercrime in general and the shift of terrorist operations from the 'real world' to the 'virtual world', in particular. It is to be hoped that they will engage more intensively with this topic in future debates about measures to combat terrorism.

Stephen Baker*

The misuse of offshore structures so as to assist the financing of terrorism

I. Introduction

The word 'offshore' is not a term of art but means different things to different people. On the broadest definition, almost every country in the world is 'offshore' to another jurisdiction. In this sense, the UK is correctly described as offshore to Kenya. In this chapter, however, the term 'offshore' is used in a narrower sense to describe financial centres which were traditionally regarded as such. Common characteristics of such centres include low or nil rates of taxation, a perception of a higher degree of client confidentiality and a proportionately higher level of financial services as a component of the economy. These offshore centres include Switzerland, Liechtenstein, Luxembourg, the Cayman Islands, the Crown Dependent Territories, the British West Indies, as well as the emerging centres such as Dubai, Qatar, Singapore and Delaware in the United States (US).

There are, of course, many ways in which these offshore centres and their services can be used honestly and honourably. However, all forms of financial services are vulnerable to misuse and the traditional offshore services are no exception. Offshore structures will often be used in economic crime. The purpose of this chapter is to give practical guidance as to the ways in which offshore services can be abused

*   Stephen Baker is an English barrister and Jersey advocate. He is a partner of BakerPlatt, a law firm based in Jersey, Channel Islands, specialising in litigation, financial crime and regulatory matters. Stephen has regularly acted for foreign governments in asset recovery actions and is frequently instructed by Jersey's Attorney General in complex fraud and money laundering cases, particularly those with an international and political dimension.

by those with a mind to do so, including the financiers of terrorism. As we shall see, the key to minimising the risk of misuse does not lie in the distinction between 'onshore' and 'offshore' jurisdictions but in ensuring that all jurisdictions have robust regulations, legislation and prosecuting authorities. In each respect, offshore centres often have better records than their larger neighbours. For this reason, it is a mistake to treat all offshore centres – or, indeed, all onshore jurisdictions – the same. To do so may even increase the vulnerability of the financial system as a whole to crime.

II. The use and abuse of trusts

Two common offshore services are the establishment and administration of trusts. A trust is a legal relationship recognised in common law jurisdictions by which one person legally owns property but holds it for the benefit of another. In a classic trust, the first person (the settlor) gives legal ownership of property to a second person (the trustee) on the condition that the trustee manages the property for the benefit of a third person (the beneficiary). Often the settlor appoints a protector to oversee the trustee's actions. Although the protector's powers may vary, he can typically remove and appoint trustees and intervene in fundamental decisions in relation to the operation of the trust.

Discretionary trusts are the most common form of trust used by criminals. Their popularity is due to their flexibility. The trustee of a discretionary trust typically has considerable freedom in dealing with the trust property. In so doing, he is under a fiduciary obligation to act in the best interests of the beneficiary. However, this may be difficult to achieve in practice if (as is often the case) the settlor retains a powerful influence over the trustee's use of the trust funds.

1. Legitimate uses of trusts

The trust concept grew out of the practice in medieval England whereby nobles fighting in the Crusades would entrust their possessions to relatives or friends (the forerunners to modern trustees) to provide for other family members in the event that they were killed in battle. The basic concepts still hold true today. There is a multiplicity of ways in which trusts are used legitimately. Estate or succession planning, tax mitigation and wealth preservation are the simplest examples of legitimate purposes, though trusts are also created to fund charitable goals.

2. Why criminals are attracted to trusts and other offshore structures

Trusts and other offshore financial services are attractive to criminals because they make it more difficult to determine the true identity of the person who owns and effectively controls assets. In this sense, offshore financial services are vulnerable to abuse by all types of criminals, not just terrorist financiers. A chief executive or chief financial officer may be diverting company profits to himself; an inside trader may be tired of watching clients make money and may look to make a 'killing' of his own; a corrupt politician may loot his treasury for millions of pounds and seek to invest the proceeds through a trust. Even drug traffickers and ordinary fraudsters may seek financial services offshore. It is perhaps the worst case scenario in which the criminal is a terrorist financier.

What all these criminals have in common is that (1) they have generated substantial amounts of property through crime and/or they want to use their legitimate assets for improper purposes and (2) they want to hide their property from law enforcement authorities whilst keeping it under their control.

3. How trusts are abused

There are various ways in which a person will seek to disguise his involvement in illicit activities. The use of overseas limited companies and bank accounts in those company names are very simple examples. Other methods are foundations, *Anstalten* and similar vehicles. However, trusts, and the various services offered by the trust industry, are particularly good vehicles for criminal investments if those involved in such industries are not alert to the risks. The trust, and the ability to manipulate it, are indeed integral to the 'smoke and mirrors' a criminal uses to disguise ownership of property while retaining control over it.

The settlor

The precise method for routing funds into the trust structure will vary. A criminal may, for example, use a 'dummy settlor' to establish the trust with a nominal amount and to avoid identifying himself as the true originator of the funds in the trust deed. In some jurisdictions not even this is necessary since there is no requirement to name a settlor and the trust can simply be created by an instrument of trust.

The settlor will often sign a letter of wishes. This is a document, not legally binding on the trustee, which expresses the manner in which he wishes the trustee to exercise his discretion. The letter of wishes may be kept in a secure location and in various versions to cater for different requests to produce.

The protector

By appointing an accomplice as protector, the criminal may be able to maintain a form of control over the assets even though he has lost legal title to them. This is of critical importance in a situation where the criminal believes the trustee is no longer doing his bidding or, as recent case law has shown,[1] the trustee becomes suspicious and the

---

1   *Basel Trust Corporation (Channel Islands) Limited v Ghirlandina Anstalt an ors* [2008] JRC013 Royal Court (Samedi Division), 28 January 2008, at paras. 106 and 107.

authorities move to freeze the assets. The actions of a friendly protector in removing the incumbent trustee can be a valuable tool to hinder law enforcement agencies.

The type of trust

The trust itself will probably have an anonymous-sounding name and peculiar features that enhance its usefulness in a criminal enterprise. It may, for example, be a blind trust (a trust with no named beneficiaries) or it may purport to be a charitable trust. Such charitable trusts are often referred to as 'Red Cross Trusts' because the Red Cross, or a similar organisation, appears as the beneficiary in the trust deed. The charities, of course, never know about their interest and in most cases they are subsequently removed as beneficiaries in accordance with the true settlor's letter of wishes. This removal often occurs immediately before the payment of a distribution to the 'real' beneficiary who is often the settlor himself or another individual or entity under his control.

The use of companies

Often, companies will be formed and their shares settled into the trust. Usually, the companies will be incorporated in a different jurisdiction to the trust and in places that do not require disclosure of the beneficial owners' identities. Typically, the person establishing the companies will appoint nominee directors (individuals who contribute nothing in practice to the management and control of the companies) and nominee shareholders (individuals or companies who hold the shares on trust for the trustee of the overlying trust). The appointment of nominee directors and shareholders further disguises the true identity of the beneficial owners. In another twist, they may issue bearer shares; these are commonly held by the true settlor. Companies thus provide a further layer of obfuscation.

Bank accounts

Bank accounts will be opened for the companies and for the trust and again these accounts will often be held in different jurisdictions. If possible, the people structuring the scheme will choose places where the trustee is not required to reveal to the bank the identity of the underlying principals – but this is an added bonus. In some rare cases, the settlor or his agent may be a signatory on the bank accounts or may arrange to have credit cards issued on behalf of the companies. This allows him and/or his associates to benefit from the property in a reasonably secure fashion since he/they have already distanced themselves from the original source of the funds.

Investing and reinvesting the assets

The funds can be paid into the structure in various ways. Funds may be paid through bank accounts in several jurisdictions before being pooled in a client account held by a trust company, i.e., a professional financial services company, which provides trustees, directors, shareholders and administration services to the trust and company structure. From there, the funds can be moved through other bank accounts held by the trust company before being paid into accounts in the names of yet other companies. These companies may then buy assets or make investments, the income from which is held with reputable institutions to add to the credibility of the arrangements.

III. Untangling the web

The trust and company structure is extremely difficult to unravel. If, for instance, real estate is purchased by the underlying companies, then all an investigator will see when he examines a land register is that the property is held in the name of a company. To discover the real owner of the company, he will need to approach another jurisdiction. If the investigator discovers that the company is owned by a trust company, he may hit another brick wall, depending upon the regulatory framework of the jurisdiction. It may be impossible to ascertain the existence of the trust. If an investigator has learned the name of the trust, it will not be registered with any regulatory authority. This will make it difficult to find the trustee. Moreover, if funds are traced into a trust structure, as described above, it will often be pooled into a client account for which the investigator only has the account number and the name of the trust company. For more information, he will have to approach the law enforcement authorities of the country in which the trust company is situated. The difficulties will be compounded if trustee services are not regulated in that jurisdiction.

Be that as it may, trust company records are likely to contain information connecting the suspect to the trust, the companies and the bank accounts. Depending on the level of regulation, the quality of the trust company's due diligence and the investigator's choice of questions, the investigator may find important evidence. In this sense, the success of the particular investigation depends on the determination of the investigator and his astuteness in understanding the information he is looking for and at.

IV. Terrorist finance offshore?

1. The financial needs of terrorists

It is frequently said by counter-terrorism experts that the financing of terrorist atrocities is relatively inexpensive. While it may be the case that specific attacks require relatively little money, it is equally true that training camps and armaments are very expensive. Young men in the North of England may spend a small amount on homemade bombs to attack London but terrorist organisations spend considerably more cultivating a climate of hate, a much more sophisticated and expensive exercise requiring funding for political, cultural and logistical purposes.

2. *Terrorist financial flows*

That said, very little is known about the precise methods used by terrorists to raise and move their money. It is not known, for example, whether the financial structures described above are frequently used to provide and disguise funds for terrorism. There is no evidence that terrorists have used these structures to any greater extent than ordinary banking services. In part, this is because information about the financing of terrorism is generally obtained after the atrocities have been committed and is used to show connections between the perpetrators.

It remains the case, however, that trusts and other such vehicles are vulnerable to misuse by all sorts of criminals. There are good reasons to assume that the financiers of terrorism will employ similar techniques, at least when large sums are at stake. It appears that those who finance terrorism need the international financial system and modern financial services to store, move and use their money. They also need to disguise their involvement in crime and to avoid detection and punishment by the prosecuting authorities – for personal reasons and to sustain the network. This gives them incentives to hide the real goal of their activities from their banks or advisers.

In this sense, the financier of terrorism is comparable to every other financial criminal. What makes the terrorist financier different is that he only needs to control the funds temporarily. At the time the funds are put to their ultimate use – i.e., when they are provided to those planning to commit an atrocity – the financier is no longer concerned with controlling the funds. So, the terrorist financier is not looking to use the assets to secure a long-term benefit to himself but to disguise any connection he has with those assets.

All the same, hiding funds behind trust and corporate structures may well assist the financier in moving large sums of money and so those providing financial services need to remain vigilant.

3.   Special problems in detecting terrorist money offshore

Both onshore and offshore jurisdictions face particular problems in dealing with the financing of terrorism. However, the offshore financial centres are vulnerable in several ways that are worth mentioning here.

Poor regulation of charities

Until very recently, most (if not all) traditional offshore financial centres lacked proper systems for registering charities. Many of the offshore centres are now passing or have passed legislation to order the registration of local charities. Until these laws come into force, charities will remain a possible avenue for money laundering and terrorist financing offshore.

Trust companies operating as unlicensed banks

Although the concept of *hawala* banking is usually associated with countries in the Middle East and Asia, there is evidence that a variation of this practice has sprung up offshore and that some trust companies are inadvertently coming to operate as a form of *hawala* bank.

The basic tenet of *hawala* banking, in whatever form, is to minimise documentary evidence of money transfers. *Hawala* banking operates on a system of trust. In a traditional *hawala* set up, cash is transferred through a network of *hawala* brokers from a depositor in one place to a recipient in another as per the following example: A customer needs to transfer funds he holds in Egyptian pounds to a relative in the US. He has no bank account nor any access to foreign currency. He approaches a *hawala* broker in Egypt and deposits his Egyptian currency. The *hawala* broker in Egypt calls a fellow *hawala* broker in the US and gives instructions to pay the US relative an equivalent sum in US dollars (minus commission and based on an unofficial exchange rate). The *hawala* brokers settle their inter-broker debts at a later date.

Transpose this to an offshore centre: it is a very simple matter for an offshore trust company to collect tens of thousands of pounds in cash from businessmen seeking to evade tax. In accepting money from the businessmen, the trust company plays the same role as the *hawala* broker and in depositing their money with the trust company, the businessmen play the role of the Egyptian customer. Soon, the trust company has amassed a very large amount of cash. Other clients of the tax evasion scheme will wish to receive cash from the trust company again and, in doing so, play the role of the American relative. In this instance, there may be no direct linkage between the depositors and the recipients of the cash but the net effect is the same: effectively, the trust company operates an unlicensed *hawala* bank.

This has implications for the uniform implementation of compliance standards in a jurisdiction. What the recipients of the cash in fact do with the money paid to them, is a matter of speculation. We know, however, that cash is often used to finance terrorism (as discussed in other chapters of this book). If the trust company maintains a casual attitude in checking the identity of the persons with whom it is doing business, the trust company has no way of ensuring that it is not inadvertently participating in money laundering or terrorist financing. Where the cash is based offshore, the risk from this form of informal banking is heightened by the fact that a client's visits onshore may be infrequent and less easy to detect.

Lack of oversight by trust companies

There is also vulnerability at the level of less reputable offshore trust companies frequently used by members of the small business community. The professional's attitude to service provision often determines how far the client's criminal objectives will be met. If the criminal client is fortunate enough to find a trust company that delivers trustee and company director services in a 'conveyor belt' fashion without due regard for the core elements of the fiduciary duty, the criminal will be able to exert real influence and control over the property and still benefit from the disguise afforded by the structure.

V. Legal and financial professions

Where criminals manage to misuse financial services, it is rarely the case that service providers have been dishonest. It is much more likely that they have been incompetent or negligent. Fear of losing the client and associated revenues can make financial institutions unwilling to probe deeply into the client's affairs. This mindset creates a culture in which financial services are more vulnerable to misuse because 're-wards' to the service provider outweigh 'risks' of violating regulatory standards and criminal prosecution. Such cultures, in turn, are most likely to emerge in jurisdictions where regulation, legislation and pro-secuting authorities are weak – whether or not the institution or juris-diction fits the classification 'offshore'. Financial institutions in all jurisdictions need to ensure that they understand the nature of the commercial relationship with the client and know and have verified the client's identity. Their key questions are: 'Who is my client and why does he need my services?' and 'What is the commercial ration-ale for the business relationship?'. A financial service provider who understands the answers to those questions is significantly less at risk of becoming involved with those who would use their services for ill.

VI. Conclusions

Many of the consumers who establish trusts and companies and use trust-related services do so for perfectly legitimate reasons. However, the features that make such products and services attractive to legit-imate consumers also make them attractive to criminals. The status of the criminal – as terrorist financier, corrupt politician, drug trafficker, insider dealer or fraudster – and the nature of the predicate criminality are basically irrelevant. In all cases, the purpose of the financial ar-rangement is to disguise the fact that the criminal effectively 'owns' property whilst allowing the criminal to keep the property within his control. Only dogged investigators who are aware of the ways in which trust and company services can be abused, will succeed in penetrating these structures and linking the suspects to the property.

The vulnerabilities of trust companies and related trustee and corporate services are readily apparent: they can be used very effectively to further a criminal enterprise. However, the risks can be managed by appropriate regulation of financial service providers and oversight of, and by, financial service professionals. Some offshore centres are more stringently regulated than their larger onshore neighbours, meaning that their services are less vulnerable to abuse. Hence, it is a mistake to treat all offshore centres the same, just as it is a mistake to assume that particular offshore centres are less well-regulated or robust than their traditional onshore counterparts. When it comes to preventing abuse of wealth management tools by terrorists and other criminals, the terms 'onshore' and 'offshore' can be irrelevant.

MARK PIETH[*] AND STEPHANIE EYMANN[**]

Combating the financing of terrorism: the 'Guantanamo Principle'

I. 'Starving' terrorists of money

During the 1990s, the financial sector became increasingly involved in combating various forms of so-called 'macro-criminality',[1] i.e., transnational economic and organised crime, serious state supported human rights violations and drug trafficking. The role of banks and financial intermediaries as 'gatekeepers' of the financial system in the effort to combat the illicit drug trade and detect money laundering had conditioned them to be particularly aware of ill-gotten gains.[2]

*   Professor of Criminal Law, University of Basel, Switzerland.
**   Research Fellow, University of Basel, Switzerland.

1   Mark Pieth, 'Criminalizing the Financing of Terrorism', *Journal of International Criminal Justice*, (4) 2006: 1074 et seq.
2   Cf., from the UN: Convention against Illicit Traffic in Narcotic Drugs and Psychotropic Substances of 19 December 1988; Council of Europe, Convention on Laundering, Search, Seizure and Confiscation of the Proceeds from Crime (COE 141) of 8 November 1990; from the Financial Action Task Force (FATF): The Forty Recommendations of the on money laundering (1990/1996/2003) of 20 June 2003; from the European Union (EU): First Directive on Prevention of the Use of the Financial System for the Purpose of Money Laundering (OJ L166) of 28 June 1991, 77–83, Second Directive on Prevention of the Use of the Financial System for the Purpose of Money Laundering (OJ L344) of 28 December 2001, 76–82, and Third Directive on Prevention of the Use of the Financial System for the Purpose of Money Laundering or Terrorist Financing (Ref. IP/05/682) of 26 May 2005; Bank for International Settlements (BIS), Basel Committee on Banking Supervision, *Customer Due Diligence for Banks*, October 2001; Wolfsberg Banking Group, *Wolfsberg Principles on Private Banking*, (2nd edn.), 2002.

With intensifying terrorist activity during the last years of the 20th Century, it seemed logical to use the techniques developed to deal with other forms of macro-criminality to prevent and detect the financing of terrorism and 'follow the money trail' of terror. Piggybacking on established concepts, international institutions sought to criminalise the funding of terrorism and the management of 'terrorist' money by freezing and confiscating terrorist assets, as well as by raising awareness in the financial sector of suspicious transactions. Rules for 'counter-terrorist financing' (CTF) were established on an international level and implemented by states into domestic law.[3]

Several years after the shocking events of 11 September 2001 (9/11), it is time to consider the effectiveness of these rules and procedures. There is a particular need to revisit the approach of the United Nations Security Council (UNSC) to CTF, by which funds may be blocked indefinitely on the basis of secret intelligence and without due process. The approach is reminiscent of the prison camps established by the United States (US) for alleged terrorists at Guantanamo Bay, Cuba. With those camps, the US government appeared to manoeuvre itself into a dead-end. The search for an exit strategy from Guantanamo and from the UNSC listing regime is now on.

This paper will first raise the issue of the effectiveness of international CTF measures (Part II), before reviewing the current international legal standards against terrorist finance (Part III) and discussing the freezing obligations according to the UNSC Resolutions with special emphasis on listing and de-listing procedures (Part IV). It ends with a few concluding remarks (Part V).

II. Uncertain effectiveness

The Commission established to investigate the 9/11 attacks against the US (9/11 Commission) estimated that those responsible spent no more

---

3   Mark Pieth, 'Financing of Terrorism: Following the Money', in Mark Pieth (ed.), *Financing Terrorism*, Dordrecht 2002: 115 ff.

than USD 500,000 in planning and executing the attacks. If this attack, which included air travel, the training of commercial pilots and student grants, cost so little,[4] it is easy to imagine how much cheaper locally organised car or suicide bombings may be.

From the perspective of financial service providers, this is a totally different world to money laundering. The funds involved in terrorism may be well below the thresholds set by private banks to detect drug money. Underground armies, like the Tamil Tigers or the Kurdistan Workers Party, may systematically collect and move large amounts of money to buy arms and fund their operations and they may structure their financial flows in ways known from other clandestine operations. However, in many other cases of terrorist financing, we are talking about small amounts moved through retail banks. The student, who opens a bank account to receive his student grant which covers his living expenses, will not necessarily appear suspicious while he is waiting for his turn to become active as a terrorist. The sums involved can be so small that they can be placed in the realm of 'microfinance'.[5] Also, the funds raised by terrorist organisations need not be ill-gotten gains; they may have been legally earned. For these reasons, bankers are reluctant to simply equate terrorist funding with money laundering.[6]

This also explains why finding terrorist funds is so much more difficult than finding laundered money. Financial service providers do use automated screening systems to pick up transactions involving persons named on lists. However, these systems work only if the names are specific, which may not be the case, e.g., if names are common or have been translated from a foreign language. It is also too much to expect bankers to proactively identify suspicious clients from their behaviour since the transactions in question are hidden among

---

4 Jonathan Winer, 'Globalization, Terrorist Finance, and Global Conflict – Time for a White List?', in Pieth, n 3: 5.

5 Ursula Cassani, 'Droit pénal économique 2003–2005: actualité législative (responsabilité pénale de l'entreprise, financement du terrorisme, corruption)', in Walter Fellmann and Thomas Poledna, *La pratique de l'avocat*, 20: 679.

6 Armand Kersten, 'Financing of Terrorism – A Predicate Offence to Money Laundering?', in Pieth, n 3: 49, is critical of the FATF's Special Recommendation II. On Special Recommendation II, see further below, n 15.

the multitude of every-day retail banking transfers. At most, a client relationship manager may be able to apply his/her professional sensitivity to make the occasional 'hit'. At the same time, it is understandable that the Wolfsberg Banking Group recommended that the Financial Action Task Force (FATF) should not apply a risk-based approach to countering the financing of terrorism.[7] In this area, secret service agencies have a monopoly on most of the crucial intelligence, making a 'risk-based approach' inappropriate.

Under these circumstances, there is an astonishing discrepancy between the rules developed by the FATF – their technical volume and detail[8] – and the likelihood that financial institutions will actually detect and prevent the transmission of terrorist funds.

III. The international standards on CTF

International bodies have created rules in three sectors to address the management of money destined or used for terrorism:

- In criminal law – regimes focusing on the criminalisation, freezing and forfeiture of suspected terrorist funds and corresponding rules on international cooperation (mutual legal assistance and extradition)
- In the law on financial supervision – regimes concentrating on client identification, the determination of beneficial ownership, customer due diligence and the notification of suspicious transactions
- In administrative law – regimes to block (i.e., freeze) suspicious funds

---

7   Wolfsberg Banking Group, *Answer to Questionnaire by FATF on Risk-Based Approach*, 2007. See, more generally on the risk based approach (RBA), Wolfsberg Banking Group, *Wolfsberg Statement: Guidance on the RBA for Managing Money Laundering Risks* of 13 December 2005, available at http://www.wolfsberg-principles.com/risk-based-approach.html.

8   See further below, III. 2.

1. Criminalising the financing of terrorism

The UN treaties on terrorism have evolved in a rather piecemeal fashion since the 1970s. At first, they addressed specific terrorist threats, i.e., threats to civil aviation or maritime navigation. Starting with conventions on hostage-taking and terrorist bombings, the UN began, over time, to develop more generalised counter-terrorist instruments.[9] In 1999, the UN adopted the International Convention on the Suppression of the Financing of Terrorism[10] (Terrorist Financing Convention), which entered into force on 10 April 2002. Regional organisations have also adopted measures on terrorism, many of them closely linked to the UN system.[11]

9   Convention for the Suppression of Unlawful Seizure of Aircraft of 16 December 1970; Convention for the Suppression of Unlawful Acts Against the Safety of Civil Aviation of 23 September 1971; Protocol for the Suppression of Unlawful Acts of Violence at Airports Serving International Civil Aviation, Supplementary to the Convention for the Suppression of Unlawful Seizure of Aircraft 1970 of 24 February 1988; Convention for the Suppression of Unlawful Acts Against the Safety of Maritime Navigation of 10 March 1988 and its Protocol for the Suppression of Unlawful Acts Against the Safety of Fixed Platforms Located on the Continental Shelf of 10 March 1988; International Convention against the Taking of Hostages of 17 December 1997; International Convention for the Suppression of Terrorist Bombings of 15 December 1997. For an analysis of the UN's response to terrorism, see also Marco Sassoli, 'Terrorism and War' and Kimmo Nuotio, 'Terrorism as a Catalyst for the Emergence, Harmonization and Reform of Criminal Law', *Journal of International Criminal Justice* (4) 2006: 959 et seq. and 998 et seq. respectively.

10   UN Doc. A/RES/54/109, 9 December 1999.

11   Cf. also the Organisation of American States Convention to Prevent and Punish the Acts of Terrorism Taking the Form of Crimes Against Persons and Related to Extortion that are of International Significance of 2 February 1971; Inter-American Convention against Terrorism of 3 June 2002; Arab Convention for the Suppression of Terrorism, League of Arab States of 22 April 1998; Organisation of African Unity Convention on the Prevention and Combating of Terrorism of 14 July 1999; Convention of the Organisation of the Islamic Conference on Combating Terrorism of 1 July 1999; Council of Europe Convention on the Suppression of Terrorism of 27 January 1977 (COE 090).

After 9/11, activities against terrorist financing in international *fora* were stepped up dramatically. In particular, the UNSC[12] declared parts of the Terrorist Financing Convention mandatory under Chapter VII of the UN Charter and the European Union (EU) enacted its EU Council Framework Decision of 13 June 2002 on Combating Terrorism. The FATF also developed more specific requirements on CTF, as discussed in further detail below.

The UN's Terrorist Financing Convention is open to criticism from two directions in particular. The first and most problematic aspect, which is shared by similar documents, is the lack of a clear delineation between 'freedom fighters' (e.g., combatants in a civil war) and terrorists. The Convention effectively ignores the philosophical debate, running since the Enlightenment, about when it is ethical to 'murder a tyrant'.[13] Second, the concept of a 'terrorist' in this Convention relies almost exclusively on an extensive *mens rea* component. Beyond acts described in the previous UN treaties,[14] whether an act is 'terrorist financing' depends largely on the nature of the alleged financier's intent:

Art. 2 (1)(b)

Any person commits an offence within the meaning of this Convention if that person by any means, directly or indirectly, unlawfully and wilfully, provides or collects funds with the intention that they should be used or in the knowledge that they are to be used, in full or in part, in order to carry out any other act intended to cause death or serious bodily injury to a civilian, or to any other person not taking an active part in the hostilities in a situation of armed conflict, when the purpose of such act, by its nature or context, is to intimidate a population, or to compel a Government or an international organisation to do or to abstain from doing any act.

---

12 UNSC Resolution 1373 on Threats to International Peace and Security Caused by Terrorist Acts of 28 September 2001.

13 See e.g., Art. 260^{quinquies} s. 4 Swiss Criminal Code or para. 278 c s. 3 Austrian Criminal Code; Marc Forster, 'Die Strafbarkeit der Unterstützung (insbesondere Finanzierung) des Terrorismus', *Schweizerische Zeitschrift für Strafrecht*, 2003: 423 et seq.; Ursula Cassani, 'Le train de mesures contre le financement du terrorisme : une loi nécessaire?', *Schweizerische Zeitschrift für Wirtschafts- und Finanzmarktrecht*, 2003: 293 et seq.

14 See above, n 9.

That the act is the financing of terrorism adds very little to the definition; it merely details acts of 'unlawfully providing and collecting funds' with the intention that they should be used or in the knowledge that they are to be used for terrorist purposes, in order to carry out the said activities

The delicate relationship between objective and subjective elements of the terrorist financing offence is highlighted by the Interpretative Note to FATF Special Recommendation II on Terrorist Financing, which demands that national 'law should permit the intentional element of the terrorist financing offence to be inferred from objective factual circumstances'.[15] Art. 6 of the Terrorist Financing Convention excludes 'considerations of a political, philosophical, ideological, racial, ethnic, religious or other similar nature' as justifications. However, state parties do make exceptions for those acting to restore democracy or human rights when implementing the provisions of the Convention. In this way, the national judiciary continues to be confronted with the full ambiguity of the notion of terrorism when making orders in relation to alleged terrorists' funds.

2.   New standards for the financial sector

As noted at the beginning of this chapter, participants in the financial sector (and some other professions) were subject to very detailed due diligence standards with regard to money laundering even before they were asked to implement standards on CTF.

After 9/11, the FATF[16] developed eight (then nine) Special Recommendations on Terrorist Financing. In force since 30 October 2001 and revised 22 October 2004, the 9 Special Recommendations require states to ensure that their financial institutions identify their clients

---

15   The FATF states that, 'The law should permit the intentional element of the terrorist financing offence to be inferred from objective factual circumstances': FATF, *Interpretative Note to Special Recommendation II (Criminalising the Financing of Terrorism and Associated Money Laundering)*, 3 October 2003, para. 11. See also, International Convention for the Suppression of the Financing of Terrorism, n 10.

16   See above, n 9.

and possibly the beneficial owners of funds, apply 'increased diligence in unusual circumstances' and notify competent authorities of suspicious transactions.[17]

The 9 Special Recommendations build on the Terrorist Financing Convention and the FATF's traditional 40 Recommendations. Special Recommendations I to V substantially replicate the requirements in the Terrorist Financing Convention, namely:

- Ratification and implementation of UN anti-terrorism conventions
- Criminalisation of the financing of terrorism and associated money laundering
- Freezing and confiscation of terrorist assets[18]
- Reporting of suspicious transactions related to terrorism
- International cooperation with regard to terrorist financing

Special Recommendations VI and VII then tackle issues more specifically relevant to terrorist financing: alternative remittance services (especially *hawala* banking) and wire transfers. In Special Recommendation VIII, the FATF calls for the registration and effective supervision of non-profit organisations (NPOs), aiming, in particular, at the enforcement of a 'know your beneficiaries and associate NPOs' rule and the enhancement of the transparency of charities. Recommendation IX, finally, is intended to increase the implementation and enforcement of declaration and disclosure systems to detect cross-border cash couriers.

The Special Recommendations are arguably no longer just 'soft law' and are enforced to some degree by peer pressure in a comprehensive mutual evaluation process.[19] Since 9/11, the FATF has developed Interpretative Notes on particular Recommendations and has

---

17   Cf. especially, the FATF's 40 Recommendations 2003, n 2.
18   FATF, *Freezing of Terrorist Assets: International Best Practices*, 3 October 2003.
19   Mark Pieth and Gemma Aiolfi (eds.), *A Comparative Guide to Money Laundering, A Critical Analysis of Systems in Singapore, Switzerland, the UK and the USA* (study by the Basel Institute on Governance commissioned by the Stiftung Finanzplatz Schweiz), Cheltenham/Northhampton 2004: 19 et seq.

added 'International Best Practices' on some key issues.[20] The FATF continues to monitor the topic.[21]

However, the FATF's 9 Special Recommendations may be a mixed blessing in the fight against terrorism. Take, for example, the concept behind Special Recommendation VIII on charities. Increasing restrictions and sanctions on charities has the potential to create strong social tensions if it means that charities are unable to play their part in the social security system and/or are excluded from the official banking system. 'Underground banking' will be the inevitable alternative (exactly what Special Recommendation VI is supposed to prevent). If applied in a generalised manner, on the other hand, Special Recommendation VIII must lead to a revolution in the secretive world of NPOs and charities (including all foundations, churches and similar institutions all over the world). The need for cooperation with the private sector is another obstacle, especially to implementing the Special Recommendations. As long as it is not possible to develop reliable 'profiles' in terrorist financing, the financial sector will be limited in its ability to detect suspicious behaviour.[22]

3. *'Targeted sanctions'*

Listing

In 1999, already two years before 9/11, the UNSC introduced a worldwide system to immediately freeze assets owned or controlled by persons or entities suspected of being associated with the Taliban, al-Qaida or Usama Bin Laden.[23] It created a Sanctions Committee, which it authorised to list persons or entities whose funds should be

---

20 FATF, *Special Recommendations on Terrorist Financing*, made October 2001 and revised version 22 October 2004; see also, the FATF's Interpretative Notes generally, and the report on best practices, n 18.

21 See further, FATF, *Terrorist Financing*, 29 February 2008, a comprehensive report on terrorist financing, exploring the range of methods used by terrorists to move funds within and between organisations.

22 Questions on this issue were raised at the Wolfsberg Forum of 29 May 2008 in the panel on terrorist financing.

23 UNSC Resolution 1267 on the Situation in Afghanistan of 15 October 1999.

frozen and whose freedom of movement should be restricted. The Sanctions Committee agreed to list at the suggestion of individual member states, provided the decision was unanimous within the Committee.[24] Since the operative UNSC Resolution 1267 is based on Chapter VII of the UN Charter, member states are obliged to implement it,[25] though they may choose whether they freeze assets in the context of a criminal investigation or create administrative (executive) freezing powers.[26]

UNSC Resolution 1373, enacted shortly after 9/11, extends the freezing obligation to all assets of persons suspected of involvement in terrorism. With this additional tool, individual countries may freeze the funds of any individual or entity listed by any other UN member state, without involving the Sanctions Committee or asking for a listing under Resolution 1267. Even though UNSC Resolution 1373 has also been enacted under Chapter VII of the UN Charter, it leaves the recipient State a certain amount of discretion in deciding whether and how to cooperate with a request.[27]

Regional bodies, such as the Council of Europe (CoE) and the EU,[28] as well as national[29] governments and parliaments, have translated these resolutions into directly applicable domestic legal rules. It is understandable, therefore, that conflicts over listing and de-listing

24 On the consensus concept, see Helen Keller, 'Antiterrormassnahmen: Verfahrensschutz bei der Sperrung von Bankkonten', in Isabelle Häner (ed.): *Nachdenken über den demokratischen Staat und seine Geschichte, Beiträge für Alfred Kölz*, Bern 2003: 302 et seq., 314.

25 Art. 25 in connection with Art. 41, 42, 48 II UN Charter.

26 FATF, *Interpretative Note to Special Recommendation III (Freezing and Confiscating Terrorist Assets)*, para. 8. c.

27 Sven Peterke, 'Die Bekämpfung der Terrorismusfinanzierung unter Kapitel VII der UN-Charta. Die Resolution 1373 (2001) des UN-Sicherheitsrates', in *Humanitäres Völkerrecht* (14) 2001: 217 et seq.; Mark Pieth, 'Criminalizing the Financing of Terrorism', in *Journal of International Criminal Justice*, December 2006: 1085.

28 Council of Europe Convention on Laundering, Search, Seizure and Confiscation of the Proceeds from Crime and on the Financing of Terrorism of 16 May 2005; European Union Council Framework Decision on Combating Terrorism of 13 June 2002 (2002/475/JHA), OJ L164/3.

29 For Switzerland, see Bundesgesetz vom 22. März 2002 über die Durchsetzung von internationalen Sanktionen, SR 946.231 (Embargo Legislation and Taliban Ordinance; al-Qaida Ordinance).

have arisen primarily at the domestic[30] and regional levels[31] when those subject to freezing orders have attempted to hold the local entity responsible for enforcing the UNSC regime to account.

The 'Guantanamo Principle'

In order to understand how the UN's 'targeted' or 'smart' sanctions are supposed to work, one has to be very clear from the outset about what they are supposed to achieve: UNSC Resolutions 1267 and 1373 are intended to impede the build-up of terrorist capabilities by freezing suspicious funds and by placing travel restrictions on suspected terrorists. Originating in police law, these measures are focused on immediate risk and are not meant to be permanent – on the contrary, the measures are only intended to last for very short periods of time. Accordingly, the UNSC Resolutions place very little emphasis on convictions and confiscation (or any other permanent measures). It would appear that rapid action is paramount and listing decisions are frequently based on little more than secret service intelligence.

At least at the national level, such police measures are subject to supervision by the courts. There is no such procedure to hear evidence by independent judges within the UN sanctions system. The Committee process is political and diplomatic. The countries agree unanimously whom they consider to be a risk to the general public, based on mere suspicion. They cannot exclude the possibility that names are

30 For Switzerland, see BGE (Federal Court Decision) 133 II 450; Stephanie Eymann, 'Bemerkung zu BGE 1A.45/2007, Embargomassnahmen – UNO Sanktionen gegen die Taliban, Youssef Nada vs. SECO', *Aktuelle Juristische Praxis* 17, 2008: 244 et seq.; Stephanie Eymann, 'Präventive Kontosperre gemäss UNO-Resolutionen – Unzulässige Vorverlagerung strafprozessualen Zwangs oder unumgängliche Massnahme im Kampf gegen den Terror?', in Salome Wolf/Marc Hürzeler/Martino Mona (eds.), *Prävention im Recht*, Basel 2008: 49 et seq.

31 In the European Court of First Instance, *Ahmed Ali Yusuf and al-Barakaat International Foundation v. Council of the European Union and Commission of the European Communities* (T-306/01), 21 September 2005; *Yassin Abdullah Kadi v. Council of the European Union and Commission of the European Communities* (T-315/01), 21 September 2005; *Faraj Hassan v. Council of the European Union and Commission of the European Communities* (T-49/04), 12 July 2006; *Chafiq Ayadi v. Council of the European Union*, (T-253/02), 12 July 2006.

put on the list undeservedly. To put it more bluntly, the UNSC does not really mind that much if it blocks the 'wrong man's' funds. In other words, there is no due process, no access to an independent body, no presumption of innocence and no mandatory consideration of national decisions: freezing is a political act. This we would call the 'Guantanamo-Principle'.

De-listing

To counter some of the criticism levelled at its sanctions system, the Sanctions Committee adopted new procedures for listing and de-listing on 7 November 2002.[32] As first introduced, the Guidelines of the Committee for the Conduct of its Work provided that an application for de-listing needed to be made by the country of residence or origin of the party subject to the freezing order. The country responsible for the listing was to be heard and the country making the motion for de-listing was to provide reasons for its application. The process was entirely inter-governmental.

In 2006, in response to further criticism and in order to counter the risk that countries would start to de-list individuals unilaterally, the UNSC enacted UNSC Resolution 1730, which created the so-called 'focal point process'.[33] The listed party is now entitled to request de-listing directly of the Council but the rest of the process remains a negotiation between states. Moreover, the de-listing decisions are still taken unanimously and the burden of persuading the Committee to accept de-listing still remains with the government proposing de-listing. Obviously, if a member state who had frozen assets concludes that there is no case, this could constitute an argument for de-listing. However, the Sanctions Committee is still not bound by a national (court) decision.

32   Helen Keller, n 24.
33   UNSC Resolution 1730 on General Issues Relating to Sanctions of 19 December 2006.

IV. How to ensure fair procedure?

1. *Deficient process*

Such diverse tribunals as the Swiss Federal Court[34] and the UN High Commission on Human Rights[35] have criticised the current listing and de-listing procedures as falling short of essential human rights standards, in particular, the right to be heard,[36] the right to access an independent court and the right to an effective appeal.[37] These criticisms found their expression in the landmark decision of the European Court of Justice (ECJ) of 3 December 2008: *Yassin Abdullah Kadi and al-Barakaat International Foundation v Council of the European Union.*[38]

2. *Unilateral de-listing by national or regional bodies*

In previous actions brought by Mr Kadi and the al-Barakaat International Foundation, the European Court of First Instance (CFI) had held that it is bound – as far as lists under UNSC Resolution 1267 are concerned – to implement the decisions of the UNSC and its subsidiary bodies without exercising discretion of its own. It held that, even if the UNSC is bound by the UN Charter itself, the competence of courts

---

34   See above, n 30.

35   Report of the United Nations High Commissioner for Human Rights on the Protection of Human Rights and Fundamental Freedoms while Countering Terrorism [A/HRC/4/ 88] of 9 March 2007.

36   International Covenant on Civil and Political Rights of 16 December 1966 (ICCPR), Art. 14 s. 1; European Convention on Human Rights, Art. 6 s. 1.

37   ICCPR, n 36, Art. 2 s. 3, European Convention on Human Rights, n 36, Art. 13, German Department for Foreign Affairs and the Swedish Ministry on Foreign Relations for Switzerland, Expert Opinion, 49; see also Advocate General Poiares Maduro's final petition of 16 January 2008 in *Kadi and al-Barakaat International Foundation* (C-402/05 P and C-415/05 P), n 38.

38   *Yassin Abdullah Kadi and al-Barakaat International Foundation v Council of the European Union and Commission of the European Communities* (Joined Cases C-402/05 P and C-415/05 P), European Court of Justice (Grand Chamber), 3 September 2008.

does not extend to the revision of its decisions. However, under UNSC Resolution 1373 they are free to ensure that the rules of fair procedure are followed[39] since this Resolution does not refer to the listing competence of the Sanctions Committee. Concerning UNSC Resolution 1267, the courts have so far restricted their right to intervene to infringements of *jus cogens* norms and have given this concept the narrowest of interpretations (it restricted it to freedom from torture, slavery and illegal imprisonment).

Therefore, the significance of the ECJ's decision of 3 September 2008 cannot be underestimated. The ECJ quashed the decision of the CFI and declared the European Commission (EC) Regulation No. 881/2002, implementing UNSC Resolution 1267, to be void. It held that the Community was based on the rule of law and that therefore the respect for human rights was a condition of the lawfulness for Community acts. Measures incompatible with the respect for human rights were not acceptable in the Community:[40]

> It must however be noted that the Charter of the United Nations does not impose the choice of a particular model for the implementation of resolutions adopted by the Security Council under Chapter VII of the Charter, since they are to be given effect in accordance with the procedure applicable in that respect in the domestic legal order of each Member of the United Nations. The Charter of the United Nations leaves the Members of the United Nations a free choice among the various possible models for transposition of those resolutions into their domestic legal order.[41]

It held that having the right to submit a request to be removed from the list to a focal point did not change the fact that the procedure before that Committee was in essence diplomatic and intergovernmental.[42] Furthermore:

> It follows from the foregoing that the Community judicature must, in accordance with the powers conferred on it by the EC Treaty, ensure the review, in principle the full review, of the lawfulness of all Community acts in the light of the fun-

---

39 *People's Mojahedin of Iran v. Council of the European Union* (T-228/02), European Court of First Instance, 12 December 2006.
40 C-402/05 P and C-415/05 P, n 38, para. 281 and 284.
41 C-402/05 P and C-415/05 P, n 38, para. 291.
42 C-402/05 P and C-415/05 P, n 38, para. 323.

damental rights forming an integral part of the general principles of Community law, including review of Community measures which, like the contested regulation, are designed to give effect to the resolutions adopted by the Security Council under Chapter VII of the Charter of the United Nations.[43]

As to the legality of the Regulations, the rights of the defence, in particular the right to be heard and the right to effective judicial review of those rights were patently not respected:[44]

> The contested regulation, in so far as it concerns Mr Kadi, was adopted without furnishing any guarantee enabling him to put his case to the competent authorities, in a situation in which the restriction of his property rights must be regarded as significant.[45]

It concluded that 'the Court of First Instance [had] erred in law' by refusing to consider the legality of the relevant EC regulations.[46] However, since voiding the regulation could lead to serious and irreversible damage, the ECJ afforded the Council of the EC a period of three months to remedy the defects. The ensuring decision by the European Commission simply reiterates that Mr Kadi and al-Barakaat International Foundation should remain on the list.[47] This does not address the fundamental problem – the lack of due process – and so the legal merry go-round is bound to start all over again.

3.   Amending the de-listing procedure of the Sanctions Committee

In light of these criticisms, the search is now on for a means to reform the UNSC listing system under UNSC Resolution 1267. In June 2008, in UNSC Resolution 1822, made its own attempt to address its procedures for listing and de-listing. In so doing, it '[took] note of challenges to measures implemented by Member States in accordance

---

43   C-402/05 P and C-415/05 P, n 38, para. 326.
44   C-402/05 P and C-415/05 P, n 38, para. 334.
45   C-402/05 P and C-415/05 P, n 38, para. 369.
46   C-402/05 P and C-415/05 P, n 38, para. 327.
47   Commission Regulation (EC) No. 1190/2008, 28 November 2008, para. 8.

with the [...] this resolution [...]',[48] however, it is yet to comment on the critique in substance. This is particularly embarrassing for an institution that hopes to stand as a 'beacon' for the protection of human rights.[49]

On 2 July 2008, Denmark, Germany, Liechtenstein, the Netherlands, Sweden and Switzerland presented the Presidents of the General Assembly and of the Security Council with a proposal for Improving the implementation of sanctions regimes by ensuring 'fair and clear procedures'.[50] Essentially, the proposal (1) calls on the UNSC to introduce a system for regular *ex officio* re-evaluations of the listings and (2) proposes the creation of an independent, impartial panel made up of judicially qualified persons to advise the Sanctions Committee on requests for de-listing. The Committee would sit together with representatives appointed on an *ad hoc* basis of the states which proposed the listing and the state(s) of residence and/or of citizenship of the listed party.

Whereas the independence of the panel would be a real progress, its advisory status is clearly insufficient and indicates that the initiating states do not really want to move away from the political nature of de-listing decisions. Furthermore, the proposal still does not clarify how a domestic acquittal or the closing of a domestic criminal case would affect the listing decision since it is based on the notion of dangerousness and risk rather than a definite judicial assessment. Such a situation arose in Switzerland when the Swiss Federal Court ordered that funds remain blocked even though the case against the owner had been closed by the Federal Attorney in 2005.[51]

---

48   UNSC Resolution 1822 on Threats to International Peace and Security Caused by Terrorist Acts of 30 June 2008, Preamble.
49   UN Charter, Art. 1 III.
50   *Identical letters dated 23 June 2008 from the Permanent Representative of Switzerland to the United Nations addressed to the President of the General Assembly and the President of the Security Council* (UNGA A/62/891–S/2008/ 428) of 2 July 2008.
51   See above, n 30.

4. *Other solutions*

Member states of the UN cannot opt out of the UNSC's listing regime. The drafters of the UN Charter intended to create a unanimous approach in endowing the UNSC with powers to maintain peace and security. However, they did not thereby give the UN competence to force member states to violate their *ordre public* or other international human rights standards, such as the European Convention on Human Rights (ECHR) and the UN's own International Covenant on Civil and Political Rights (ICCPR).[52] Rather, UN Charter has to be viewed holistically: member states are only bound up to the point where UN bodies violate essential human rights themselves.[53] If we went back in the history of the *jus commune* for a moment, we would find that the notion of 'social contract' was immediately qualified by a 'submission contract'. At that time, the right to refuse compliance in the face of illegal requests was not yet accepted.[54] We have since moved far from this attitude.

V. Conclusion

Much energy has gone into combating terrorism and the financing of terrorism since 1999 and especially since 2001. Nonetheless, the effectiveness of the steps taken is more than doubtful. Furthermore, the lack of flexibility of the UNSC in creating listing and de-listing procedures that respect fundamental human rights is casting its shadow over the UN's 'smart sanctions' regime. In waging the 'War on Terror', it seems that many policy-makers have come to think that restricting the right to a fair hearing and other human rights will enhance the effectiveness of counter-terrorism measures. This is a dubious

---

52   Eymann, n 30.
53   Frank Meyer, 'Lost in Complexity – Gedanken zum Rechtsschutz gegen Smart Sanctions in der EU', *Zeitschrift für Europarechtliche Studien*, 2007: 25 et seq.
54   Thomas Hobbes, *De Cive*, Oxford ed., 1998: 1642.

assumption and not one, in any case, that the UN can afford to make if it wants to retain its position as the guardian of peace and human rights. If you cannot prove why somebody's funds need to be frozen, then they need to be released. This is the message that the ECJ conveyed in its landmark decision of September 2008: if the UNSC is unable to provide for a fair process and if the necessary information to allow the defence is not made available within a reasonable time, regional or national agencies will have to free the funds unilaterally.

JACQUES RAYROUD*

The UN listing system: challenges for criminal justice authorities

I. Introduction

The United Nations' (UN) strategy of combating terrorism by adopting a system of lists and sanctions against al-Qaida, the Taliban and Usama Bin Laden has placed particular emphasis on crime prevention and the protection of victims at the expense of listed parties. These administrative sanctions proved very efficient immediately after their adoption and the publication of the lists. However, they suffer from serious flaws as they only act through provisional (temporary) measures, such as asset freezes and travel bans, and are applied without regard to their consequences – for the human rights of the listed individual or the efficacy of a subsequent criminal investigation. As these temporary measures may continue indefinitely, do they not take on the colour of a criminal sentence?

Admittedly, the UN Security Council (UNSC) has implemented a procedure, by which the Sanctions Committee may de-list an individual after consulting the governments concerned. However, the UNSC has provided no legal remedy to the listed party in the case of a refusal.[1] By default, one of the principal means of rectifying the unlimited effect of the sanctions is to systematically refer listings to an authority within a national criminal justice system which has the power

* Federal Attorney at the Office of the Attorney General (OAG) of Switzerland. The contents of this article does not commit the OAG. Many thanks to Patrick Lamon, Federal Attorney and Anne Rochat, Assistant Federal Attorney, of the OAG's Section on Terrorism, Financing of Terrorism, Organised Crime and Money Laundering for their judicious suggestions.
1   UNSC Resolution 1730, 19 December 2006.

to investigate each case with due respect to fundamental rights. Paradoxically, this attempt at rectification is of limited effect because the withdrawal of legal proceedings at the national level is not automatically linked to a parallel and equivalent examination in the de-listing process at the international level.[2]

The UN's emphasis on preventive measures also invites potential terrorist financiers to take countermeasures. This considerably restricts the ability of the criminal justice authorities to use of the full range of investigation techniques. As a result, it becomes more uncertain that they will be able to bring the truth to light. It is indeed the case that the interest at stake in the field of counter-terrorist financing (CTF) demand extreme prudence in determining the right moment to freeze assets. These difficulties make it even more important that we further efforts to optimise the means available to criminal justice authorities when examining these cases. In so doing, we confront more questions: Do the classical rules of mutual legal assistance (MLA) offer a sufficient basis for the disruption of terrorist activity? Are they efficient enough to counteract modern media communications? Is the solution to this exceedingly critical situation of potentially indefinite asset freezes necessarily the reinforcement of the jurisdictional rules governing the power of courts or competent authorities to confiscate assets?

More questions arise if we accept the UN's recommendation that member states adopt mechanisms to ensure compensation for victims of acts of terrorism and their families.[3] Would it be adequate for each state to adopt such a system individually, rather than on an international basis? Is there not a danger that each state will favour compensation for its own citizens to the detriment of victims elsewhere in the world, whose only error is failing to recognise that they have a rightful cause of action in another jurisdiction?

---

2   Swiss Federal Court Decision of 14 November 2007 (FCD 133 II 450): In spite of the suspension of a criminal procedure opened against a person on the UN list on 31 May 2005, Switzerland could not de-list him from the annex 2 of the Federal Ruling Against the Taliban since it is bound to the sanctions system developed by the UN Security Council. To achieve the aim of de-listing, Switzerland must support this person in the de-listing procedure provided by the Sanction Committee of the Security Council.

3   Art. 8 § 4 of the International Convention for the Suppression of Terrorism.

I. Preventive measures taken by the UN: unwanted consequences for the administration of justice?

It is accepted that the publication of international terrorist lists contributes to the effective transmission of suspicions and that these suspicions weigh heavily on those listed. What is perhaps less well appreciated is the impact of the lists on investigations: publishing the lists also prompts terrorists around the world to take countermeasures. Listed parties become aware that they are under suspicion. If in possession of valuable information, they will be able to take precautions, e.g., by destroying evidence, using extra prudence in contacting collaborators and modifying their usual channels for financial transfers.

All of this undermines the work of the criminal justice authorities. Law enforcement agencies generally try to investigate with a maximum degree of discretion so as to preserve the efficacy of the measures, some of which may be very intrusive, e.g., undercover investigations or wire taps. Effectively, by alerting parties to the fact that they are suspected of an association with terrorism, lists may make it even more difficult for law enforcers to obtain proof that those investigated are taking part in terrorism or assisting an international terrorist organisation: they render the most effective investigative tools useless. How can successful investigations be undertaken – and the truth be brought to light – if it is not possible to use the most effective means of investigation?

Unable to use a large number of the most appropriate investigation techniques, law enforcement authorities will enquire as rapidly as possible into the source and the contents of the information which motivated the listing. They may receive this information but not the authorisation to use it in criminal proceedings. And, even if disclosure is authorised, they may need to interpret the information so that it can be considered by the court in accordance with local rules of criminal procedure or evidence. The exercise of translating intelligence into evidence will be laborious – perhaps impossible – if the source is a government (intelligence) agency whose rules on collecting, compiling and assessing information are fundamentally different to those of police, prosecutors and courts.

Assuming that the information which gives rise to the listing cannot be used, the law enforcement authority will be faced with another problem: that of the empty file. It will lack any basis for its suspicion, even though the allegations that caused it to open the file are particularly serious. Such a situation is extremely tricky; it can turn out to be completely at odds with the rules of criminal procedure that require there be sufficient evidence to warrant the commencement of proceedings against an individual.[4] Under time pressure and with limited means, the prosecuting authority will have to collect enough proof to support the allegations and justify continuing the investigation. Such a case is almost doomed from the start.

Regarded from this angle, the UN's preventive strategy takes on a new dimension. Admittedly, it has deprived terrorist organisations of some of their resources and restricted the movements of some of their sympathisers. But it risks limiting the chances of success of criminal investigations and prosecutions which could lead to a severe sentence and to the confiscation of all financial assets belonging to an organisation.[5] Thus, the fact remains that the UN strategy may be jeopardising important measures under national law which also strikes home against terrorism.

Even so, should this cause us to doubt the UN strategy? Was it a mistake to emphasise prevention at a time when terrorism appeared so seriously threatening? To answer these questions properly would necessitate a thorough analysis of the results of the UN sanctions and listing system – total amounts frozen, number of persons placed under house arrest, number of criminal convictions, etc. – and their comparison with the expected results of a classical criminal investigation, in which the suspects have not been 'tipped off' by a listing. This would be a difficult process given the differences between the legal systems of all UN member states. But this analysis can be put to one side as we may find a solution via another – more pragmatic – approach: that of

---

4   Art. 101 of the Swiss Federal Criminal Procedure Law.
5   Art. 72 of the Swiss Criminal Code reverses the burden of proof for forfeiture in
     the case of criminal organisations.

asking whether law enforcement authorities really do possess additional latitude when choosing the right moment to freeze the assets of someone who is not on the lists but is a member of a terrorist organisation, such as al-Qaida.

II. Freezing assets: a Cornelian dilemma for law enforcement authorities

It is common knowledge that the funds used to finance terrorism can be of both unlawful (e.g., when they are the proceeds of an offence) and lawful origin (e.g., when they are funds collected as donations to a charity). In the first case, in which funds are illegitimate, law enforcers have a somewhat easier task since they may use a dual approach. On the one hand, they may investigate the financing of terrorism, following the financial flows 'downstream' to their destination. On the other hand, they may undertake a classical money laundering investigation, analysing the financial flows 'upstream' to pinpoint the predicate offence. The possibility of using two approaches increases the chances of success. In the second case, in which the funds have a legitimate source, law enforcers may need to follow the financial flows until the funds appear within a terrorist's sphere of influence. If the terrorist group is not well-known, the prosecuting authority will retain the burden of proof. This burden may be difficult to discharge as the concept of 'terrorism' is imprecise and international collaboration can sometimes be weak with some countries in this area. However, unless the prosecution can prove that the accused at least knew and accepted that the assets were potentially destined for terrorism, a conviction for handling the assets will be impossible.

Before seizing the funds, the law enforcement authority must have enough suspicion to warrant the opening of an investigation. This subtle difference to the UNSC's *fait accompli* is of some importance. Even in better cases, where the authority has collected sufficient clues and is convinced of their pertinence, the time for determining the right point at which to freeze the assets is limited. It is, in fact, a particularly delicate choice which gives rise to an important dilemma. The immediate freezing of assets ruptures the paper trail and so can deprive the authority of its one chance to reach the terrorist organisation. Without this link, the possibility of obtaining a sentence and a confiscation order decreases considerably as confessions are not to be expected in this area. Worse still, if the prosecution fails or an appeal succeeds because of the lack of evidence, there is a significant risk that the seized funds will be put back into circulation. In such a case, authorities responsible for the administration of justice can unwittingly serve the interests of terrorism by 'laundering' assets of illegal origin or destination; the persons concerned will certainly point to the court's decision to show their 'good faith' in raising and moving the money.

Thus, there is a considerable temptation for prosecutors to delay the application for the freezing order so that they can keep following the financial flows and gathering evidence. The risk that they will lose the funds is indeed significant when one considers the speed of international money transfers. Moreover, if the investigation has been opened against persons associated with al-Qaida, the prosecutor runs the much greater risk (and accepts the much greater responsibility) that these funds will be used to pay for a deadly terrorist attack. Before law enforcement authorities decide to delay the freezing order, the public interest requires them to ensure that sufficient safeguards are in place to prevent the funds from being used for such an end. But is this always possible, considering that large-scale bombings often cost so little?

For criminal justice authorities, the limited room for manoeuvre in dealing with the financiers of al-Qaida and the Taliban and the fear of seeing such a case go unresolved may seem to justify the perverse consequences of the UNSC's listing strategy. They may see it as the lesser evil, which simultaneously ensures the rapid worldwide transmission of information, the public interest in security and better self-regulation by financial institutions in the domain of money laundering. But should such a system, which is limited to temporary measures and does not offer appropriate legal remedies, be backed without reservation? Ten years after the introduction of the UN strategy, do we need to reflect further on different ways of improving the situation? One option would be to intensify efforts to improve the measures at the disposal of law enforcement authorities in combating terrorism.

III. More efficient tools for law enforcement authorities

As previously mentioned, criminal investigations in the field of terrorism and the financing of terrorism are among the most complex and tricky that a prosecutor can encounter. However, they have an important role to play in the system adopted by UN as they can provide a final answer for or against an asset freeze or a travel ban. But criminal justice authorities cannot efficiently play their role if insufficient international cooperation or outdated or unsuitable tools hinder them in their work. Everything must be done to improve the present system. With the following examples, we briefly consider the situation under Swiss domestic law and illustrate some of the loopholes and difficulties which might remain even if Switzerland were to ratify the different UN conventions on terrorism.

1. Optimisation of international cooperation: joint investigation teams

Joint investigation teams are one of the most important improvements made in the area of international cooperation of the last few years. They give law enforcement authorities investigating the same case in two different countries the opportunity to work together more closely, to communicate directly and to share the same offices without informing the suspect. They reduce, as far as possible, the impediments created by national borders and the usual rules of MLA and are clearly targeted at certain types of cross-border criminality, such as terrorism and the financing of terrorism.

Under current Swiss law, joint investigations are only possible with Italy,[6] the states which have ratified the Second Additional Protocol to the European Convention on Mutual Assistance in Criminal Matters (APII ECMA)[7] and the United States (since 1 December 2007, when the bilateral agreement focusing on this subject came into force).[8] This creates a paradox: in dealing with requests for assistance from the great majority of western European countries, Switzerland must apply its ordinary rules of MLA as those states have not yet ratified the APII ECMA. Yet, these standard rules are inappropriate to counter-terrorism investigations, which require confidentiality. In giving the person concerned the right to object to the presence of foreign officials or the transmission of evidence or intelligence abroad, the standard Swiss rules actually require the disclosure of the request. The present situation is therefore unsatisfactory, particularly with respect to the fight against terrorism. Unfortunately, Art. 48–53 of the Convention of 19 June 1990 on the implementation of the Schengen Agreement, which came into force for Switzerland on 12 December 2008, will not rectify the situation.

6   Art. XXI of the Agreement between Switzerland and Italy in order to complete the European Convention on Mutual Assistance in Criminal Matters (SR 0.341.945.41).

7   Albania, Bosnia-Herzegovina, Bulgaria, Croatia, Denmark, Estonia, Latvia, Lithuania, Poland, Portugal, Czech Republic, Rumania, Serbia, Slovakia and Israel.

8   Arrangement on 12 July 2006 between the Federal Department of Justice and Police of the Swiss Confederation and the Department of Justice of the United States of America on the creation of joint investigation teams concerning the fight against terrorism and the financing of terrorism (SR 0.362.336.1). According to Art. 2: 'The joint investigation teams carry out their duties in accordance with the domestic law of the host country. Officers assigned to the joint investigation teams have access to all information necessary to perform their tasks, to the extent permitted by the applicable laws of the host country and their security clearance statutes'.

2. Cybercrime

It is no coincidence that the only conviction in Switzerland in the area of counter-terrorism was in a case of 'cyberterrorism'.[9] In 2007, the Swiss Federal Criminal Court convicted operators of websites and discussion forums that allowed organisations attached to al-Qaida and other radical Islamists (Jihadists) to transmit violent messages and threats, to claim responsibility for terrorists attacks and hostage-takings and to exchange information on the manufacture of explosives. The website had made available pictures of corpses and linked to other pages from which users could view or download pictures depicting the killing of defenseless civilians.

This is proof (were it still needed) that terrorist organisations have understood the advantages of working with this new form of communication, the Internet. However, Switzerland, like many countries, lacks adequate provisions to counter this new type of criminality. In 2001, it signed the Council of Europe's (CoE) Convention on Cybercrime.[10] The Convention on Cybercrime expands considerably on present measures for cooperation, providing competent authorities in some cases with direct access to data stored in other states[11] and a highly efficient means for spontaneously disclosing information.[12] It

---

9   Decision of 21 June 2007 of the Court of Criminal Affairs of the Federal Criminal Court in Bellinzona (SK.2007.4), confirmed by the Federal Court on 2 May 2008 (6B_645/2007 and 6B_650/2007).

10 Council of Europe, Convention on Cybercrime signed in Budapest on 23 November 2001.

11 Convention on Cybercrime, Art. 32: cross-border access to stored computer data with consent or where publicly available: 'A Party may without the authorisation of another Party [...] access or receive, through a computer system in its territory, stored computer data located in another Party, if the Party obtains the lawful and voluntary consent of the person who has the lawful authority to disclose the data to the Party through that computer system', n 10.

12 Art. 30 anticipates that, under certain conditions, some data retained in another state can rapidly be disclosed. This differs from other dispositions concerning the spontaneous information in the field of mutual assistance in the sense that it does not require the opening of a criminal procedure in the country which transmits the information. It is a question of anticipated transmission of information, n 10.

also recommends that states introduce a range of criminal provisions and arrangements for effective international cooperation in relation to cybercrime. Without doubt, the CoE's Convention on Cybercrime is a tool which would further the interest of fighting terrorism and certain new types of criminality. However, Switzerland has not yet ratified the Convention and neither has a good half of the European Union's member states. The measures proposed go well beyond what is customary for countries, such as Switzerland, and this creates difficulties relating to the enforcement of the Convention. But is it not essential to oppose certain types of serious criminality? Would the new methods have been introduced more rapidly if the provisions had been focused exclusively on terrorism and its financing?

3. Universal confiscation: quid juris?

Swiss criminal law, in conformity with the relevant UN conventions,[13] uses standard methods for determining jurisdiction, concentrating on the principle of territoriality, active and passive personality and relative universality (i.e., it is assumed that the perpetrator is on Swiss territory and is not to be extradited). There is no provision giving Switzerland jurisdiction as the *forum rei sitae*, i.e., the formal location of the object to be confiscated (an exception is Art. 24 of the Federal Law on Narcotics, which is limited to the proceeds of drug trafficking).[14] This means that Switzerland cannot prosecute a person and restitute funds simply because it is the place where the funds are held. A further connection – to the offender, offence or victim – is necessary.

---

13 Art. 6 of the UN Convention for the Suppression of Terrorist Bombings, Art. 7 of the UN Convention for the Suppression of the Financing of Terrorism, Art. 9 of the UN Convention for the Suppression of Acts of Nuclear Terrorism.

14 Art. 24 of the Federal Law on Narcotics: 'Unlawful profits lying in Switzerland are forfeited to the State even if the offence was committed abroad. If there is no jurisdiction according to article 348 of the Swiss Criminal Code, the Canton where the assets lie shall be competent'.

In two recent cases,[15] this serious loophole led to the release of funds allegedly belonging to criminal organisations and, in a third case,[16] to the release of funds originating from the arms trade. The situation would be no different in the case of terrorist financing as Switzerland puts terrorist organisations in the same category as any other criminal organisation. In the absence of a connecting factor with Switzerland, there is likewise no way by which Swiss authorities could retain the funds, even though terrorism is a particularly delicate matter.

It is surprising that neither international institutions nor the Swiss legislator were able to perceive this important defect and to pave the way for universal jurisdiction to confiscate at the place where the object is formally located in the case of organised crime or terrorist financing prosecutions; Switzerland, at least, had understood the need for confiscation *forum rei sitae* in relation to drug trafficking. This loophole cannot be explained by a fear on the part of lawmakers of creating conflicts of laws. In fact, it would be simple to close the gap by implementing a hierarchical mechanism, in which classical rules on jurisdiction were granted priority. This would allow the state that convicts the perpetrator to simultaneously order the confiscation of the assets used or intended for terrorism.

4. Statute of limitations for confiscations

Again, Switzerland is not properly equipped to deal with situations in which there is a long delay between the act of terrorism or the financing of terrorism and the criminal proceedings. The Swiss Criminal Code provides a statute of limitations for confiscations of seven years, unless the offence itself may be prosecuted more than seven years after it was committed. This means that the time limit for initiating confiscation proceedings in terrorist financing and organised crime cases is fifteen years. Whatever deadline is enforced, the situation is

---

15 Decisions of the Swiss Federal Court of 8 May 2008 (FCD 134 IV 185: 2.1) and of 7 February 2005 (6P.142/2004: 4.2).
16 Decisions of the Swiss Federal Court (FCD 128 IV 145).

unsatisfactory. How can the passing of time explain a decision to allow terrorist groups to recover their funds? Is the removal of the statute of limitations not the only solution?

5. *Contributing confiscated terrorist assets to an international
    investment fund in favour of victims of terrorism*

A final problem is the lack of a universal system for ensuring the just
allocation of funds to compensate the victims of terrorism. Art. 8(4) of
the UN Convention for the Suppression of the Financing of Terrorism
addresses the implementation by the state parties of mechanisms allowing confiscated terrorist assets to be used to compensate victims
and their families. In addition to the provisions in the criminal law,
which permit civil actions by injured parties, most European countries
have adopted specific laws for the compensation of victims. This legislation is generally based on the principle of territoriality according to
which a country only compensates for offences that took place within
its territory.[17] For some time, Switzerland applied broader criteria and
accepted the payment of damages to citizens who were victims of an
offence in a foreign country in as much as they were resident in Swiss
territory at the time of the act and had not already received compensation from another State.[18] However, the Swiss legislator has decided to
be more restrictive and to revert to the principle of territoriality in a
complete amendment of the law, which came into force on 1 January
2009.[19] Can any state claim that its citizens will not be exposed to

---

17   Message of the Swiss Federal Council of 9 November 2005 concerning the total
     revision of the Law on Assistance to Victims of Offences (FF 2005: 6710),
     which resumes the study of the Swiss Institute of Compared Law (Avis 04-016
     of 12 March 2004, updating the Avis 97-125 of 27 February 1998).
18   Art. 11 §3 of the Federal Law on Assistance to Victims of Offences, in force
     until 31 December 2008: 'When a person of Swiss nationality resident in Swit-
     zerland is victim of an offence in a foreign country he can ask the Canton in
     which he is resident for compensation or legal redress if he has not received suf-
     ficient benefit from the foreign State'.
19   FF 2005: 6704: Victims of offences in a foreign country who are resident in
     Switzerland at the time of the criminal act will, however, continue to benefit

terrorist acts outside its own territory and can it guarantee that they will receive compensation in all situations? Is it worth allowing a state in which a confiscation has been pronounced to keep the funds to the detriment of foreign victims, whose only fault is to fail to understand that they have a right to claim and the proper procedure in that state for making a claim?

Undoubtedly, one of solution is to create an international compensation scheme funded predominantly by the assets confiscated under counter-terrorist financing legislation. Art. 10 of UNSC Resolution 1566[20] lays the foundation for the creation of such a fund and shows that the UNSC perceives the importance of such a scheme. It is to be hoped that implementation will proceed quickly and that regulations will ensure that damages will be distributed to the right persons. However, is this really sufficient? Would the creation of a legal consultation centre within the UN structure not be a better means of ensuring support for the victims of terrorist acts whatever their nationality?

IV. Conclusion

At this stage in history, no state can promise its citizens that they will not be the victims of a terrorist attack – at home or abroad. And yet, it seems easier to impose a standardised system of administrative sanctions on all UN member states than to undertake a real harmonisation of national criminal laws and rules on international cooperation, even though the importance of such efforts has already been acknowledged. It is essential to develop a real interdisciplinary approach so that the gaps in administrative law can be rectified through the criminal law and, if necessary, through the civil law and *vice versa*. Efforts toward harmonisation, especially in the area of MLA and financial support for victims need to be pursued in a spirit of anticipation and innovation

---

from the present facilities put in place to ensure psychological support in overcoming the consequences of the offence.
20   S/RES/1566 (2004).

rather than as a hurried response to tragic incidents. Only in this way will the fight against terrorism, which cannot tolerate the slightest mistake, have the desired effect and only in this way will it be possible to elaborate a system for compensating victims for the tragic consequences of terrorist attacks.

YARA ESQUIVEL SOTO*

An autonomous offence for the financing of terrorism: notes from an Ibero-American perspective

I. Introduction: reinventing the wheel?

On 29 June 2000, twenty-year-old Marwan al-Shehhi received USD 5,000 at a Western Union facility in New York. The remittance was sent from the United Arab Emirates (UAE) Exchange Centre in Dubai by a man who identified himself as Isam Mansar. Less than a month later, al-Shehhi received a second remittance from Mansar: on 18 July 2000, Mansar sent USD 10,000 via another bank transfer from the same exchange centre in Dubai to al-Shehhi's account in Suntrust Bank, Florida; the joint account holder was Mohammed Atta. On 5 August 2000, Mansar made yet a third remittance of USD 9,500, again from the same exchange centre to the same account at the Suntrust Bank. Three weeks later, on 29 August 2000, a man by the name of Ali Abdul Aziz Ali transferred by wire USD 20,000 to the account owned jointly by al-Shehhi and Atta, using a phone number which differed from the number provided by Mansar in previous transactions

* Yara Esquivel Soto worked as an Anti Corruption Public Prosecutor in Costa Rica, where she was in charge of the investigation and trial of several high profile corruption cases. Later she took a position as a regional investigator in the Office of Internal Oversight Services of the United Nations in Kenya, where she investigated fraud, corruption and malfeasance within the organisation. Currently, she works as an Asset Recovery Specialist for the International Centre for Asset Recovery, helping developing countries recover stolen assets. She has worked with over 20 countries in criminal investigations and providing technical assistance. She is also pursuing a Master's Degree at Oxford University in the field of International Human Rights Law.

by only one digit. On 17 September 2000, Hani Fawaz Trading transferred USD 70,000 to the Suntrust account, using the same exchange centre in Dubai and the same phone number as Ali Abdul Aziz Ali. In less than one month, USD 90,000 went unnoticed through the UAE Exchange Centre, although the transactions were clearly linked by the recipient, the phone numbers and the place of transmission. The Suntrust Bank of Florida received, over a period of three months, a total of USD 109,400 in the al-Shehhi-Atta account.[1] Only one year later, at 08.46 am on 11 September 2001, Mohammed Elamir Atta flew American Airlines Flight 11 into the North Tower of the World Trade Centre in New York City. At 09.02 am Marwan Yusef al-Shehhi flew United Airlines Flight 175 into the South Tower of the World Trade Centre. These shocking incidents became known as the 9/11 attacks or 9/11.

The 9/11 attacks had been in the planning since 1996. According to the US Department of Homeland Security,[2] before the year 2000 al-Qaida had operated with an annual budget of thirty million USD. The USD 114,500 received by al-Shehhi during this period paid for English lessons, jet pilot training and living expenses for some of the al-Qaida terrorists.[3] The attack itself cost roughly USD 400,000 of which 25% was received into the Suntrust account. This translated into the deaths of over 3,000 people and an impact of USD 11 trillion on the US economy, a loss that could perhaps have been prevented if appropriate counter-terrorist financing (CTF) measures had been in place in 2000.[4]

Immediately after the attacks, on 12 September 2000, the United Nations Security Council (UNSC) passed Resolution 1368, condemn-

---

1   US Department of Defense, 'Verbatim Transcript of Combatant Status Review Tribunal Hearing for ISN 10018' in *Press Resources*, 29 September 2008, available at http://www.defenselink.mil/news/transcript_isn10018.pdf#1.

2   Thomas H. Kean, Lee H. Hamilton, Richard Ben-Veniste, Bob Kerrey, Fred F. Fielding, John F. Lehman, Jaime S. Gorelick, Timothy J. Roemer, Slade Gorton, and James Thompson, *The 9/11 Commission Report*, National Commission on Terrorist Attacks upon the United States, available at www.9-11commission.gov/report/911Report.pdf.

3   Ibid, n 2.

4   Tom Templeton and Tom Lumley, '9/11 in numbers', The Observer 18 August 2002, in *The Guardian*, 16 March 2009 http://www.guardian.co.uk/world/2002/aug/18/usa.terrorism.

ing the attacks and calling on the international community to prevent and suppress terrorist acts.[5] Shortly afterwards, through Resolution 1373, the UNSC reaffirmed that terrorism constitutes a threat to international peace and security and called upon states to criminalise the financing of terrorism.[6] Terrorist financing was not, however, a new concern for the international community. Already in 1999, the UN had opened the International Convention for the Suppressing of the Financing of Terrorism (Terrorist Financing Convention) for signature. The preamble to this convention refers to the threat to international peace and security posed by terrorist activities. The Convention then criminalises the collection or provision of funds with the knowledge and intention that they are to be used to carry out a terrorist offence as defined.[7]

The inclusion of a specialised offence of terrorist financing in the UN Convention raises the issue of whether domestic laws truly need a new and independent criminal offence of the financing of terrorism or whether existing laws adequately criminalise this type of behaviour. This chapter considers this issue by looking at the approaches taken by a number of Ibero-American states (i.e., states in Latin America and Spain). In so doing, it addresses several questions. First, what is the protected value underlying the offence of financing terrorism? Second, is terrorist financing an 'offence of danger'? Third, if so, is the danger concrete or abstract? Each of these questions will be addressed in order to establish whether there is a need for the creation of a separate offence of financing of terrorism. Although the approach is Ibero-American, the topic's relevance is universal as the trend seems to be the creation of new offences dealing with financing of terrorism.

---

5   UNSC Resolution 1368 of 12 September 2001.
6   UNSC Resolution 1373 of 28 September 2001.
7   UN Convention on the Suppression of the Financing of Terrorism, Art. 2.

II. An Ibero-American perspective

The position in Ibero-American countries reflects both approaches. Some countries that have been dealing with terrorist offences for a longer time, such as Spain, have modified existing legal concepts to accommodate the new concept of terrorist financing. Others in Latin America have opted to adopt new laws specifically on terrorist financing into their criminal statutes.

Given Spain's long history of dealing with Basque terrorism and its influence amongst Ibero-American states, Spanish counter-terrorism legislation provides important insights into these issues. In Spain, the concept of terrorism was embedded in the 1978 Constitution through references to the acts of armed gangs or terrorist cells. The Spanish Supreme Court has tried to differentiate terrorism from organised crime by establishing clear criteria both in the *actus reus* (a sufficiently large group with a structure and a hierarchy in possession of arms and explosives) as well as in the *mens rea* (the intention to create fear and subvert the political order).[8] The Spanish Criminal Code has reserved an entire title for terrorism offences. However, there is no autonomous terrorist financing offence. Rather, acts of terrorist financing are dealt with as 'participating in a terrorist organisation', which is contained in Art. 576 of the Criminal Code.[9] The same is true of Argentina, which punishes terrorist financing through the offence of illicit association (Art. 210 of the Argentine Criminal Code)[10] and Colombia, which treats 'terrorist financing' as agreement to commit crimes (Art. 340 of the Colombian Criminal Code).[11]

---

8   José De la Cuesta, 'Anti-Terrorist Penal Legislation and the Rule of Law: Spanish Experience', in *Electronic Review of the International Association of Penal Law*, 2007, available at http://www.penal.org/new/publications.php?Doc_zone=PUB&langage=gb&ID_doc=351. Clearly, a *dolus specialis* (or special intent) is needed for an act to be considered 'terrorist'.

9   Ibid, n 8.

10   Grupo de Acción Financiera de Sudamérica (GAFISud), *Sistemas Nacionales contra el Lavado de Activos*, 29 September 2008, available at www.gafisud.com.

11   Ibid, n 10.

On the other hand, Chile, Brazil and Peru have opted for the creation of entirely new terrorist financing offences. Chile incorporated the offence of terrorist financing through Law 19906, which modified Art. 8 of Law 18314 and criminalised the act of directly or indirectly soliciting, collecting or providing with funds to be used in the commission of terrorist acts. Following the Terrorist Financing Convention, this offence is committed regardless of whether the funds are destined for one person or many, whether they are sent to an organisation or an association, whether a terrorist act is indeed committed and, if so, which act is committed.[12] In Brazil, terrorist financing was criminalised through Art. 20 of Law 7170 as the act of obtaining funds destined to support subversive or clandestine political organisations. This, however, is a much more restrictive definition than that proposed in the UN Convention.[13]

In Peru, counter-terrorism legislation has been in place since 1992, reflecting that country's long battle against the 'Shining Path'. Law 25,475 contains a detailed description of what is considered terrorism and Art. 4 deals with the offence of collaboration with terrorist acts. Among the different conduct described, para. (f) establishes that it is an offence to provide economic action, aid or mediation voluntarily or with the aim of financing the activities of elements of terrorist organisations. This offence is completed even if the financial support does not result in the commission of a terrorist act.

III. The Theory of the Offence and the importance of the protected legal value

The Theory of the Offence is the foundation for most criminal laws in Ibero-American countries. As first developed by Carrara and von Jhering in the 19th Century, the Theory treated an offence as an unlawful action resulting in a sanction. The classical version of the Theory re-

---

12   Ibid, n 10.
13   Ibid, n 10.

ferred to a physical action, which resulted in a subsequent alteration of the external world.

Currently, the Theory of the Offence looks to systematically understand the elements that justify the imposition of a legal consequence (a sanction) on human conduct.[14] Criminal law is conceived as the *ultima ratio* or last resort against an action that is so damaging that society imposes a severe punishment. The Theory of the Offence is based on the idea that a valid criminal law will always protect a certain legal value. The 'protected legal value' is implicit within the legal text itself and is both the purpose and the limit of the law. Before even beginning to analyse a certain offence, the protected value must be identified in order to establish whether the offence was justified and whether it is constitutional.

The Theory of the Offence should be used to analyse terrorism offences. For example, in the offence of 'membership to an illegal organisation', the protected legal value is the appropriate exercise of the right of association, which is a fundamental right. As explained by Zúñiga Rodríguez, following Antonio García Pablos and Klaus Roxin,

> [...] whoever associates to commit homicides is exercising his right to freedom of association in excess, this person acts outside of any freedom or right: he or she acts against the law.[15]

According to Zúñiga Rodríguez, some offences, like this one, lack an autonomous protected legal value and they are intended to repress actions that endanger other protected values. In other words, if by criminalising terrorism we intend to protect public order as a legal value, criminalising the participation in a terrorist organisation aims to repress threats to public order.[16]

Terrorism itself has been considered an offence that affects several protected values, such as life, physical integrity, property or free-

14　Raúl Plascencia Villanueva, *Teoría del Delito*, Albuquerque, Universidad Nacional Aut, 1998.

15　Laura Zúñiga, 'Redes Internacionales y Criminalidad: a Propósito del Modelo de Participación en Organización Criminal', in L. Zúñiga r./ c. Méndez R./ R. Diego Díaz Santos (eds.), *El derecho penal ante la globalización*, Colex, Madrid, 2002: 51–71.

16　Ibid, n 15.

dom. It has been said that the protection of public order serves to prevent concrete acts of aggression against persons, property or public services, which affect the life of a community.[17] Ocrospoma Pella understands public order as security.[18] This is in keeping with UNSC Resolutions 1368 and 1373, which reaffirm that terrorism constitutes a threat to international peace and security.

Following this train of thought, the underlying protected value behind terrorism offences should be domestic or international public order. The financing of terrorism, however, could be easily considered a preparatory act for the commission of terrorist attacks. Is there a reason why it should be turned into an autonomous offence? If we did so, would it risk becoming an offence of danger?

Von Rohland once said that criminal law must not only deal with concrete grievances caused to the protected value but also with the possibility of harm; hence *danger* itself becomes the object of the criminal investigation.[19] As a consequence, many actions that are normally considered preparatory acts become criminal offences themselves. Eduardo Corigliano has mentioned that certain values – due to their higher relevance or to their special vulnerability – require protection even beyond an actual attack to their integrity.[20] These are known as 'offences of danger'. Offences of danger are committed with the mere threat to the protected value and they differ from 'offences of result' in the sense that the latter require concrete damage to the protected value. For example, homicide is a typical offence of result as it requires the loss of life.

---

17   Enrique Ocrospoma Pella, 'El bien jurídico como criterio modificador del delito de terrorismo' in *Derecho.com Productos y Servicios Jurídicos: Contratos Libros Legislación*, 16 March 2009, available at http://www.derecho.com/articulos/2001/07/01/el-bien-jur-dico-como-criterio-modificador-del-delito-de-terrorismo/.

18   Ibid, n 17.

19   Von Rohland as quoted by Mario Eduardo Corigliano, *La Frontera de lo Punible en el Derecho Penal*. 29 September 2008, available at http://www.monografias.com/; Mario Eduardo Corigliano, 'Delitos de peligro. La frontera de lo punible en el Derecho penal', *Monografías*, available at http://www.monografias.com/trabajos21/delitos-de-peligro/delitos-de-peligro.shtml.

20   Ibid, n 19.

There are two types of danger: concrete and abstract. In the first case, the action itself is dangerous (an *ex ante* danger), whereas in the second case it is the result of the action that is dangerous (an *ex post* danger).[21] Jakobs considers that abstract danger offences are by nature offences of disobedience, as the norm demands that the subject must obey the norm even when the threat has passed.[22] Road offences demonstrate the distinction between the categories: manifestly reckless driving is a dangerous action in and of itself (i.e., a concrete danger). However, driving under the influence of alcohol could result in a dangerous action as the subject may or may not be able to drive his vehicle carefully in his/her physical condition (i.e., an abstract danger). The distinction is of no small importance since abstract danger offences have been deemed unconstitutional in many jurisdictions due to a lack of real or imminent threat to the protected value.

Looking at this analysis and the various national approaches discussed above, we see that terrorist offences are 'multi offensive' in that they affect many protected values, such as the life, physical integrity, property, freedom of movement, national security and so on. As stated before, the concept that best encompasses all these values is that of public order and security – whether at a national or an international level. The conduct of financing terrorist organisations poses an *ex ante* threat to public order. Terrorist activities are offences of result, the result being concrete damage to any of the protected values listed above and contained by the concept of public order and security. The financing of terrorist organisations threatens by itself these protected values, as it allows terrorist acts to become a reality. In other words, without financial support, terrorist organisations cannot exist and cannot commit terrorist acts. For this reason, the financing of terrorism should be an autonomous criminal offence.

---

21 Ibid, n 19.
22 Rafael Márquez Piñero, 'Delitos de Peligro Abstracto'. *Biblioteca Jurídica Virtual*, available at http://www.bibliojuridica.org/libros/2/997/12.pdf.

IV. The need for an autonomous offence of 'terrorist financing'

At the beginning of this paper three questions were posed: which is the protected value behind the criminalisation of the financing of terrorism, should it be criminalised independently and, if so, would it be an offence of concrete or abstract danger? Terrorism needs financial support and a financial platform to survive. The threat that these actions pose must be evaluated *ex ante*: financing terrorism is dangerous in and of itself. If the financing of terrorism poses an *ex ante* threat, it is clearly an offence of concrete danger. As such, there is enough justification to take terrorism financing out of the *iter criminis* and transform it into an autonomous and independent offence, which can be prevented and repressed even if no terrorist activities have yet been committed. The threat to basic and fundamental values, such as life, is too high for the legislator to remain passive and allow terrorist organisations to raise and move money at will. The criminalisation of the financing of terrorism is more than a repressive tool but a preventive weapon in the fight against terror.

SCOTT VESEL*

Combating the financing of terrorism while protecting human rights: a dilemma?

Human rights and fundamental freedoms are the birthright of all human beings, are inalienable and are guaranteed by law. Their protection and promotion is the first responsibility of government. Respect for them is an essential safeguard against an overmighty State. Their observance and full exercise are the foundation of freedom, justice and peace.

Organisation for Stability and Cooperation in Europe (OSCE)
Charter of Paris for a New Europe (1990)

Peace and security in our region is best guaranteed by the willingness and ability of each participating State to uphold democracy, the rule of law and respect for human rights....
We reaffirm that respect for human rights and fundamental freedoms, democracy and the rule of law is at the core of the OSCE's comprehensive concept of security.

OSCE Charter for European Security (1999)

I. Introduction

One occasionally encounters the view that, when it comes to combating terrorism, human rights and security are in conflict and that human rights must give way before the imperatives of security. As a matter of

* Human Rights and Anti-Terrorism Project Officer, Organisation for Security and Cooperation in Europe (OSCE) Office for Democratic Institutions and Human Rights. The views expressed in this paper are those of the author and do not represent the views of the ODIHR, the OSCE or its participating states.

principle, this view is inconsistent with the commitments of the OSCE
and the United Nations Global Counter-Terrorism Strategy.
In adopting the 2002 OSCE Charter on Preventing and Combating Terrorism, OSCE participating States affirmed:

> [We] [u]ndertake to implement effective and resolute measures against terrorism
> and to conduct all counter-terrorism measures and cooperation in accordance
> with the rule of law, the United Nations Charter and the relevant provisions of
> international law, international standards of human rights and, where applicable,
> international humanitarian law [...].

> [We] [a]re convinced of the need to address conditions that may foster and sus-
> tain terrorism, in particular by fully respecting democracy and the rule of law, by
> allowing all citizens to participate fully in political life, by preventing discrimi-
> nation and encouraging intercultural and inter-religious dialogue in their socie-
> ties, by engaging civil society in finding common political settlement for con-
> flicts, by promoting human rights and tolerance and by combating poverty.[1]

The same point was made succinctly in the UN Global Counter-
Terrorism Strategy:

> We resolve to undertake the following measures, reaffirming that the promotion
> and protection of human rights for all and the rule of law is essential to all com-
> ponents of the Strategy, recognising that effective counter-terrorism measures
> and the promotion of human rights are not conflicting goals but complementary
> and mutually reinforcing.[2]

The international community clearly agrees, in principle, that the protection and promotion of human rights is essential to the success of
any counter-terrorism strategy.

Nevertheless, policy makers are (perhaps understandably) tempted
to look first to repressive measures when trying to achieve security
while neglecting the more subtle task of incorporating human rights
protections. Such an approach, however, is short-sighted and inher-

---

1   OSCE Charter on Preventing and Combating Terrorism, MC(10).JOUR/2
     (7 December 2002), available at http://www.osce.org/documents/odihr/2002/12/
     1488_en.pdf.
2   Global Counter-Terrorism Strategy, GA Res 60/288, UN GAOR, 60th session,
     Agenda Items 46 and 120, UN Doc A/RES/60/288 (20 September 2006), Annex
     [9], available at http://www.un.org/terrorism/strategy-counter-terrorism.shtml.

ently self-defeating. As the United Nations (UN) Secretary General wrote in his 2006 report:

> Terrorism often thrives in environments in which human rights are violated and where political and civil rights are curtailed, [...] Past cases show that Govern-ments that resort to excessive use of force and indiscriminate repression when countering terrorism risk strengthening the support base for terrorists among the general population. Such measures generally invite counter-violence, undermine the legitimacy of counter-terrorism measures and play into the hands of terrorists [...].
>
> Only by placing counter-terrorism within a rule-of-law framework can we safe-guard the internationally valued standard that outlaws terrorism, reduce the con-ditions that may generate cycles of terrorist violence and address grievances and resentment that may be conducive to terrorist recruitment. To compromise on the protection of human rights would hand terrorists a victory they cannot achieve on their own.[3]

Indeed, a statistical analysis, performed by two prominent economists apparently confirmed a correlation between poor human rights protec-tions and extremist violence, the authors noting that 'the data seems to suggest that a lack of civil liberties is associated with higher participa-tion in terrorism [...]'.[4]

Clearly, respecting human rights while countering terrorism is not only a matter of principle but is in fact vital to the success of counter-terrorism measures. Indeed, far from being a hindrance, human rights provide useful guideposts to the development of an effective counter-terrorism strategy.

In addition, as is set out in more detail below, a failure to incorpo-rate adequate due process protections can render counter-terrorism measures unenforceable and, hence, ineffective. There is, thus, no 'dilemma' in the sense of an opposition between the aims of providing security and protecting human rights. Instead, both aims must be pur-sued simultaneously, as integral components of counter-terrorism

3   UN Secretary General, *Uniting against Terrorism: Recommendations for a Global Counter-Terrorism Strategy*, United Nations General Assembly Official Rec-ords (UNGAOR) 60th session, Agenda Items 46 and 120, UN DOC A/60/825 (27 April 2006) [7, 22].

4   Alan Krueger and Jitka Malesckova, 'Education, Poverty and Terrorism: Is There a Causal Connection?', *Journal of Economic Perspectives* 17/4, 2003: 142.

strategies. As this chapter illustrates, the challenges of doing so are considerable but not insurmountable.

While a broad range of human rights are engaged by efforts to suppress terrorist financing, this chapter will focus on the due process rights implicated by international, regional and national terrorist blacklisting regimes. The experiences of national governments, the European Communities and the UN itself have all demonstrated that the failure to integrate adequate due process protections seriously undermines the effectiveness of these efforts. At the same time, the development and implementation of adequate due process protections has remained elusive.

II. Human rights in practice

In order to understand how rights work in practice, it is essential to recognise that, while all human rights are 'universal, indivisible and interdependent and interrelated',[5] they are not identical. In particular, rights differ in the degree to which they may be permissibly interfered with by governments. Civil and political rights can be categorised as follows:

- Absolute rights permit no qualification or interference under any circumstances
- Limited rights can be limited within constraints that are spelled out in the article of the international convention that provides for the right
- Qualified rights permit restrictions intended to strike a balance either between the individual and the community or between two competing rights. Any restriction on these rights has to be a proportionate means for achieving a legitimate purpose

5   World Conference on Human Rights, *Vienna Declaration and Programme of Action*, 12 July 1993, UN Doc A/Conf.157/23, available at http://daccessdds. un.org/doc/UNDOC/GEN/G93/142/33/PDF/G9314233.pdf?OpenElement.

1. Absolute rights

There can never be a justification for violating an absolute right. The classic example is the right to freedom from torture, inhuman or degrading treatment. Thus, the European Court of Human Rights (ECtHR) held in *Ireland v. UK* that certain interrogation techniques in relation to suspected terrorists in Northern Ireland amounted to inhuman and degrading treatment. As a result, not even national security could justify those measures.[6]

Another example is the *Chahal* case, in which the ECtHR held that the UK Government could not extradite someone in circumstances where it was likely that the person would be exposed to torture. Due to the absolute nature of the right to protection from torture, this rule applied even when national security interests were at stake.[7] This approach was recently confirmed with the ECtHR's decision in *Saadi*.[8]

Other examples of absolute rights include the protection from slavery and elements of the obligation to protect life.

2. Qualified rights

Sometimes, rights can conflict with each other. For example, one person's right to private life may conflict with another person's right to freedom of expression. In such cases, a fair balance has to be struck between the two competing rights, which necessarily entails some restriction on one or both rights. Hence, qualified rights can be lawfully restricted provided that the restrictions satisfy the legality, necessity, proportionality and non-discrimination tests.

In most cases, qualified rights are easily identified in the human rights treaties. Typically, the relevant provision first asserts the right and then provides that it can be lawful to qualify the right if it is necessary in a democratic society to do so and that there is a legal basis

---

6   ECtHR, *Ireland v. UK*, Application No. 5310/71, 18 January 1978, §§ 162–164.
7   ECtHR, *Chahal v. UK*, Case No. 70/1995/576/662, 25 October 1996.
8   ECtHR, *Saadi v. Italy*, Application No. 37201/06, 28 February 2008.

for such limits. A typical example of such a formulation is the right of association in Art. 22(1)–(2) of the International Covenant on Civil and Political Rights:

> 1. Everyone shall have the right to freedom of association with others, including the right to form and join trade unions for the protection of his interests.
>
> 2. No restrictions may be placed on the exercise of this right other than those which are prescribed by law and which are necessary in a democratic society in the interests of national security or public safety, public order (*ordre public*), the protection of public health or morals or the protection of the rights and freedoms of others. This article shall not prevent the imposition of lawful restrictions on members of the armed forces and of the police in their exercise of this right.

There are well-established procedural rules for addressing claims that a qualified right has been violated. The claimant bears the burden of establishing an interference with the right and the state has the burden of proving the interference was justified.

In *Olsson v. Sweden*,[9] the ECtHR articulated the standard test according to which an interference will be justified only if it is:

– 'In accordance with the law' (i.e., there must be a sufficiently precise legal basis which contains a measure of protection against arbitrariness)
– In pursuit of one of the legitimate aims defined in the second paragraph of the relevant article of the Convention (e.g., national security)
– 'Necessary in a democratic society', (i.e., 'that an interference corresponds to a pressing social need and, in particular, that it is proportionate to the legitimate aim pursued')

In practice, when a case is brought before the ECtHR, the Court applies a three-pronged proportionality test which asks: (1) whether the measure is likely to be effective in achieving the government's stated purpose (the 'suitability' test), (2) whether there are less restrictive ways of achieving the purpose (the 'necessity' test) and (3) whether the negative impact on the right is justified by the benefits to the

---

9   ECtHR, *Olsson v. Sweden*, No. 10465/83, Judgment of 24 March 1988, § 67.

pressing social need (the test for 'proportionality in the narrow sense').

3. *Limited rights*

Some rights are absolute in principle but may be subject to certain limits in practice. The relevant treaty provisions will typically assert such rights in absolute terms, before stating that they may be subjected to certain enumerated limits. For example, the right to liberty can be taken away from an individual following conviction by a competent court.[10]

Similarly, the right to a fair trial is absolute to the extent that the trial as a whole must be fair; however, the separate elements of the fair trial right can be limited in certain circumstances in the public interest, so long as the right as a whole is not compromised. For example, a defendant's right to confront the prosecution's witnesses may be limited where a particular witness is the alleged victim or has been threatened by the defendant. In such circumstances, the methods and content of cross-examination can be limited to protect the witness' rights and the integrity of the proceeding. However, such modifications must be balanced to ensure a fair trial for the defendant.

III. Due process and terrorist financing blacklists

1. *Targeted sanctions, the 1267 Committee and the 'Consolidated List'*

The cornerstone of the international counter-terrorist financing regime consists of the compilation of international and national blacklists of individuals and organisations involved in terrorism in order to freeze

---

10   See, e.g., European Convention on Human Rights, Art. 5(1)(a).

their assets and prohibit the provision of any further resources to such organisations or individuals.

The introduction of the UN's terrorist blacklists must be seen historically as an evolution in the use of sanctions by the United Nations Security Council (UNSC).[11] The UN sanctions power, provided for under Art. 41 of the UN Charter, was designed to be used against states, although, in practice, individuals (including government officials) were often targeted. The frequency of the use of comprehensive sanctions against states increased significantly in the 1990s but gave rise to serious humanitarian concerns. Accordingly, it was hoped that 'smart' or 'targeted' sanctions could provide a better alternative; UN Security Council (UNSC) Resolution 1267 (1999) represented the first attempt to put such targeted sanctions into practice at the UN level.[12]

Through Resolution 1267, the UN Security Council imposed financial sanctions on the Taliban and established the 1267 Committee – composed of the members of the Security Council – to maintain the Consolidated List of proscribed organisations and individuals. These targeted sanctions were extended to al-Qaida by Resolution 1333 (2000). At present, any Member State may submit a name to the 1267 Committee and if all Committee members agree, the name is added to the list. Where a person or group appears on the list, all UN Member States are obligated to (a) freeze his or her or their assets, (b) bar the individual from travelling and (c) prevent the supply of arms to such a group or individual.

The creation of the 1267 Committee and the maintenance of the Consolidated List, placed the Security Council in the new and unusual

---

11   See generally Thomas Biersteker and Sue Eckert, 'Strengthening Targeted Sanctions through Fair and Clear Procedures', *Watson Institute Publications*, 2006, available at http://watsoninstitute.org/pub/Strengthening_Targeted_Sanctions.pdf; Noah Birkhauser, 'Sanctions of the Security Council against Individuals – Some Human Rights Problems', *European Society of International Law*, available at http:// www.esil-sedi.org/english/pdf/Birkhauser.PDF.

12   See Conor Gearty, 'Situating Human Rights Law in an Age of Counter-Terrorism', *John Kelly Memorial Lecture*, delivered at University College Dublin Law Faculty, 13 March 2008, available at http://www.conorgearty.co.uk/pdfs/EU_UN _textFINAL.pdf.

position of dealing with individual cases, a role which one commentator described as follows:

> [...] the Security Council is now behaving as a 'quasi-criminal' investigating, prosecuting and sentencing agency. It is starting to do things which were previously only done by national judges, police, prosecutors and intelligence officials.[13]

Moreover, Resolution 1267 did not provide the Committee with guidance as to the legal standards for inclusion on the list or safeguards or remedies for individuals or organisations claiming to have been included erroneously on the list. As the Secretary General's High Level Panel on Threats, Challenges and Change observed in its 2004 report:

> The way entities or individuals are added to the terrorist list maintained by the Council and the absence of review or appeal for those listed raise serious accountability issues and possibly violate fundamental human rights norms and conventions. The Al-Qaida and Taliban Sanctions Committee should institute a process for reviewing cases of individuals and institutions claiming to have been wrongly placed or retained on its watch lists.[14]

Since then, the Security Council has implemented some improvements. Most notably, Resolution 1730 (2006) established a focal point within the UN Secretariat to receive de-listing requests directly from concerned parties and Resolution 1735 (2006), called on Member States to provide a statement of case when proposing names for inclusion on the list. More recently, Resolution 1822 (2008) directed the 1267 Committee to make available on its website 'a narrative summary of reasons for listing for the corresponding entry or entries on the Consolidated List'. However, as will be seen below, these changes have not persuaded regional or national courts that the 1267 Committee's procedures adequately protect due process rights.

---

13   Iain Cameron, 'Protecting Legal Rights: on the (In)security of Targeted Sanctions', in Peter Wallensteen and Carina Staibano, *International Sanctions: Between Words and Wars in the Global System,* Routledge, London, 2005: 189.
14   UN Secretary General, *A More Secure World: Our Shared Responsibility, Report of the High-level Panel on Threats, Challenges and Change,* UNGAOR 59th session, Agenda Item 55, UN Doc. A/59/565 (2 December 2004) [50], available at http://daccessdds.un.org/doc/UNDOC/GEN/N04/602/31/PDF/N0460231.pdf.

2. *Procedural rights implicated by terrorist financing blacklists*

While the details of the blacklisting process are different in each country and at the regional and UN levels, the process typically involves the compilation of a dossier by an administrative agency, which supports the agency's conclusion that a group or individual is involved in 'terrorism'. This dossier may include both public and confidential information. The group is then added to the blacklist, at which point its assets are frozen, its members[15] are forbidden to travel and it becomes a criminal offence for third parties to provide support to the group or its members. Normally, the group in question does not have an opportunity to participate in the administrative process leading to its inclusion on the list, though it will ordinarily have some opportunity to appeal its inclusion through an administrative or a court proceeding. Even in these appeal proceedings, however, the confidential materials are typically withheld from the applicant and provided only to the court or administrative tribunal reviewing the listing.

As can be seen from this brief description, terrorist blacklists engage a range of human rights concerns, including the right to privacy, the right to property, the freedom of association and the right to travel (or freedom of movement). This chapter focuses primarily on due process complaints raised in relation to the listing process in selected national and regional court cases. The selection is intended to be illustrative rather than comprehensive and therefore other important issues may have been omitted.

In a report issued in March 2007, the UN High Commissioner for Human Rights (UNHCHR) summarised the procedural rights implications of the UN's targeted sanctions:

> While the system of targeted sanctions represents an important improvement over the former system of comprehensive sanctions, it nonetheless continues to pose a number of serious human rights concerns related to the lack of transpar-

---

15   Identifying the 'members' of a proscribed organisation is a separate problem. There are divergent views as to the strength of connection required between an individual and the organisation, as well as the extent to which an individual must know of an organisation's involvement in terrorism, in order for the individual to be blacklisted on the basis of their membership alone.

ency and due process in listing and delisting procedures. [...] [I]n brief, they include questions related to:

- Respect for due process rights: Individuals affected by a United Nations listing procedure effectively are essentially denied the right to a fair hearing.
- Standards of proof and evidence in listing procedures: While targeted sanctions against individuals clearly have a punitive character, there is no uniformity in relation to evidentiary standards and procedures.
- Notification: Member States are responsible for informing their nationals that they have been listed but often this does not happen. Individuals have a right to know the reasons behind a listing decision, as well as the procedures available for challenging a decision.
- Time period of individual sanctions: Individual listings normally do not include an 'end date' to the listing, which may result in a temporary freeze of assets becoming permanent. The longer an individual is on a list, the more punitive the effect will be.
- Accessibility: Only States have standing in the current United Nations sanctions regime, which assumes that the State will act on behalf of the individual. In practice, often this does not happen and individuals are effectively excluded from a process which may have a direct punitive impact on them.
- Remedies: There is a lack of consideration to remedies available to individuals whose human rights have been violated in the sanctions process.[16]

Some (but not all) of these due process issues also arise in the context of regional and national terrorist blacklists.

In this connection, it is important to note that although listing is linked, at some level, with involvement in criminal activity ('terrorism' – although there is still no internationally agreed definition of terrorism), a criminal trial is not a feature of the blacklisting process. As the 1267 Committee explains,

---

16 UN High Commissioner for Human Rights, *Report of the United Nations High Commissioner for Human Rights on the Protection of Human Rights and Fundamental Freedoms while Countering Terrorism*, UN Doc A/HRC/4/88, 9 March 2007: 10–11, available at http://daccessdds.un.org/doc/UNDOC/GEN/G07/117/52/PDF/G0711752.pdf.

A criminal charge or conviction is not necessary for inclusion on the Consolidated List as the sanctions are intended to be preventive in nature.[17]

Because there are no criminal trials, the full range of fair trial rights available to a criminal defendant is not available in such proceedings.[18] The terrorist blacklists represent new and highly unusual legal regimes. Conceived as 'preventive' rather than 'punitive' in nature, they nonetheless have serious consequences on listed parties as well as their family members. The use of administrative or civil procedures, rather than criminal trials, necessarily impacts the due process rights of the parties concerned, including by weakening (and in some cases reversing)[19] the burden of proof, limiting (or ignoring) the presumption of innocence, modifying evidentiary rules to permit secret evidence,[20] as well as other types of evidence that would not be admissible in criminal trials, and lowering the standards for determining guilt.[21]

---

17   Al-Qaida and Taliban Sanctions Committee, *Guidelines of the Committee for the Conduct of its Work*, updated as of 12 February 2007: 3, available at http://www.un.org/sc/committees/1267/pdf/1267_guidelines.pdf.

18   For example, the protections set out in Art. 6(2) and Art. 6(3) of the European Convention on Human Rights and in Art. 14(2)–(7) of the International Covenant on Civil and Political Rights apply only to defendants in criminal proceedings. However, Iain Cameron has argued that, '[t]he effects of blacklisting may be sufficiently serious to be a "determination of a criminal charge", triggering the application of Art. 6 in its entirety. If this is not the case, then blacklisting fits into the Convention framework of disputes over "civil rights" under Art. 6 (1), i.e. the rights to property and to reputation': Iain Cameron, *The European Convention on Human Rights, Due Process and UN Security Council Counter-Terrorism Sanctions*, report prepared for the Council of Europe, 6 February 2006: 2, available at http://www.coe.int/t/e/legal_affairs/legal_co-operation/Public_international_law/Texts_&_Documents/2006/I.%20Cameron%20Report%202006.pdf.

19   Laura Donohue, *Anti-Terrorist Finance in the United Kingdom and United States*, 27 *Michigan Journal of International Law*, L 303, 2006: 375–376 (discussing asset forfeiture provisions under the USA PATRIOT Act).

20   Secret evidence in this context refers to evidence, such as intelligence, that is available to the administrative decision maker and (ordinarily) presented to the tribunal, but not disclosed to the group or individual concerned.

21   The normal standard for criminal cases is proof beyond a reasonable doubt, whereas in civil cases a lower, 'balance of probabilities' standard is ordinarily

In January 2008, the Parliamentary Assembly of the Council of Europe (PACE) issued a resolution emphasising that, whatever the precise nature of the sanctions, minimum due process protections were required:

> Whilst it is not at all clear and still being debated whether such sanctions have a criminal, administrative or civil character, their imposition must, under the European Convention on Human Rights (ECHR) (ETS No. 5) as well as the United Nations International Covenant on Civil and Political Rights (UNCCPR), respect certain minimum standards of procedural protection and legal certainty.[22]

Similarly, the Monitoring Team established to support the 1267 Committee (Monitoring Team) noted in its November 2007 report:

> [...] there is continued concern that sanctions have a punitive effect, whatever is said about them as a preventive measure and that the listing process should therefore incorporate higher standards of fairness.[23]

In its January 2008 resolution, the PACE concluded that:

> [...] the procedural and substantive standards currently applied by the UNSC and the Council of the European Union, despite some recent improvements, in no way fulfil the minimum standards laid down above [i.e. right to notice, a statement of reasons, a hearing, judicial review and compensation for any rights violation as well as a clear definition of the grounds for the imposition of sanc-

applied to basic findings of fact. However, in many blacklisting cases, the parties concerned had no participation in the original, administrative, fact-finding proceedings, in which case the operative standard is the standard of judicial review applied by the reviewing court. In the US cases discussed below, the reviewing courts apply a 'substantial evidence' standard according to which listing would be upheld so long as it was supported by substantial evidence, which could include evidence that would be inadmissible in criminal proceedings (i.e., hearsay), as well as secret evidence not disclosed to the party.

22 Parliamentary Assembly of the Council of Europe (PACE), *Resolution 1597* (2008), adopted 23 January 2008, available at http://assembly.coe.int/Documents /AdoptedText/ta08/ERES1597.htm.

23 *Report of the Analytical Support and Sanctions Monitoring Team pursuant to resolution 1735 (2006) Concerning Al-Qaida and the Taliban and Associated Individuals and Entities*, UN Doc S/2007/677: 11, available at http://daccessdds. un.org/doc/UNDOC/GEN/N07/606/64/PDF/N0760664.pdf.

tions and relevant evidence] and violate the fundamental principles of human rights and the rule of law.[24]

The PACE went on to urge both the European Union (EU) and the UN bodies 'to implement procedural and substantive improvements aimed at safeguarding individual human rights and the rule of law, in the interest of the credibility of the international fight against terrorism'.[25] This call was echoed in the Reply by the Council of Europe's Committee of Ministers on 21 July 2008 in which it 'reiterates that it is essential that these sanctions be accompanied by the necessary procedural guarantees'.[26]

The institutions of the Council of Europe are not alone in expressing concern that the due process problems in the listing/de-listing process risk undermining the credibility and effectiveness of the international counter-terrorism financing regime. Indeed, the report issued by the Monitoring Team stated in May 2008:

> The Consolidated List remains the cornerstone of the sanctions regime. However, as the Team has noted in all its previous reports, the List has serious defects. It requires all Member States, under the active leadership of the Committee and with the help of the Team, to put this right; until that happens, the impact of the sanctions regime will continue to fade.[27]

In particular, the Monitoring Team emphasised problems with the quality of the information on the list, noting that 'some entries lack the basic identifiers necessary to make any check against them worthwhile'.[28] However, it also noted due process criticisms relating to the

24 PACE, n 22.
25 PACE, 'United Nations Security Council and European Union Blacklists', *Recommendation 1824* (2008), available at http://assembly.coe.int/Documents/ AdoptedText/ta08/EREC1824.htm.
26 Committee of Ministers of the Council of Europe, *Reply to Recommendation 1824* (2008), (Reply adopted by the Committee of Ministers on 9 July 2008), available at https://wcd.coe.int/ViewDoc.jsp?id=1325221.
27 *Report of the Analytical Support and Sanctions Monitoring Team pursuant to resolution 1735 (2006), concerning al-Qaida and the Taliban and associated individuals and entities*, UN Doc S/2008/324, 13 May 2008: 12, available at http://daccessdds.un.org/doc/UNDOC/GEN/N08/341/88/PDF/N0834188.pdf.
28 Monitoring Team Report, n 27: 12.

fact that 'listed parties do not know why they have been placed under sanctions and have no opportunity to challenge the evidence against them'[29] as well as the absence of any right of appeal.

While the need for fair procedures is universally acknowledged, considerable debate remains as to the nature of listing/de-listing proceedings and the proper scope of due process rights in such proceedings. Meanwhile, as the debate continues, dissatisfaction with the existing procedural safeguards has grown to the point that it risks undermining the entire sanctions regime. As states lose confidence in the process and doubts persist about the credibility of the lists, states will be increasingly unwilling to provide names or information to the 1267 Committee or to vigorously implement the sanctions within their domestic legal orders. Moreover, successful legal challenges to the current procedures in national and regional courts make it increasingly difficult to implement the regime. Although the decisions are only locally binding, they threaten a regime which must be implemented globally in order to be effective.

Nonetheless, the cases discussed in the remainder of this paper, point to an emerging consensus on at least two points. The first point is that the basic due process requirements for blacklisting include, at a minimum:[30]

–   Notice to the listed party of the case against it (although confidential material may in some cases be withheld)
–   An opportunity for the party to be heard and challenge the case for listing
–   An opportunity to appeal the listing decision to an independent tribunal that has access to the confidential materials and is empowered to grant an effective remedy

The second point of consensus is that existing blacklisting processes at the UN, regional and national levels frequently fall short of these

---

29   Monitoring Team Report, n 27: 17.
30   A 2006 study commissioned by the UN Office of Legal Affairs also included a right of the party to be advised and represented. See Bardo Fassbender, *Targeted Sanctions and Due Process*, 20 March 2006: 8 and 28–32, available at http://www.un.org/law/counsel/Fassbender_study.pdf.

minimum standards. At the same time, there does not appear to be consensus regarding the standards of proof applicable to initial listing decisions nor regarding the standard of judicial review to be applied by a reviewing court or tribunal.

IV. Review of selected cases concerning blacklists

1. Cases reviewing implementation of UNSC Resolution 1267

As a technical matter, it is not open to any national, regional or international court to review the compatibility of the UN sanctions regime itself with due process norms because the regime was established by way of Security Council resolutions under Chapter VII of the UN Charter. As the Court of First Instance of the European Communities (CFI) explained,

> [T]he resolutions of the Security Council at issue were adopted under Chapter VII of the Charter of the United Nations. In these circumstances, determining what constitutes a threat to international peace and security and the measures required to maintain or re-establish them is the responsibility of the Security Council alone and, as such, escapes the jurisdiction of national or Community authorities and courts [...].[31]

Nonetheless, in the cases discussed in this section, courts in the European Communities (EC) and the UK have struck down implementing measures on human rights and rule of law grounds and in the process have expressed severe criticisms of the limited procedural protections afforded at the UN level.

---

31   *Yassin Abdullah Kadi v. Council of the European Union*, Case T-315/01 (Judgment, Court of First Instance, 21 September 2005) § 219, reversed on other grounds, *Yassin Abdullah Kadi & Al Barakaat Int'l Fdn v Council of the European Union*, Cases C-402/05 P and C-415/05 P (Judgment of the Court, Grand Chamber, 3 September 2008).

European Communities

In a decision rendered on 3 September 2008 in the cases of *Kadi* and *Al Barakaat*, the Court of Justice of the European Communities annulled measures taken to implement UNSC Resolution 1267 at the European level for failing to comply with due process norms. The Court emphasised that such implementing measures needed to be subjected to strict judicial review precisely because the due process protections afforded by the 1267 Committee were so poor:

> The Guidelines of the Sanctions Committee, as last amended on 12 February 2007, make it plain that an applicant submitting a request for removal from the list may in no way assert his rights himself during the procedure before the Sanctions Committee or be represented for that purpose, the Government of his State of residence or of citizenship alone having the right to submit observations on that request.
>
> Moreover, those Guidelines do not require the Sanctions Committee to communicate to the applicant the reasons and evidence justifying his appearance in the summary list or to give him access, even restricted, to that information. Last, if that Committee rejects the request for removal from the list, it is under no obligation to give reasons.
>
> It follows from the foregoing that the Community judicature must, in accordance with the powers conferred on it by the EC Treaty, ensure the review, in principle the full review, of the lawfulness of all Community acts in the light of the fundamental rights forming an integral part of the general principles of Community law, including review of Community measures which, like the contested regulation, are designed to give effect to the resolutions adopted by the Security Council under Chapter VII of the Charter of the United Nations.[32]

The rationale for the Court of Justice's conclusion here is not made explicit but may be more clearly understood through the Court's reference to the decision by the ECtHR in the *Bosphorus* case. In that case, the ECtHR was called upon to consider whether the seizure of an aircraft by the Irish authorities, pursuant to Ireland's obligations under European Community law to implement sanctions against the Federal

---

32   *Yassin Abdullah Kadi & Al Barakaat Int'l Fdn v. Council of the European Union*, European Court of Justice (ECJ), Cases C-402/05 P and C-415/05 P (Judgment of the Court, Grand Chamber, 3 September 2008) §§ 324–326.

Republic of Yugoslavia, was consistent with Ireland's human rights' obligations.[33] The ECtHR stated:

> [...] State action taken in compliance with such legal obligations is justified as long as the relevant organisation is considered to protect fundamental human rights, as regards both substantive guarantees offered and the mechanisms controlling their observance, in a manner which can be considered at least equivalent to that for which the Convention provides [...].[34]

Given the dim view the Court of Justice on the due process protections afforded at the UN, the Court evidently did not consider that the actions taken to implement Resolution 1267 – which involved the mere transposition of names from the 1267 Committee's list into the Annex of the regulation, without any further process for the affected persons and entities[35] – were justified. The Court stated:

> [I]n the light of the actual circumstances surrounding the inclusion of the appellants' names in the list of persons and entities covered by the restrictive measures contained in Annex I to the contested regulation, it must be held that the rights of the defence, in particular the right to be heard and the right to effective judicial review of those rights, were patently not respected. [...] Because the Council neither communicated to the appellants the evidence used against them to justify the restrictive measures imposed on them nor afforded them the right to be informed of that evidence within a reasonable period after those measures were enacted, the appellants were not in a position to make their point of view in that respect known to advantage. [...] In addition [...] the appellants were also unable to defend their rights with regard to that evidence in satisfactory conditions before the Community judicature, with the result that it must be held that their right to an effective legal remedy has also been infringed.[36]

---

33   At issue was an aircraft belonging to Yugoslav Airlines (JAT) which had been leased to a Turkish company. When the aircraft was sent to Ireland for servicing, it was seized by Irish authorities pursuant to UNSC Resolution 820 (1993) which provided that states should impound all aircraft within their territories 'in which a majority or controlling interest is held by a person or undertaking in or operating from the [FRY]'. Resolution 820 was implemented in the European Communities through Regulation (EEC) No. 999/93.

34   *Bosphorus Hava Yollari v Ireland*, Application No. 45036/98 (Judgment, Grand Chamber, 30 June 2005), § 155.

35   See ECJ, *Kadi*, n 32, §§ 32–33.

36   ECJ, *Kadi*, n 32, §§ 334: 348–349.

Accordingly, the Court has effectively held that, in circumstances where the 1267 Committee does not afford adequate due process protections, the European authorities cannot simply take the names provided by the 1267 Committee and add them to the European list: they must provide any listed party with an opportunity to be informed of and respond to the evidence against them. The Court suspended the effectiveness of its ruling temporarily in order to afford the European Communities with an opportunity to rectify the problems with the existing regulation but it is unclear how the problem can be resolved without changes at the UN level. Thus, the limited due process rights afforded by the 1267 Committee have jeopardised the successful implementation of the sanctions at the European level and this may have serious consequences for the regime as a whole.

United Kingdom

Prior to the decision of the European Court of Justice (ECJ) in *Kadi* discussed above, five individuals subject to asset freezing orders made by the UK government in connection with the implementation of UNSC Resolutions 1267 and 1373, brought an action before the High Court. They raised various due process and human rights issues. On 24 April 2008, the High Court issued a decision that struck down the orders on the basis, *inter alia*, that the orders had the effect of overriding a listed person's fundamental human rights and only Parliament had the power to authorise such measures.[37] The Court also found that the criminal offences created by the statute were impermissibly vague and therefore violated the principle of legal certainty.[38] It noted that 'The very wide definition of economic resources makes it impossible for members of the family of the designated person in particular to

---

37   *A, K, M, Q & G v. Treasury*, [2007] EWHC 869 (Admin) at § 38, see also §§ 24–25.

38   'Legal certainty' incorporates the principles of legitimate expectations and of non-retroactivity. In this case, the High Court quoted the definition provided by the House of Lords in *R v Rimmington* [2006] 1 AC 459 § 33: 'no one should be punished under a law unless it is sufficiently clear and certain to enable him to know what conduct is forbidden before he does it; and no on should be punished for any act which was not clearly and ascertainably punishable when the act was done': *A, K, M, Q & G v. Treasury*, [2007] EWHC 869 at § 43.

know whether they are committing an offence or [whether] a licence was needed'.[39]

The Court also considered at some length the claim that the order implementing Resolution 1267 (the AQO or Al Qaida Order) denied the listed person a right to be heard and to judicial review. Justice Collins described the delisting procedure established by the 1267 Committee and stated:

> It is, I think, obvious that this procedure does not begin to achieve fairness for the person who is listed. Governments may have their own reasons to want to ensure that he remains on the list and there is no procedure which enables him to know the case he has to meet so that he can make meaningful representations.[40]

However, the Judge also found that this claim had to be considered in light of the decision rendered by the CFI in the *Kadi* case, which rejected a similar claim against the applicable EC regulation. Although bound by the CFI's decision, the High Court strongly disagreed with it and quoted approvingly from the Opinion of the Advocate General which urged the ECJ to grant Kadi's appeal. The High Court noted that 'the acceptance [by the ECJ] of the Advocate General's views would inevitably lead to the quashing of the AQO'.[41] As discussed above, the ECJ did in fact grant the appeal in the *Kadi* case, thereby confirming the High Court's view that due process concerns were of sufficient weight to require the quashing of both the UK order and the EC regulation.

Thus, the High Court and the Court of Justice are now in agreement that, given the absence of due process protections at the UN level, administrative authorities at the national and regional level may not simply implement freezing orders on the basis of the Consolidated List. Rather they must also provide listed parties with an opportunity to be heard and to challenge the case against them. The message is clear: if the blacklisting regime under Resolution 1267 is to survive and be effective, it must integrate adequate due process protections for listed parties.

---

39 *A, K, M, Q & G v. Treasury*, n 38, at §§ 42–46.
40 *A, K, M, Q & G v. Treasury*, n 38, at § 18.
41 *A, K, M, Q & G v. Treasury*, n 38, § 32.

2. Cases concerning national and regional listing/de-listing procedures

The 1267 Sanctions Committee, however, is not alone in struggling to integrate due process protections into blacklisting regimes: courts and administrations around the world are dealing with challenges to other terrorist blacklisting regimes, such as those established pursuant to UNSC Resolution 1373 (2001). While some countries had established terrorist blacklists prior to 11 September 2001 (9/11), these efforts were given significant impetus by Resolution 1373, which called upon all states, *inter alia*, to enact measures to freeze the assets of persons or entities involved in terrorism and to criminalise the provision of resources to such persons or entities. The cases discussed below involve challenges brought by a single organisation, the People's Mojahadeen Organisation of Iran (PMOI) against its inclusion in the US, UK and EC lists. They illustrate just some of the approaches to due process and security taken by national and regional governments and courts, particularly on the use of secret evidence, the standard for determining guilt and the proper scope of judicial review.

United States

US statutory law[42] empowers the Secretary of State to designate an organisation as a 'foreign terrorist organisation' if the Secretary finds that the organisation (a) is foreign, (b) 'engages in terrorist activity' which (c) 'threatens the security of US nationals or the national security of the United States'. When an organisation is so designated, its assets are frozen, its members cannot enter the United States (and may be deported) and it becomes a criminal offence to provide that organisation with any 'material support or resources'.

PMOI was designated as a 'foreign terrorist organisation' in 1997 and brought a challenge before the Court of Appeals for the District of

---

42   8 USC § 1189 (2006), available at http://uscode.house.gov/pdf/2006/2006usc08. pdf. It should be noted that this is only one of several terrorist blacklists maintained by the US government.

Columbia Circuit.[43] The DC Circuit expressed clear misgivings about how proceedings were conducted under the statute:

> The statute before us is unique, procedurally and substantively. On the basis of an 'administrative record', the Secretary of State is to make 'findings' that an entity is a foreign organisation engaging in terrorist activities that threaten the national security of the United States. [...] But unlike the run-of-the-mill administrative proceeding, here, there is no adversary hearing, no presentation of what courts and agencies think of as evidence, no advance notice to the entity affected by the Secretary's internal deliberations. [...] Any classified information on which the Secretary relied in bringing about these consequences may continue to remain secret, except from certain members of Congress and this court. [...] There is a provision for 'judicial review' confined to the material the Secretary assembled before publishing the designation. [...] Because nothing in the legislation restricts the Secretary from acting on the basis of third hand accounts, press stories, material on the Internet or other hearsay regarding the organisation's activities, the 'administrative record' may consist of little else.

The Court further emphasised that the limited scope of its review did not permit it to take any position as to the veracity of the underlying facts:

> At this point in a judicial opinion, appellate courts often lay out the 'facts'. We will not, cannot, do so in these cases. What follows in the next two subsections may or may not be facts. The information recited is certainly not evidence of the sort that would normally be received in court. It is instead material the Secretary of State compiled as a record, from sources named and unnamed, the accuracy of which we have no way of evaluating [...].

However, because PMOI had no presence or assets within the United States, the Court concluded that the organisation 'has no constitutional rights, under the due process clause or otherwise' and that the only rights PMOI had, were those contained in the statute itself, namely, the right to judicial review of whether the designation was 'arbitrary, capricious, an abuse of discretion 'in excess of statutory jurisdiction' or 'lacking substantial support in the administrative record taken as a whole or in classified information' or not made 'in accord[ance] with the procedures required by law'. Consequently, despite the Court's evident misgivings, it felt compelled to conclude that the Secretary

---

43   *People's Mojahedin Org of Iran v. Dep't of State*, 182 F3d 17 (DC Cir 1999).

had not violated the statute in designating PMOI a foreign terrorist organisation:

> We [...] believe that the record, as the Secretary has compiled it, not surprisingly contains 'substantial support' for her findings that the [PMOI] engage in terrorist activities' within the meaning of 8 USC § 1182(a)(3)(B). [...] We reach no judgment whatsoever regarding whether the material before the Secretary is or is not true. [T]he record consists entirely of hearsay, none of it was ever subjected to adversary testing and there was no opportunity for counter-evidence by the organisations affected. As we see it, our only function is to decide if the Secretary, on the face of things, had enough information before her to come to the conclusion that the organisations were foreign and engaged in terrorism. Her conclusion might be mistaken but that depends on the quality of the information in the reports she received – something we have no way of judging.

Two years later, however, PMOI was offered a second opportunity to challenge its designation when the Secretary of State re-designated PMOI as a foreign terrorist organisation and also concluded that the National Council of Resistance of Iran (NCRI) was an alter ego or *alias* of the PMOI and therefore also liable to designation. Unlike PMOI, the NCRI had a bank account in the United States and was therefore able to invoke the due process protections of the US Constitution. Since the Secretary of State had found that the two organisations were one and the same, these due process protections also extended to PMOI.

In the second case,[44] the Court reiterated its concerns over the procedures in place:

> Despite the seriousness of the consequences of the determination, the administrative process by which the Secretary makes it, is a truncated one. [...] The unique feature of this statutory procedure is the dearth of procedural participation and protection afforded the designated entity. At no point in the proceedings establishing the administrative record is the alleged terrorist organisation afforded notice of the materials used against it or a right to comment on such materials or the developing administrative record. [...] The Secretary may base the findings on classified material, to which the organisation has no access at any point during or after the proceeding to designate it as terrorist.

---

44 *Nat'l Council of Resistance of Iran v. Dep't of State*, 251 F3d 192 (DC Cir 2001).

The scope of judicial review is limited as well. [...] Again, this limited scope is reminiscent of other administrative review but again, it has the unique feature that the affected entity is unable to access, comment on or contest the critical material. Thus the entity does not have the benefit of meaningful adversary proceedings on any of the statutory grounds, other than procedural shortfalls so obvious a Secretary of State is not likely to commit them.

The Court concluded that this manner of proceeding did not respect PMOI's due process rights and went on to describe the sort of procedure which might be satisfactory:

[T]he fundamental norm of due process clause jurisprudence requires that before the government can constitutionally deprive a person of the protected liberty or property interest, it must afford him notice and hearing. [...]

The notice must include the action sought but need not disclose the classified information to be presented in camera and *ex parte* to the court under the statute. This is within the privilege and prerogative of the executive and we do not intend to compel a breach in the security which that branch is charged to protect. [...] We therefore require that as soon as the Secretary has reached a tentative determination that the designation is impending, the Secretary must provide notice of those unclassified items upon which he proposes to rely to the entity to be designated. There must then be some compliance with the hearing requirement of due process jurisprudence – that is, the opportunity to be heard at a meaningful time and in a meaningful manner recognised in *Mathews*, *Armstrong* and a plethora of other cases. We do not suggest 'that a hearing closely approximating a judicial trial is necessary': *Mathews*, 424 US at 333. We do, however, require that the Secretary afford to entities considered for imminent designation the opportunity to present, at least in written form, such evidence as those entities may be able to produce to rebut the administrative record or otherwise negate the proposition that they are foreign terrorist organisations.

At present, it is unclear precisely what procedures have been put in place by the State Department to comply with the requirement that designated entities be provided notice of the unclassified evidence and a hearing. However, the governing statute was modified after the court's decision by the Intelligence Reform and Terrorism Prevention Act (IRTPA) of 2004. Whereas previously, a designation would lapse after two years unless it was renewed, under the IRTPA, the burden is now upon the designated organisation to initiate a revocation proceeding at the expiry of the two-year period. Moreover, the organisation bears the burden of proof:

PROCEDURES – Any foreign terrorist organisation that submits a petition for revocation under this subparagraph must provide evidence in that petition that the relevant circumstances described in paragraph (1) are sufficiently different from the circumstances that were the basis for the designation such that a revocation with respect to the organisation is warranted.[45]

Given that a designation may be based entirely or primarily on secret evidence, it is at least theoretically possible that an organisation would have no knowledge of the basis for its original designation and therefore would have considerable difficulty in presenting contrary evidence.

European Communities

The minimal due process requirements of notice and a hearing were affirmed in similar terms by the CFI in another case involving PMOI. In addition, the CFI highlighted the requirement that a blacklisting decision must be accompanied by a statement of reasons in order to afford the affected party a reasonable opportunity to challenge the designation.

On 27 December 2001, the Council of the European Union sought to implement UNSC Resolution 1373 (2001) by establishing its own list of terrorist organisations and providing for the freezing of their assets. It did so, through the adoption of Common Position 2001/931/CFSP on the application of specific measures to combat terrorism and Council Regulation (EC) No. 2580/2001 on specific restrictive measures directed against certain persons and entities with a view to combating terrorism. On 2 May 2002, PMOI was added to the list; it subsequently brought a challenge before the CFI.[46]

---

45   Intelligence Reform and Terrorism Prevention Act (IRTPA) of 2004, § 7119(a)(2), codified at 8 USC § 1189(a)(4)(B)(iii). A similar burden of proof for revocation of designation applies to other US terrorism-related blacklists, see 31 CFR §§ 501.807 (describing procedures for removal of names from lists of specially designated nationals, specially designated terrorists or specially designated narcotics traffickers maintained by the US Department of the Treasury).

46   *Organisation des Modjahedines du peuple d'Iran v. Council of the European Union*, Case T-228/02 (Judgment of Court of First Instance, 12 December 2006). See further, the discussion in the Epilogue below.

The Court described the PMOI's due process rights in terms largely similar to those employed by the US Court of Appeals:

> It follows from that case-law that, subject to exceptions (see paragraph 127 et seq. below), the safeguarding of the right to be heard comprises, in principle, two main parts. First, the party concerned must be informed of the evidence adduced against it to justify the proposed sanction ('notification of the evidence adduced'). Second, he must be afforded the opportunity effectively to make known his view on that evidence ('hearing'). [...]

> 127 At the same time, however, certain restrictions on the right to a fair hearing, so defined in terms of its purpose, may legitimately be envisaged and imposed on the parties concerned, in circumstances such as those of the present case, where what are in issue are specific restrictive measures, consisting of a freeze of the financial funds and assets of the persons, groups and entities identified by the Council as being involved in terrorist acts.

Given the importance of surprise to the effectiveness of assetfreezing orders, the Court accepted that the affected party need not be notified or heard before the freeze. It was a legitimate restriction on the right to a fair hearing to provide notice and a hearing 'either concomitantly with or as soon as possible after the adoption of the initial decision to freeze funds' (§§ 128–129). The Court similarly found (§ 133) that confidential information could be withheld from the concerned party:

> [O]verriding considerations concerning the security of the Community and its Member States or the conduct of their international relations, may preclude the communication to the parties concerned of certain evidence adduced against them and, in consequence, the hearing of those parties with regard to such evidence, during the administrative procedure.

However, the Court also went beyond the decision of the US Court of Appeals in two respects. First, it emphasised the importance of a statement of reasons in order to afford the concerned party a reasonable opportunity to contest its inclusion on the list (§ 140):

> If the party concerned is not afforded the opportunity to be heard before the adoption of an initial decision to freeze funds, compliance with the obligation to state reasons is all the more important because it constitutes the sole safeguard enabling the party concerned, especially after the adoption of that decision, to make effective use of the legal remedies available to it to challenge the lawfulness of that decision.

Second, the Court also observed that judicial review of a decision to list an organisation would extend to an assessment of the underlying facts as well as any confidential materials (§§ 154–155):

> [T]he judicial review of the lawfulness of the decision in question extends to the assessment of the facts and circumstances relied on as justifying it and to the evidence and information on which that assessment is based. [...] The Court must also ensure that the right to a fair hearing is observed and that the requirement of a statement of reasons is satisfied and also, where applicable, that the overriding considerations relied on exceptionally by the Council in disregarding those rights are well founded.

> In the present case, that review is all the more imperative because it constitutes the only procedural safeguard ensuring that a fair balance is struck between the need to combat international terrorism and the protection of fundamental rights. Since the restrictions imposed by the Council on the right of the parties concerned to a fair hearing must be offset by a strict judicial review which is independent and impartial [...] the Community Courts must be able to review the lawfulness and merits of the measures to freeze funds without it being possible to raise objections that the evidence and information used by the Council is secret or confidential.

In light of the foregoing, the Court concluded that PMOI's rights to a fair hearing had been violated. In particular, the Court found that 'at no time before this action was brought was the evidence adduced against the applicant notified to it' and that, 'it had not been apprised of the specific evidence adduced against it in order to justify the sanction envisaged and was not, therefore, in a position effectively to make known its views on the matter' (§§ 160–161). As a result, the Court annulled the contested decision of the Council in so far as it applied to PMOI.

United Kingdom

The United Kingdom has set up a specialised administrative tribunal known as the 'Proscribed Organisations Appeal Commission' (POAC) to which organisations can appeal a refusal of the Secretary of State for the Home Department to remove the organisation from the UK's list of terrorist organisations. Either the Secretary or the listed party may appeal the POAC's decision to the English Court of Appeal. Where a case involves confidential material, such material is dealt with in a closed session in which the appellant is not present but is represented by a 'special advocate' appointed by the Attorney General. An unusual application was brought before the POAC on behalf of PMOI by a group composed of 35 members of the two Houses of Parliament. The application was successful and the POAC concluded that PMOI was not an organisation concerned in terrorism. The Secretary appealed the decision of the POAC but the Court of Appeal affirmed.

In its decision, the Court of Appeal considered that both the POAC and the Court should undertake an intensive scrutiny of the facts relating to a determination by the Secretary of State that a particular organisation was concerned in terrorism:

> Thus the question for the [Secretary of State for the Home Department] was whether she believed that PMOI was 'otherwise concerned in terrorism' within the meaning of section 3(5)(d) [of the Terrorism Act 2000]. [...]
>
> The question of whether an organisation is concerned in terrorism is essentially a question of fact. Justification of significant interference with human rights is in issue. We agree with POAC that the appropriate course was to conduct an intense and detailed scrutiny of both open and closed material in order to decide whether this amounted to reasonable grounds for the belief that PMOI was concerned in terrorism. [47]

After reviewing both the open and closed material, the Court concluded that there was no basis to find that PMOI was concerned in terrorism, within the meaning of the Terrorism Act 2000:

> The reality is that neither in the open material nor in the closed material was there any reliable evidence that supported a conclusion that PMOI retained an intention to resort to terrorist activities in the future. [48]

Accordingly, the Court affirmed the conclusion of the POAC:

> In those circumstances, the only belief that a reasonable decision maker could have honestly entertained, whether as at September 2006 or thereafter, is that the PMOI no longer satisfies any of the criteria necessary for the maintenance of

---

47   *Secretary of State v. Lord Alton of Liverpool & Ors*, [2008] EWCA Civ 443, §§ 26, 43.
48   *Secretary of State v. Lord Alton of Liverpool & Ors*, [2008] EWCA Civ 443, § 53.

their proscription. In other words, on the material before us, the PMOI is not and, at September 2006, was not concerned in terrorism.[49]

Thus the Court of Appeal, echoing the CFI, offered an unambiguous affirmation of the principle that courts must exercise 'intense and detailed scrutiny' over attempts by state authorities to justify a significant interference with human rights.

V. Conclusion

Terrorist financing is a global problem and its suppression clearly requires concerted action at the international level. However, as the cases reviewed in this chapter show, where such action fails to incorporate adequate human rights protections, the credibility and, ultimately, the effectiveness of these efforts is seriously undermined.

It remains to be seen how the relevant actors at the United Nations, European and national levels will respond to the recent court decisions discussed in this chapter. The Monitoring Team has acknowledged that 'the sanctions are at a legal crossroads'.[50] Referring to the *Kadi* case, then pending before the ECJ, it observed that the invalidation of the European implementing measures, could lead to further challenges both within and outside the EU that would 'quickly erode enforcement'.[51] The Monitoring team was pessimistic about the prospect of national measures filling the legislative gap at the European level:

> [...] [I]t is unclear what options would exist for a long term fix. Advocate General Maduro suggested that it would be difficult for individual European Union

---

49   *Secretary of State v. Lord Alton of Liverpool & Ors*, [2008] EWCA Civ 443, § 54, quoting *Lord Alton of Liverpool & Ors (In the Matter of the People's Mojahadeen of Iran) v. Secretary of State*, [2007] POAC, Appeal No: PC/02/2006, Judgment of 30 November 2007, § 349, available at http://www.statewatch.org/terrorlists/PC022006%20PMOI%20FINAL%20JUDGMENT.pdf.
50   Monitoring Team Report, n 27.
51   Monitoring Team Report, n 27: 16.

Member States to replace the Community's regulation with domestic legislation, since any such measures likewise would be subject to the same European due process standards.[52]

Indeed, the fact that individual EU member states will have difficulty in replacing the EC regulations, was alluded to by the English High Court.[53]

Any solution, it seems, will need to address the procedural problems at the UN level but, as the Monitoring Team has emphasised, the unique position and role of the Security Council make it extraordinarily difficult to rectify the procedural deficiencies, particularly with regard to the right of judicial review:

> The Committee has made a series of incremental improvements to its procedures which have addressed many of the concerns expressed about the fairness of the sanctions but one major issue remains: the suggestion that listing decisions by the Committee be subject to review by an independent panel. It is difficult to imagine that the Security Council could accept any review panel that appeared to erode its absolute authority to take action on matters affecting international peace and security, as enshrined in the Charter. This argues against any panel having more than an advisory role and against publication of its opinions, to avoid undercutting Council decisions.[54]

In fact, a proposal for an 'advisory panel' was formally submitted to the UNSC in mid-2008 by the governments of Denmark, Germany, Liechtenstein, the Netherlands, Sweden and Switzerland.[55] Notable features of this proposal include:

– 'Independent, impartial and judicially qualified' panel members to be proposed by the Secretary General and appointed by the Security Council

---

52 Monitoring Team Report, n 27: 17.
53 *A, K, M, Q & G v. Treasury*, [2007] EWHC 869 at § 32.
54 Monitoring Team Report, n 27: 17.
55 *Identical Letters dated 23 June 2008 from the Permanent Representative of Switzerland to the United Nations Addressed to the President of the General Assembly and the President of the Security Council*, UN Docs A/62/891 & S/2008/428, 2 July 2008, available at http://daccessdds.un.org/doc/UNDOC/GEN/N08/411/57/PDF/N0841157.pdf.

- Member states and international organisations to provide information to the panel, including, to the extent possible, confidential information
- The panel may disclose non-confidential information
- Procedures before the panel would be 'governed by general principles of international law concerning fair procedure' (although these are not specified)
- The panel should recommend de-listing 'where the information and evidence available to the panel members does not justify the listing'
- A 'summary report with the recommendation(s) of the panel shall be published together with the decision(s) taken by the Security Council [...]'

The fate of this particular proposal – and its compliance with due process norms – remains to be determined. A 2006 study commissioned by the UN Office of Legal Affairs suggested several additional options, including:

- An independent international court or tribunal
- An ombudsman's office
- An inspection panel following the model of the World Bank Inspection Panel
- A commission of inquiry
- A committee of experts following the model of Art. 28 of the ICCPR[56]

Clearly, significant changes are necessary at the UN and EU level, if the sanctions regime is to be effective in the wake of the decisions by the ECJ and the High Court in England. In the absence of improvements, the Monitoring Team's prediction of 'quickly eroding' enforcement of the sanctions may well come to pass. Indeed, this review

---

56   Bardo Fassbender, *Targeted Sanctions and Due Process: The responsibility of the UN Security Council to ensure that fair and clear procedures are made available to individuals and entities targeted with sanctions under Chapter VII of the UN Charter*, 20 March 2006, available at http://www.un.org/law/counsel/Fassbender_study.pdf.

of cases concerning terrorist blacklisting regimes demonstrates that counter-terrorism practitioners ignore human rights at their peril: a failure to pursue security and human rights jointly and concomitantly can result in the degradation of both human rights and security.

VI. Epilogue

This chapter was prepared for delivery on 2 October 2008. Since then, there have been a number of developments related to the cases and issues discussed.

1. EC responds to Kadi

In the *Kadi* decision issued on 3 September 2008, the ECJ gave the Commission three months in which to remedy the annulled regulation. The Commission responded on 28 November 2008 by issuing Regulation (EC) No. 1190/2008. The Regulation reports that:

> In order to comply with the judgment of the Court of Justice, the Commission has communicated the narrative summaries of reasons provided by the UN Al-Qaida and Taliban Sanctions Committee, to Mr Kadi and to Al Barakaat International Foundation and given them the opportunity to comment on these grounds in order to make their point of view known.[57]

The Commission further reports that it received comments from both parties, considered them and concluded in each case that inclusion of both parties on the list was justified by reason of their association with the al-Qaida network.

The regulation is terse, at just over a page in length and provides no details regarding the quantity or quality of information provided to the parties, the nature of their comments or the procedures and stan-

---

57 Commission Regulation (EC) No 1190/2008 of 28 November 2008, 2008 OJ (L322): 25.

dard of review applied by the Commission. It is therefore difficult to determine whether this limited proceeding satisfies the requirements set out by the ECJ. Presumably, further litigation will clarify the point and the PMOI case, discussed next, may provide a useful reference point.

2. European CFI delists PMOI

As discussed above, the Court of First Instance of the European Communities (CFI) had ordered the removal of PMOI from the blacklist in light of the absence of adequate procedural protections, in particular the lack of a statement of reasons for their inclusion on the list. On 23 October 2008, the CFI issued a decision in a subsequent proceeding in the case. The CFI notes that on 30 January 2007, the Council provided PMOI with a statement of reasons for its inclusion on the blacklist, relying *inter alia* on the Order of the UK Home Secretary proscribing PMOI, which was then still in effect.[58] The CFI further notes that some (but not all) of the documents relied upon as evidence were provided to PMOI, whereas others were withheld by the state which had provided them.[59] PMOI submitted comments and evidence and Decision 2007/445 was taken to retain PMOI on the list.

With respect to that decision, the CFI rejected PMOI's claim that the Council had violated its rights of defence and its obligation to state reasons, noting the 'limitations'[60] of the observance of the rights of defence in the context of asset freezing set out in its previous decision and observing:

> [I]n its letter of 30 January 2007, the Council sent to the applicant a statement clearly and unambiguously explaining the reasons which, in its opinion, justified the applicant's continued inclusion in the list at issue [...] That statement contained specific examples of acts of terrorism as referred to in the relevant provi-

58 *People's Mojahedin Organization of Iran v. Council of the European Union,* Case T-256/07 (Judgment, Court of First Instance, 23 October 2008) §§ 5–6.

59 *Id.,* n 58, §§ 8–11.

60 *Id.,* n 58, §§ 88, 99, citing *Organisation des Modjahedines du peuple d'Iran v Council* [2006] ECR II-4665, §§ 114–151.

sions of Common Position 2001/931 for which the applicant was said to be responsible.[61]

PMOI did not challenge the withholding of certain evidence, so the CFI did not address that issue.[62]

However, by the time the case was argued, that decision had been superseded by Decision 2007/868, adopted on 20 December 2007. That decision was taken *after* the POAC's decision of 30 November 2007 in which it held that there was no basis to conclude that PMOI was involved in terrorism and ordered its removal from the UK blacklist. The Council did not take account of the POAC's decision, other than to note that the Home Secretary had sought to bring an appeal and simply repeated the statement of reasons previously provided.[63]

In this context, the CFI held that Decision 2007/868 did not satisfy the requirement of a statement of reasons because it failed to take into consideration the facts found by the POAC, as well as its conclusion that:

[T]he only belief that a reasonable decision maker could have honestly entertained, as from September 2006, was that the applicant no longer met any of the criteria necessary for the maintenance of its proscription as a terrorist organisation.[64]

Accordingly, the CFI annulled Decision 2007/868 insofar as it concerned PMOI.

On 26 January 2009, the Council complied with this decision and removed PMOI from the EU blacklist – the first time that a group had been removed from the list.[65]

---

61 *Id.,* n 58, §§ 87–90.
62 *Id.,* n 58, § 91.
63 *Id.,* n 58, § 176.
64 *Id.,* n 58, § 180.
65 See Stephen Castle, 'EU lifts ban on Iranian group', *International Herald Tribune,* 26 January 2009, at http://www.iht.com/articles/2009/01/26/europe/terror.4-416313. php.

3.   *English Court of Appeal overturns* A,K, M, Q, & G v. HMT

On 30 October 2008, a divided Court of Appeal reversed the High Court's decision striking down the Terrorism Order and the al-Qaida Order.[66] While acknowledging the defects in the Orders, including the absence of adequate procedural protections, the Court found that the defects in the orders could be overcome through judicial review and oversight.

Thus, in the lead opinion, the Master of the Rolls acknowledged that the Terrorism Order (TO) exceeded the government's authority to act without involving parliament to the extent that it allowed the government to freeze a person's assets solely on a reasonable suspicion that the person 'may be' involved with terrorism.[67] Nonetheless, the Master of the Rolls concluded that the Court could excise the offending words rather than quashing the entire order.[68]

On the issue of procedural safeguards, the Master of the Rolls observed that 'the thinking underlying the applicants' case has considerable force' and noted that the blacklisting system lacked the sort of procedural protections, such as provision for special advocates, included within regimes devised by Parliament for control orders.[69] However, rather than quash the order, he called upon the courts to remedy this failing by appointing special advocates under their own authority.[70]

The Master of the Rolls further acknowledged the problems associated with the use of undisclosed intercept evidence, noting that 'it is tempting, in these circumstances, to hold that the TO is unlawful on the ground that better safeguards could have been provided for those in the same position as the of the applicants.[71] Nonetheless, he concluded that, rather than quash the order as a whole, the proper course of action would be to quash the direction in any individual case in which closed source material was relied on. This would still permit the

---

66   *A, K, M, Q, & G v. H.M. Treasury*, [2008] EWCA Civ 1187.
67   *Id.*, n 66, §§ 48–49.
68   *Id.*, n 66, § 51.
69   *Id.*, n 66, § 57.
70   *Id.*, n 66, § 60.
71   *Id.*, n 66, § 65.

government to make listing decisions based solely on open source materials or based on certain closed materials that could be disclosed to a special advocate.[72]

In sum, the Master of the Rolls concluded as follows:

> My answer to the question 'what is the effect of the lack of procedural safe-guards?' is that the courts must be relied upon to ensure that there are sufficient procedural safeguards to protect applicants under article 5(4) [of the TO], that it should be possible to do so and that, if it proves impossible in a particular case, the direction must be set aside. In these circumstances [...], it would be wrong to quash the TO itself. The problems must be resolved, not by taking that dramatic step but on a case by case basis.[73]

With respect to the Al-Qaida Order, the Master of the Rolls likewise declined to quash the order but instead called upon the courts to exercise full judicial review, notwithstanding the fact that they lacked the power to order the removal of a particular individual from the UN list:

> I would accept the submission that the court has power to consider an application for judicial review by a person to whom the AQO applies as a result of designation by the Committee and, on such an application, to ask the court, so far as it can, to consider what the basis of the listing was. This will not be a challenge to the AQO itself but if [...] it were to be held that G should not have been listed, I see no reason why HMT (or the relevant Government body) should not, as the judge put, be bound to support delisting. I feel sure that if it were so held, HMT would wish to have G delisted and take appropriate steps to that end.[74]

However, the Master of the Rolls was vague about the procedures that should apply in such a judicial review proceeding:

> There must be procedures to enable [a listed party], again so far as possible, to discover the case against him, so that he may have an opportunity to meet it. This may involve, as in the case of the TO, appropriate use of a special advocate. How the system will work in a particular case will depend upon the circumstances, as the House of Lords held is appropriate in the control order cases in *MB and AF*. There may be greater difficulties in a case where HMT knows

---

72   *Id.,* n 66, §§ 72–75.
73   *Id.,* n 66, § 78.
74   *Id.,* n 66, § 119.

nothing of the facts upon which the designation was made by the Committee. I would leave the possible problems in such a case to be solved when they arise.[75]

The Court of Appeal's decision thus relied heavily on the courts to remedy the defects in the orders and to create *ad hoc* procedures in individual cases. This drew a dissenting view from Lord Justice Sedley, who wrote:

> I am unable to accept that it is the role of the courts to devise such a system in order to save delegated legislation from invalidity. It was one thing for their Lordships' House in *Roberts v Parole Board* [2005] UKHL 11 to authorise the Parole Board to resort to the use of a special advocate where a particularly sensitive case prevented their affording a prisoner the open hearing to which he would otherwise have been entitled. It is another for the courts to devise a surrogate system for securing fair hearings, at what will be considerable public expense, for individuals for whom the executive has not – or not so far – found it expedient to provide a fair hearing. [...] [I]s it the role of the courts not simply to ensure that what is lawfully enacted is fairly administered but to fill the gaps in enactments in order to make them valid?[76]

It is difficult to assess the precise import of the Court of Appeal's decision, for while it affirmed the need for better procedural safeguards for those subjected to national or international blacklisting, it provided little guidance as to the precise scope of such protections.

4. UNSC 1267 Committee amends its procedures

On 9 December 2008, the 1267 Committee adopted amendments to the guidelines[77] governing its work to reflect the requirements of Resolution 1822 (2008). In particular, the new guidelines describe the statement of case which member states must provide when submitting a new name for listing:

---

75   *Id.*, n 66, § 120.
76   *Id.*, n 66, §§ 133, 141.
77   *Guidelines of the Committee for the Conduct of its Work*, http://www.un.org/sc/committees/1267/pdf/1267_guidelines.pdf.

Member States shall provide a detailed statement of case in support of the proposed listing that forms the basis or justification for the listing in accordance with the relevant resolutions. The statement of case should provide as much detail as possible on the basis(es) for listing indicated above, including: (1) specific findings demonstrating the association or activities alleged; (2) the nature of the supporting evidence (eg, intelligence, law enforcement, judicial, media, admissions by subject, etc) and (3) supporting evidence or documents that can be supplied. States should include details of any connection with a currently listed individual or entity. States shall identify those parts of the statement of case that may be publicly released, including for the use by the Committee for development of the summary described in paragraph (h) below or for the purpose of notifying or informing the listed individual or entity of the listing and those parts that may be released upon request to interested States.[78]

While this change clearly represents a step forward, the Committee's website does not yet contain any examples of publicly available statements of case, so it is difficult to assess the extent to which this new requirement addresses the concerns which gave rise to it. Moreover, the new guidelines do not address the provision of statements of case for individuals or groups already on the list, although this was also required by §. 13 of Resolution 1822 (2008). However, the guidelines do call for a one-time review of all of the names on the list by 30 June 2010 and the procedures set out for this review clearly contemplate the use of narrative statements of case.[79] Accordingly, in order for the review to take place, such statements of case will need to be prepared; nonetheless, it remains to be seen what sort of information they will contain and to what extent they will be made available to the affected parties and the public.

---

78   *Id.*, n 77, § 6(d).
79   *Id.*, n 77, § 9.

RADHA IVORY*

Recovering terrorist assets in the United Kingdom: the 'domestication' of international standards on counter-terrorist financing

I. Introduction

Though states have long recognised their common interest in combating 'terror' as a form of political communication, ideological and political divisions prevented a united and comprehensive international response to terrorism for most of the 20th Century. International action on terrorism was characterised by disagreement over the initial question, 'Who is a 'terrorist?', quite apart from the issue of what should be done to prevent and suppress terrorist acts.[1]

The collapse of political bipolarity reignited concerns about terrorism at the end of the Cold War, concerns apparently confirmed in the East African embassy bombings in 1998 and the attacks on the World Trade Centre and the Pentagon in the United States (US) on 11 September 2001 (9/11). These events seemed to produce a new sense of unity on counter-terrorism, particularly on counter-terrorist financing. States expressed their common resolve through a United Nations (UN) convention on terrorist financing, targeted sanctions from the UN Security Council (UNSC) and 'special recommendations' from the Financial Action Task Force (FATF).

---

*   Research Fellow, Basel Institute on Governance, Switzerland.

1   Sean Anderson and Stephen Sloan, *Historical Dictionary of Terrorism* (Scarecrow Press, London 2002), 6–10. There is, perhaps, no greater evidence of this than the lack of a unified convention on terrorism and universal definition of 'terrorism' under international law.

The resulting 'soft' and 'hard' international standards required states *inter alia* to freeze, and sometimes seize and confiscate, terrorist assets. Similar asset recovery measures had been employed in the 'war on drugs' and, it was thought, could play a useful role in waging the 'war on terror'. As it happened, the nature of terrorism and the logic of counter-terrorism necessitated adaptations to existing asset recovery models. This chapter looks at how the United Kingdom (UK) has incorporated asset recovery into its domestic counter-terrorism laws and how these measures reflect and contribute to the development of international laws on the recovery of terrorist assets.

II. Key concepts: defining terrorism, counter-terrorist financing and asset recovery

1. Terrorism

Our discussion of asset recovery in terrorist financing starts with a definition of the term 'terrorism'. As noted above, there is no universal definition of 'terrorism' under international criminal law, states having opted to criminalise acts commonly perpetrated by terrorists rather than a specific activity of 'terrorism'. Nonetheless, there is an emerging consensus that 'terrorism' involves, at the very least, the use of physical violence against civilians to intimidate a population or coerce a government or an international organisation. This definition accords with the formulation in the International Convention for the Suppression of the Financing of Terrorism (1999) (UN) (Terrorist Financing Convention) and finds support among international policy-makers and political philosophers.[2] It is in this sense that we will be discussing 'terrorism' here.

---

2   Art. 2(1)(b) International Convention for the Suppression of the Financing of Terrorism (1999) (UN) (Terrorist Financing Convention); Christian Walter, 'Defining Terrorism in National and International Law' in Christian Walter *et al.* (eds), *Terrorism as a Challenge for National and International Law: Security*

2. Counter-terrorist financing

The 'financing of terrorism', for its part, is defined in the Terrorist Financing Convention as 'wilfully, provid[ing] or collect[ing] funds with the intention that they should be used or in the knowledge that they are to be used [...] in order to carry out' specified acts of terrorism,[3] whether or not the funds were actually used for a terrorist offence.[4] 'Counter-terrorist financing' (CTF) describes measures which aim at decreasing terrorists' ability to raise, move and use financial resources.[5] The measures include increased regulation in the formal financial sector and so-called vulnerable sectors, mandatory suspicious transaction reporting and asset recovery, including targeted economic sanctions.[6]

3. Asset recovery

Though not defined expressly under international law, the term 'asset recovery' is used in international instruments and in the literature[7] to

versus Liberty (Springer, Berlin 2004), 42; Ilias Bantekas, 'The International Law of Terrorist Financing' (2003) 97(2) *The American Journal of International Law*, 315–333, 315; Igor Primoratz, 'Terrorism' in Edward N. Zalta (ed.), *The Stanford Encyclopedia of Philosophy* (forthcoming), available at http://plato. stanford.edu/archives/fall2008/entries/terrorism, accessed October 2008.

3   Terrorist Financing Convention, Art. 2(1).

4   Terrorist Financing Convention, Art. 2(3).

5   Financial Action Task Force (FATF), *Terrorist Financing* (FATF/OECD, Paris 2008) (FATF 2008), 28–33. See also the FATF's Interpretive Note to Special Recommendation II, para. 2(d) and 3.

6   FATF 2008 n 5, 27–33. See further Mark Pieth and Stephanie Eymann, 'Combating the financing of terrorism: the "Guantanamo Principle"?' in this volume; Kristel Poh, 'Measures to counter the financing of terrorism', in this volume.

7   The United Nations Convention against Corruption (UN Corruption Convention), Chap. V, was the first international convention to use the term 'asset recovery' to describe this process. Other conventions which deal with the identification, freezing, seizing and confiscation of assets are the UN Convention against the Illicit Traffic in Narcotic Drugs and Psychotropic Substances (1988) (UN Narcotics Convention), the Council of Europe's Convention on Laundering, Search, Seizure and Confiscation of the Proceeds from Crime (1990)

mean measures that enable the confiscation and repatriation of assets on the grounds that they are attributable to, or connected with, criminal (or potentially criminal) conduct. In this chapter, we consider steps to freeze, seize and confiscate assets. However, asset recovery can include measures to identify and trace assets, as well as the legal processes that enable cooperation between states to achieve freezing, seizure and confiscation.

III. Asset recovery as a tool for countering the financing of terrorism

1. The logic of asset recovery

During the 1970s and 1980s, asset recovery was promoted in national and international fora as a means of combating transnational 'macro-criminality', such as drug trafficking, organised crime and corruption.[8] By depriving individuals of the benefits of otherwise profitable offences, it was thought possible to increase deterrence, prevent reinvestment in criminal enterprises and compensate society for the cost of criminal behaviour.[9] International organisations generally advocated asset recovery mechanisms that targeted both the proceeds and

---

(OECD Money Laundering Convention), the OECD Convention on Combating Bribery of Foreign Public Officials in International Business Transactions (1997) (OECD Bribery Convention) and the UN Convention on Transnational Organised Crime (2000) (UN Organised Crime Convention). From the literature see, Mark Pieth, 'Introduction' in Mark Pieth (ed.), *Recovering Stolen Assets* (Peter Lang, Bern 2007), 3–18.

8   See further, Pieth and Eymann, n 6.
9   Pieth and Eymann n 6; Mark Pieth (ed.), *Recovering Stolen Assets* (Peter Lang, Bern 2007), 6–8; Claire Daams, *Criminal Asset Forfeiture: One of the most effective weapons against (organised) crime? A Comparative Analysis* (Wolf Legal, Nijemgen 2003), 13–40.

the instrumentalities of crimes.[10] However, they promoted mechanisms that required competent national authorities to establish that an offence had been committed[11] or, at least, that the state had a valid civil claim to the assets.[12] Measures to freeze or seize property to prevent the commission of an offence were better known in the form of economic sanctions against states that threatened international peace and security.

2. The logic of asset recovery as a tool for counter-terrorist financing

Used for counter-terrorism, asset recovery came to be as much a preventive as a repressive measure: by freezing, seizing and/or confiscating funds intended for terrorism (i.e., the instrumentalities of terrorism), it was thought possible to stop terrorist attacks or disrupt terrorist operations.[13] This development can be linked to at least two features of terrorism and counter-terrorist strategies. First, the charac-

---

10   I.e., property derived from or obtained through the commission of the offence or used in the commission of offences: see, e.g., UN Narcotics Convention, Art. 1(q) and 5(1)(b); UN Organised Crime Convention, Art. 2(e) and 12(1)(b); UN Convention against Corruption, Art. 2(b) and (e) and 31(1)(b).

11   UN Narcotics Convention, Art. 5(1)(a) and (b); UN Organised Crime Convention, Art. 12(1); UN Corruption Convention, Art. 54.

12   See, e.g., UN Corruption Convention, Art. 53 and 54(1)(c).

13   Thomas Kean and Lee Hamilton, *The 9/11 Commission Report* (National Commission on Terrorist Attacks upon the United States, Washington (DC) 2004), 14 and 381–383; Maurice Greenberg, William Wechsler and Lee Wolosky, *Terrorist Financing: Report of an Independent Task Force Sponsored by the Council on Foreign Relations* (Council on Foreign Relations, New York 2002), 12–21; FATF 2008 n 5, 27–32. When used as an economic sanction, freezes may also aim to coerce the object of the measure to change his/her behaviour. The United Kingdom and the United States used such asset freezes prior to 9/11 against alleged state sponsors of terrorism and belligerent individuals in regional conflicts: Gary Clyde Hufbauer, Jeffery Schott and Barbara Oegg, *Using Sanctions to Fight Terrorism* (Peterson Institute for International Economics, Washington (DC) 2001), available at www.petersoninstitute.org, accessed October 2008; House of Lords Select Committee on Economic Affairs, *The Impact of Economic Sanctions: Volume 1* (The Stationary Office, London 2007).

terisation of terrorism as a 'crime of ideology' – rather than of passion or profit – can be associated with the view that terrorists cannot be deterred from violence.[14] This is reflected, in the area of asset recovery, in an emphasis on the interception rather than the confiscation of funds.[15] Second, as terrorist organisations are said to draw funds from a mixture of legitimate and illegitimate sources,[16] legislation targeting the 'proceeds' of offences would only operate against a portion of terrorist income. For both these reasons, establishing the criminal origin of funds through criminal or civil proceedings could be seen to be comparatively less important in terrorist financing law than it is in other areas of economic crime. This view is apparent from the international instruments that use asset recovery as a means of countering terrorist financing.

IV. International instruments on asset recovery and counter-terrorist financing

1. The Terrorist Financing Convention

The link between asset recovery and terrorist financing was made initially in the UN's Terrorist Financing Convention, which called on state parties to criminalise the financing of terrorism and institute measures to enable the confiscation of terrorist property.[17] Art. 8 re-

---

14 See generally, on the relation between terrorism and deterrence, Wyn Q. Bowen, 'Deterring Mass-Casualty Terrorism' 31 (2002) *Joint Force Quarterly*, 25–29, available at http://www.dtic.mil/doctrine/jel/jfq_pubs, accessed 6 April 2009.

15 Interestingly, this approach reverses the traditional logic for applying economic sanctions, namely, to persuade the target of the sanctions to change his, her or its behaviour: House of Lords Select Committee on Economic Affairs, n 13, para. 7–11 and 20; Peter Fitzgerald, 'Smarter "Smart" Sanctions' 26(1) *Penn State International Law Review*, 37 to 56.

16 FATF 2008, n 5.

17 Terrorist Financing Convention, Arts. 2(1), 4 and 8. See further, Bantekas n 2, 324.

quired state parties to enable the identification, detection, freezing, seizure and forfeiture of 'any funds used or allocated for the purpose of committing [...] [terrorist] offences [...], as well as the proceeds derived from such offences'.

2. Initiatives by the UNSC

UNSC Resolutions 1267

The counter-terrorist financing regime, as we know it, emerged in response to events in East Africa and Afghanistan in the late 1990s. The Afghan government's refusal to hand over or prosecute Usama Bin Laden, prompted the UNSC to introduce targeted financial sanctions against him, al-Qaida and the Taliban, as well as people and entities associated with any of those parties. Such associates were to be listed by a committee established under Resolution S/RES/1267 (1999) (UNSC Resolution 1267) and Chapter VII of the UN Charter (Sanctions Committee).[18] Criticisms of the listing system as unaccountable and unfair prompted the UNSC to allow humanitarian exemptions and derogations, as well as an intergovernmental delisting procedure. These procedures have recently been reformed.[19] Still, to this day, the Sanctions Committee remains the final power on listing, its diplomatic and political processes providing limited opportunity for a fair hearing, disclosure of reasons or judicial review.[20]

18　The Sanctions Committee formally manages the list but member states are said to control the nomination process in practice: Iain Cameron, *Targeted Sanctions and Legal Safeguards: Report to the Swedish Foreign Office* (Swedish Institute of International Law, Stockholm 2002) at 8; UN Security Council, *Guidelines of the Committee for the Conduct of its Work*, adopted on 7 November 2002 as amended; see further, Pieth and Eymann in this volume, n 6.

19　On 9 December 2008, the Sanctions Committee amended its *Guidelines of the Committee for the Conduct of its Work* to (amongst other things) stipulate what information states should provide in submitting names for inclusion in the UNSC Resolution 1267 list: see further, Scott Vesel, 'Combating the financing of terrorism while protecting human rights: a dilemma?' in this volume.

20　See further, Pieth and Eymann, n 6.

UNSC Resolution 1373

In the wake of the 9/11 attacks, the UNSC created a second regime against terrorist financing. Under S/RES/1373 (2001) (UNSC Resolution 1373), it required UN member states to freeze all terrorist assets and to ensure these are not made available for terrorism. In contrast to UNSC Resolution 1267, UNSC Resolution 1373 is not limited to people or organisations involved in the Afghan conflict and does not establish a 'blacklist'. Rather it relies on member states to establish their own lists, their own procedures for listing and their own legal arrangements for enforcement of foreign lists.[21]

3. European measures

UNSC Resolutions implemented within Europe

Using its powers with regards to the Common Foreign and Security Policy, the European Union and Communities (EU) implemented UNSC Resolutions 1267 and 1373 through a series of Common Positions, Regulations and Decisions.[22] Regulation 881/2002[23] incorporated the listing regime under UNSC Resolution 1267 into European law,

---

21 Indeed, UNSC Resolution 1373 does not even mention listing. However, it calls on states to identify and freeze the assets of a very wide group of people and organisations involved in or associated with terrorism. Listing is a favoured tool for implementing these sanctions as its enables governments and financial institutions to more easily distinguish terrorists from legitimate assets: Fitzgerald n 14, 38–56; FATF 2008, n 5.

22 See in particular Common Position 2001/154/CFSP and 2001/931/CFSP and EC Regulations 881/2002 and 2580/2001.

23 Council Regulation (EC) No. 881/2002 of 27 May 2002 imposing certain specific restrictive measures directed against certain persons and entities associated with Usama Bin Laden, the al-Qaida network and the Taliban, and repealing Council Regulation (EC) No. 467/2001 prohibiting the export of certain goods and services to Afghanistan, strengthening the flight ban and extending the freeze of funds and other financial resources in respect of the Taliban of Afghanistan.

whilst Regulation 2580/2001[24] established the list envisaged by UNSC Resolution 1373 for Europe (the European list). Under the EC Treaty, these Regulations are directly applicable in the municipal law of EU member states. They have been challenged in the European courts, over time with different results in relation to the different listing regimes.

Challenges to measures implementing UNSC Resolution 1267

Initially, challenges to measures implementing UNSC Resolution 1267 were unsuccessful in the European courts. As is well known, the European Court of First Instance (CFI) held in *Kadi* and *Yusuf and Al Barakaat*[25] that the UNSC Resolution 'clearly' prevailed over obligations in domestic and international treaty law, as it was made under Chapter VII of the UN Charter and did not leave any discretion in implementation to member states. Therefore, it held that the Court's substantive powers of review were limited to checking compliance with *jus cogens* norms.[26]

Though this position was slightly modified in subsequent cases, it was not until the decision of the European Court of Justice (ECJ) in *Kadi and Al Barakaat International Foundation*[27] (*Kadi and Al Barakaat*) that the European judiciary finally clarified the relationship between EU law and the UN measures. As recommended by Advocate General Maduro, the ECJ overturned the decisions at first instance, holding that member states and Community institutions were required

24 Council Regulation (EC) No. 2580/2001 of 27 December 2001 on specific restrictive measures directed against certain persons and entities with a view to combating terrorism.

25 Case T-315/01, *Kadi v. Council of the European Union and Commission of the European Communities* (Court of First Instance, 21 September 2005), para. 209–232; Case T-306/01, *Ahmed Ali Yusuf and Al Barakaat International Foundation v. Council of the European Union and Commission of the European Communities* (Court of First Instance, 21 September 2005), para. 231–254.

26 *Kadi* n 25, para. 209–232; *Yusuf and Al Barakaat International Foundation* n 25, para. 231–254.

27 Joined cases C-402/05 P and C-415/05 *Yassin Abdullah Kadi and Al Barakaat International Foundation v. Council of the European Union* (Court of Justice, Grand Chamber, 3 September 2008) (*Kadi and Al Barakaat*).

to implement the UNSC Resolution in accordance with general principles of Community law, including fundamental rights, such as the right to a defence and effective judicial protection. At the same time, the ECJ acknowledged that counter-terrorism remained an important objective and that asset recovery measures could be appropriate if implemented with proper safeguards. Thus, it stayed the effect of its decision until December 2008 to allow the institutions and member states time to reconsider their positions.

Challenges to measures implementing UNSC Resolution 1373

Challenges to the measures imposed pursuant to UNSC Resolution 1373, have enjoyed more consistent – though not unqualified – success in the Community courts. Even before the appeal decision in *Kadi and Al Barakaat*, the CFI had found that measures implementing UNSC Resolution 1373 were subject to review for compliance with general principles of Community law. It reasoned in *Organisation des Modjahedines du people d'Iran v. Council of the European Union (OMPI)* that UNSC Resolution 1373 left UN member states considerable discretion in creating an asset freezing regime and so that it did not benefit from any rule of primacy or immunity from review.[28] In that case, the Court overturned the listing of an organisation opposed to the Iranian government because the Council had failed to sufficiently state its reasons and provide the organisation with a fair hearing.[29] All the same, it found that Community institutions would normally be deemed to respect fundamental rights if they acted on the basis of decisions from competent national authorities. Further, the Community courts would usually recognise the validity of municipal decisions and municipal restrictions on rights, particularly the right to reasons.[30]

---

28   Case T-228/02, *Organisation des Modjahedines du people d'Iran v. Council of the European Union* (Court of First Instance, 12 December 2006) (*OMPI*).

29   *OMPI* n 28, para. 173.

30   *OMPI* n 28, para. 121–125 and 123–124.

The Council responds

The Council's response to these challenges is apparent in the successor cases to *OMPI*. Rather than end its efforts to list OMPI, the Council made a new Decision by which it relisted the organisation after applying a seemingly corrected procedure.[31] The legal basis for the new listing was again said to be the UK Home Secretary's decision of December 2001 to proscribe the organisation under UK law;[32] this remained the alleged legal basis for the listing, in fact, until the organisation successfully challenged its UK proscription in November 2007.[33] From then on, the purported basis for the listing was the decision of a French prosecutor to bring charges against the organisation and initiate a judicial inquiry relating to terrorism and terrorist financing.[34]

The organisation challenged its relisting in two decisions: *People's Mojahedin Organisation of Iran v. Council of the European Communities* of 23 October 2008 (*PMOI No. 1*)[35] and *People's Mojahedin Organisation of Iran v. Council of the European Communities* of 9 December 2008 (*PMOI No. 2*).[36] In *PMOI No. 1*, the CFI found that the Council could rely on the 'same matters of fact and law' as had been at issue in the *OMPI* case 'provided that [...] it observed the formal and procedural rules whose breach gave rise to the annulment [...]'.[37] However, once the POAC had found the Home Secretary's

---

31   Decision 2006/1008/EC of 21 December 2006. See further, Case T256/07, *People's Mojahedin Organisation of Iran v. Council of the European Communities* (Court of First Instance, 23 October 2008) (*PMOI No. 1*), para. 1–15.

32   On proscription under the Terrorism Act 2000 (UK), see further below, 'Statutory terrorism offences – proscription and terrorist property offences'.

33   In the UK, two events had effectively invalidated the Home Secretary's decision to add the organisation to the UK list: first, in November 2007, the Proscribed Organisations Appeal Commission (POAC) had ordered the removal of the organistion from the UK list and, second, in May 2008, the English Court of Appeal had refused the Home Secretary's application for leave to appeal the POAC's decision: *PMOI No. 1* n 31, para. 22–37.

34   See further, Case T-284/08, *People's Mojahedin Organization of Iran v. Council of the European Union* (Court of First Instance, 4 December 2008) (*PMOI No. 2*).

35   N 31.

36   *PMOI No. 2*, n 34.

37   *PMOI No. 1*, n 31, para. 65 and 75.

decision was unsustainable,[38] the Council could not maintain the organisation on the list without a fresh decision and a fair procedure.[39] In that respect, in *PMOI No.* 2, the CFI found that the Council had not respected the organisation's procedural rights[40] in relisting it on the basis of the French investigations; in any case, that the French prosecutor's decision was probably not sufficient evidence of the organisation's involvement in terrorism.[41] Citing the decision in *PMOI No.* 2, the Council finally removed PMOI from the European list on 26 January 2009.[42]

In relation to the measures implementing UNSC Resolution 1267, the Council also responded by retaining Mr. Kadi and the Al Barakaat International Foundation (the applicants) on the European list. In Regulation 1190/2008 passed just five days before the decision in *Kadi and Al Barakaat* was due to take effect,[43] the Commission attempts to demonstrate that it has afforded the applicants a fair procedure. Nonetheless, it relies on the same evidence for the listing (the Sanctions Committee's decision) and concludes that neither party should be removed from the European list. The Commission states:[44]

> In order to comply with the judgment of the Court of Justice, the Commission has communicated the narrative summaries of reasons provided by the [Sanction's Committee] to Mr. Kadi and to Al Barakaat International Foundation and given them the opportunity to comment on these grounds in order to make their point of view known. [...]

38   N 33.
39   *PMOI No. 1*, n 31, para. 167–186; see also para. 130–139.
40   *PMOI No. 2*, n 34, para. 27–47 and 60–79.
41   *PMOI No. 2*, n 34, para. 48–59.
42   See Council Common Position 2009/67/CFSP of 26 January 2009 updating Common Position 2001/931/CFSP on the application of specific measures to combat terrorism and repealing Common Position 2008/586/CFSP, in particular, para. 4.
43   Commission Regulation (EC) No. 1190/2008 of 28 November 2008 amending for the 101st time Council Regulation (EC) No. 881/2202 imposing certain restrictive measures directed against certain persons and entities associated with Usama Bin Laden, the al-Qaida network and the Taliban.
44   Commission Regulation (EC) No. 1190/2008, n 43, para. 3–4, para. 6 (for Mr. Kadi) and para. 7 (for Al Barakaat International Foundation).

> After having carefully considered the comments received from [the Mr. Kadi and Al Barakaat International Foundation], and given the preventative nature of the freezing of funds and economic resource, the Commission considers that the listing of the parties is justified for reasons of [their] association[s] with the Al-Qaida network.

Mr. Kadi and the Al Barakaat organisation were therefore added to the list in Annex 1 of Regulation 881/2002 again.[45]

Future developments

It remains to be seen whether the European courts will be prepared to apply the same approach to listings under Regulation 881/2002 as they applied to listings under Regulation 2580/2001. The question is whether a decision of the Sanctions Committee to list an individual or entity under UNSC Resolution 1267 is sufficient evidence of the party's association with al-Qaida, the Taliban or Usama Bin Laden. Given the procedural defects identified by the ECJ in *Kadi and Al Barakaat*, this would seem at first highly doubtful. However, the Committee has recently revised its procedural guidelines and changed (amongst other things) provisions regarding the statement of case (reasons).[46] The sufficiency of this process – and the willingness of the European courts to further adjudicate on the fairness of the UNSC procedures – will be determined in any future appeal against Regulation 1190/2008 or other similar instruments.

4.   The FATF's Special Recommendations

Finally, the FAFT's Special Recommendation III calls on states to confiscate, as well as freeze and seize, property that is 'used in, or intended or allocated for use in, the financing of terrorism, terrorist acts or terrorist organisations'. In requiring states to confiscate as well as freeze and seize terrorist assets, the FATF goes beyond the other international terrorist financing instruments. This is a significant de-

---

45   Commission Regulation (EC) No. 1190/2008, n 43, para. 8 and Art. 1.
46   UNSC, *Guidelines of the Committee for the Conduct of its Work*, 9 December 2008, n 19, para. 6.

velopment since the FATF is regarded as a highly persuasive source of soft law and implements its Recommendations through mutual evaluations and its own listing regime.

V. Counter-terrorism in a common law system: the United Kingdom

Support from powerful nations, international review mechanisms and the persistence of terrorism, have created strong pressure for compliance with counter-terrorist financing standards. Nonetheless, in an anarchic system, individual states remain primarily responsible for the interpretation, implementation and enforcement of international norms. So, for the rest of this chapter, we consider how one common law state – the UK – has approached the implementation of these counter-terrorist financing standards in domestic law.

1. Adherence to international standards on counter-terrorism and counter-terrorist financing

In terms of its international obligations, the UK has ratified (without reservation) the Terrorist Financing Convention and all the counter-terrorist conventions it mentions.[47] As an EU and UN member state, a member of the UNSC and a founding member of the FATF, it has both legal and political obligations to implement the measures on counter-terrorist financing and asset recovery mentioned above.

---

47 Rainer Grote, 'Country Report on the United Kingdom' in Walter *et al.* (eds), *Terrorism as a Challenge for National and International Law: Security versus Liberty* (Springer, Berlin 2004), 591–631 and 597–598; HM Treasury and the Home Office, *Combating the financing of terrorism: A report on UK action* (HM Stationary Office, London 2002), 13 and 23–24.

2. Domestic laws on counter-terrorism and counter-terrorist financing

A major financial centre and former imperial power with a large and diverse population, the UK is no stranger to terrorism and terrorist financing. From the beginning of the 1960s through to the 1990s, the UK witnessed the 'Troubles' in Northern Ireland. And, though the Good Friday peace agreement generally stymied Irish terrorism, the threat from other quarters increased, as demonstrated by the attacks on the London transport system in 2005.

The changing terrorist threat prompted the UK to reform its counter-terrorism legislation. 'Emergency legislation' targeting Irish unrest was largely replaced in February 2001 with the Terrorism Act 2000 (TACT).[48] Now the legislative centrepiece for counter-terrorism in the United Kingdom, the TACT was amended and strengthened by the Anti-terrorism, Crime and Security Act 2001 (ATCS Act) and the Terrorism Act 2006 (TACT 2006); it was amended again (after some uncertainty) by the Counter-Terrorism Act (CT Act) in November 2008.[49] With regard to assets recovery, it is supplemented by the Proceeds of Crime Act 2002 (POCA).

---

48 Grote n 47, 592 and 595–596.

49 After the bombings of the London transport system in 2005, the British Labor government proposed amendments to the TACT and related legislation in the Counter-Terrorism Bill (CT Bill). The initial draft of the CT Bill included controversial provisions on secret inquests and detention without trial. The Bill was passed by the Lower House with minority support and rejected in the House of Lords, before being amended and returned to the Lower House. The amended Bill was eventually passed and received Royal Assent on 26 November 2008: see further, UK Parliament, *Business: Counter-Terrorism Bill 2007–08*, available at http://services.parliament.uk/bills/2007-08/counterterrorism.html, accessed on 11 March 2009; 'House of Lords deals fatal blow to 42-day terror detention plans' *The Times* (14 October 2008), available at http://www.timesonline.co.uk/tol/news/politics/article4938637.ece, accessed on 11 March 2009; Sam Coates, 'Another U-turn sees "secret inquests" axed from Counter-Terrorism Bill', *The Times* (15 October 2008), available at http://www.timesonline.co.uk/tol/news/politics/article 4944551.ece, accessed on 11 March 2009.

3. How the UK defines terrorism

The TACT defines 'terrorism' as:

> [...] the use or threat of action [...] designed to influence the government or an international governmental organisation or to intimidate the public or a section of the public, and [...] made for the purpose of advancing a political, religious, racial or ideological cause.[50]

As this definition has been discussed elsewhere,[51] we note simply that it is much broader than its *de facto* international counterpart in the Terrorist Financing Convention,[52] geographically and in terms of its subjective and objective elements[53] and that it has been further expanded by the passage of the CT Act into law.[54]

---

50 TACT, s. 1(1). The definition is incorporated into other UK counter-terrorism laws, such as the CT Act, the ATCS and the UN Orders: see e.g., CT Act, s. 75.

51 See e.g. *R v. F* [2007] EWCA Crim 243, para. 13–32, per Forbes P.

52 Terrorist Financing Convention, Art. 2(1)(b), applies to acts 'intended to cause *death or serious bodily injury* to a civilian [...], when the purpose of such act [...] is to intimidate a population, or to *compel* a government or an international organisation to do or to abstain from doing any act' (emphasis added).

53 In terms of the subjective (mental) elements, s. 1 requires a mere intention to 'influence' a government rather than an intention to 'compel' or 'coerce'. Moreover, the objective (physical) elements of the offence are not restricted to (intentional) physical violence against persons but extend to actions which endanger another person's life, actions against property and actions which create a serious risk to public health or safety. Finally, the definition of 'terrorism' is geographically broad, with provisions that the 'government' and 'public', 'action', 'property' and 'persons' may all be situated in a country other than the UK.

54 With the passage of the CT Act, the definition was extended to the use or threat of action for purposes of advancing a racial cause: CT Act, s. 75(1).

4. Terrorism offences in the UK

No general offence of terrorism

Though UK counter-terrorist legislation relies heavily on its definition of terrorism,[55] it does not contain a distinct offence of 'terrorism', by which conduct is criminalised as 'terrorist' if it is committed with a certain state of mind.[56] Instead, the UK deals with political violence via the general common law offences (e.g., murder, manslaughter) and specialist statutory offences (e.g., causing bodily injury by explosives, dealing with terrorist property). It reflects its particular disapprobation of terrorism by giving law enforcers special powers in investigating terrorist acts and by enabling the courts to take into account a 'terrorist connection' when considering the seriousness of certain offences at sentencing.[57]

Specific offences: proscription and terrorist property offences

Of the statutory offences targeting terrorism, those related to proscribed organisations and terrorist property are most relevant to terrorist financing and asset recovery.[58] Proscription is dealt with under Part II TACT. It empowers the Secretary of State of the British Home Office to proscribe organisations 'concerned in' terrorism, i.e., organisations that commit or participate in acts of terrorism or prepare, promote, encourage or are otherwise concerned in terrorism.[59] Once an organisation has been proscribed, others are prohibited from providing it with various forms of non-financial support[60] and – importantly for us – there is a legal basis for EC listing and the freezing of assets under the relevant EC Regulations and Decisions. Notably, the Act also contains a 'de-proscription' procedure,[61] which has been used to suc-

---

55   See *R v. F* [2007] EWCA Crim 243, per Forbes P, para. 13.
56   See Pieth and Eymann, n 6.
57   CT Act, s. 30, 31, 33, 35 and 42 and Schedule 2; Grote n 47, 609–610.
58   Grote n 47, 610–612.
59   TACT, s. 3(3) to (5).
60   TACT, s. 11–13.
61   TACT, s. 4 to 7.

cessfully challenge proscriptions in the UK[62] and subsequent listings at the European level,[63] as discussed above in relation to the organisation, OMPI.[64]

Part III TACT then establishes offences dealing with terrorist property, according to the FATF, the core offences related to the financing of terrorism.[65] S. 14 defines 'terrorist property':

> (1) In this Act 'terrorist property' means—
>
>   (a) money or other property which is likely to be used for the purposes of terrorism (including any resources of a proscribed organisation)
>   (b) proceeds of the commission of acts of terrorism, and
>   (c) proceeds of acts carried out for the purposes of terrorism.
>
> (2) In subsection (1)—
>
>   (a) a reference to proceeds of an act includes a reference to any property which wholly or partly, and directly or indirectly, represents the proceeds of the act (including payments or other rewards in connection with its commission), and
>   (b) the reference to an organisation's resources includes a reference to any money or other property which is applied or made available, or is to be applied or made available, for use by the organisation.

Hence, 'terrorist property' is not merely the direct instrumentalities of the terrorist act (e.g., money dedicated to buying explosives) but also the proceeds of the attack (e.g., compensation paid to families of suicide bombers) and instrumental funds which have a more distantly

---

62   *The Secretary of State for the Home Department v. Lord Alton of Liverpool and Others* [2008] EWCA Civ 443.

63   *PMOI No. 1*, n 31.

64   See further, n 38.

65   FATF, *Third Mutual Evaluation Report: Anti-Money Laundering and Combating the Financing of Terrorism – The United Kingdom of Great Britain and Northern Ireland* (FATF / OECD, Paris 2007) (dated 29 June 2007) (FATF 2007), 41; Grote n 47, 610. Since the CT Act became law in November 2008, the UK may also take criminal action against financial institutions which do not comply with directions in relation to countries suspected (amongst other things) of 'terrorist financing': CT Act 2008, Schedule 7. The directions may be an important tool for gathering intelligence about terrorist operations and their financial activities. However, as they do not deal with the freezing, seizing and confiscation of terrorist assets, they will not be considered further here.

causal relationship to the act of terrorism itself (e.g., donations intended to fund an organisations accused of terrorism).

In s. 15–18 TACT, certain activities involving terrorist property are criminalised:

'fund raising' for terrorism, i.e., receiving, providing or inviting others to provide for money or other property for the purposes of terrorism[66]

– 'use and possession' of terrorist property, i.e., the use and possession of money or other property for the purposes of terrorism[67]

– 'funding arrangements' for terrorism, i.e., entering into or becoming concerned in an arrangement which results in money or other property being made available to a person for the purposes of terrorism[68] with the requisite *mens rea*[69]

– 'money laundering' for terrorism, i.e., entering into or becoming concerned in an arrangement which facilitates the retention or control of terrorist property by or on behalf of someone else[70]

In each case, the accused must have acted with the requisite state of mind. Broadly, s. 15–17 require proof that the accused intended, knew or had reasonable cause to suspect that the property would or may be used 'for the purposes of terrorism'.[71] S. 18, by contrast, requires the defendant to show that he/she did not know and did not have reasonable cause to suspect that the arrangement related to terrorist property.[72] The reversed burden of proof is one reason why prosecutors

---

66 TACT, s. 15.
67 TACT, s. 16.
68 TACT, s. 17.
69 TACT, s. 17.
70 TACT, s. 18, i.e., this does not include self-laundering: see TACT, s. 18(1), and, further, FATF 2007 n 65, 33–35.
71 This includes an action taken for the benefit of a proscribed organisation: Terrorism Act 2000, s. 1(5). According to the FATF, it would encompass such actions for non-proscribed individuals and organisations, provided there was a 'reasonable cause to suspect' that the funds may be used for terrorism: FATF 2007 n 65, 42–43.
72 TACT, s. 18(2). In other words s. 18(2) TACT reverses the burden of proof in relation to the mental elements of laundering.

may chose to rely on s. 18 TACT instead of the equivalent provisions of the POCA.[73]

VI. Recovering terrorist assets in the UK

As the FAFT notes in its third evaluation of the UK, British law provides diverse avenues for the freezing, seizing and confiscation of terrorist assets pursuant to criminal and civil proceedings and executive direction.[74]

1. Recovery under the TACT and the CT Act

The TACT establishes a conviction-based forfeiture regime for terrorist offences. As the CT Act introduced a number of changes to this regime, we consider the two acts together, with particular emphasis on the recent changes.[75]

---

73 S. 17 and 18 TACT have two advantages over the equivalent offences in the POCA. The first, as noted above, is the reversal of the burden of proof in relation to the mental elements of money laundering. The second is the restriction of the POCA to 'criminal property' (i.e., the proceeds of past offences): cf. the definition of 'terrorist property' in s. 14(1) TACT. However, the offences in the POCA may be easier to establish as the TACT requires evidence of 'terrorism', whereas the POCA applies to all criminal conduct over which the UK has jurisdiction: TACT, s. 327–340.

74 FATF 2007 n 65, 47.

75 TACT, s. 11A and 120A, as inserted by CT Act, s. 38, allow for forfeiture upon conviction of offences relating to weaponry and the misuse of information for terrorism. They will not be considered further here as they are not directly relevant to asset recovery in the counter-terrorist financing context.

Revised power to forfeit terrorist property

First, the CT Act amends s. 23 TACT, which allows courts to order the forfeiture of property[76] after terrorist property convictions.[77] The CT Act slightly changes the property which may be confiscated pursuant to convictions for terrorist property offences. As a result of the amendments, a conviction for any terrorist property offence allows the courts to confiscate the instrumentalities of terrorist financing, i.e.,

> any money or other property which, at the time of the offence, the person had in their possession or under their control and which [...] had been used for the purposes of terrorism [...].[78]

In addition, the court may confiscate the potential or intended instrumentalities of terrorism, in other words, 'any money or other property which, at the time of the offence, the person had in their possession or under their control and which [...]':

- For convictions under s. 15(1), 15 (2) and 16 TACT – 'they intended should be used, or had reasonable cause to suspect might be used, for those purposes'[79]
- For convictions under s. 15(3) TACT – 'which, at that time, they knew or had reasonable cause to suspect would or might be used for those purposes'[80]
- For convictions under s. 17 and 18 – 'was, at that time, intended by them to be used for those purposes'[81]

Moreover, for funding arrangement or money laundering convictions under s. 17 and 18, the court may order the forfeiture of 'money or

---

76 'Property' includes property wherever situated, whether real or personal, heritable or moveable and things in action and other intangible or incorporeal property: s. 122 TACT.
77 CT Act, s. 34.
78 TACT, s. 23(2)(a), 23(3)(a), 23(4)(a) as amended by CT Act, s. 34.
79 TACT, s. 23(2)(b). As a result of the amendment, it is no longer necessary to show that the person intended to use the property for terrorist purposes *at the time of the offence.*
80 TACT, s. 23(3)(b).
81 TACT, s. 23(4)(b).

other property to which the arrangement in question related'.[82] In the case of convictions under s. 17, however, the prosecution must also show that the property:

(a) had been used for the purposes of terrorism, or

(b) at the time of the offence, the person knew or had reasonable cause to suspect would or might be used for those purposes.[83]

Finally, the TACT makes it possible to confiscate the proceeds of terrorism, i.e.,

[...] any money or other property which wholly or partly, and directly or indirectly, is received by any person as a payment or other reward in connection with the commission of the offence.[84]

New power to forfeit property after convictions for other offences

Second, the CT Act adds s. 23A to the TACT,[85] which allows the courts to order forfeiture of property when a person has been convicted of specified offences,[86] an ancillary offence[87] or an offence in Schedule 2 for which there is a 'terrorist connection'.[88] Any money or other property is liable for forfeiture, provided it was in the convicted person's possession or control at the time of the offence and it has been, is intended to be used, for the purposes of terrorism or the court believes it will be used for the purposes of terrorism unless it is forfeited.[89]

---

82 TACT, s. 23(5) and 23(6), as amended by CT Act, s. 34.

83 TACT, s. 23(5) as amended by CT Act, s. 34.

84 TACT, s. 23(7) as amended by CT Act, s. 34.

85 S. 23A(1) and (2) TACT as amended by CT Act, s. 35.

86 S. 23A(2) i.e., weapons training, possessing things and collecting information for the purposes of terrorism, inciting terrorism outside the UK, dissemination of terrorist publications, preparation of terrorist acts, training for terrorism, offences involving radioactive devices or materials.

87 CT Act, s. 23A(3).

88 See above, part V.4., 'Terrorist Offences in the UK: No General Offences of Terrorism'.

89 TACT, s. 23A(2)(b) as amended by CT Act, s. 35(1).

Rights in forfeiture proceedings

Third, a new s. 23B in the TACT provides further procedural safe-guards for the convicted person and third parties in forfeiture proceed-ings. It confirms that owners or other third parties with an interest in the property must be given an opportunity to be heard before the prop-erty is forfeited.[90] And, it requires the court to consider the value of the property and the effect of forfeiture on the convicted person in decid-ing whether to make a forfeiture order.[91]

Application of terrorist funds

Fourth, an amendment to Schedule 4 TACT allows the court to apply confiscated funds in compensating the victims of terrorism where the offence resulted in personal injury, loss or damage.[92]

2. Recovery under the Proceeds of Crime Act

The specific conviction-based forfeiture regime in the TACT is com-plemented by the general regime in the POCA. This allows the courts to order a convicted offender to pay an amount equal to the benefit from his/her criminal conduct.[93] The POCA is relevant where law en-forcement authorities can prove general criminal conduct but not a connection to terrorism. In addition, the POCA's civil forfeiture pro-visions could be used to recover assets which are, or represent, prop-erty obtained through unlawful conduct, if the person is not or cannot be convicted of an offence (including a terrorist property offence).[94] Finally, decisions on the POCA's cash confiscation provisions may be relevant to the interpretation of parallel provision under the ATCS Act.[95]

---

90   TACT, s. 23B(1), as amended by CT Act, s. 36.
91   TACT, s. 23B(2), as amended by CT Act, s. 36.
92   CT Act, s. 37.
93   POCA, s. 6(5).
94   POCA, s. 240(1).
95   POCA, Part 5, Chap. 3.

3.   *Recovery under the ATCS Act*

The ATCS Act provides for the executive seizure and the civil forfeiture of terrorist cash, as well as for the freezing of certain assets to protect the UK economy, nationals or residents.[96]

Seizure and forfeiture of 'terrorist cash'

The provisions on the seizure and forfeiture of cash apply to 'terrorist cash', i.e., cash which is intended to be used for the purposes of terrorism, consists of resources of a proscribed organisation or represents property obtained through terrorism, as well as property earmarked as terrorist property.[97] They allow an authorised officer to seize cash if she/he has reasonable grounds for suspecting that it is terrorist cash in whole or part,[98] retaining it for an initial period of 48 hours.[99] A judicial officer[100] may extend the orders for three months at a time for up to two years[101] provided he/she is satisfied that one of three conditions is met.[102] In all cases, the applicant authority must show that continued detention is justified while authorities investigate or consider initiating proceedings or that proceedings in connection with the cash are underway.[103] The judicial officer may then, on application, order forfeiture. Notably, none of these powers requires that proceedings have

---

96   Grote n 47, 601–603.

97   S. 1(1) and Schedule 1, para. (1)(a) and (b).

98   ATCS Act, Schedule 1, para. 2.

99   ATCS Act, Schedule 1, para. 3(1). See also, CT Act, s. 83, which specifies how the period for detaining terrorist cash is to be determined.

100 Since the passage of the CT Act, appeals are heard by the Crown Court in England, the Sheriff Principal in Scotland and the County Court in Northern Ireland and Scotland: ATCS Act, Schedule 1, para. 7, as amended by CT Act, s. 84(1). Previously, in England and Wales, a Magistrate heard these applications.

101 ATCS Act, Schedule 1, para. 3(2).

102 These are: (1) that there are reasonable grounds for suspecting that the cash is intended to be used for the purposes of terrorism; (2) that there are reasonable grounds for suspecting that the cash consists of resources of a proscribed organisation; and (3) that the cash is property earmarked as terrorist property: ATCS Act, Schedule 1, para. 3(6)–(8).

103 ATCS Act, Schedule 1, para. 3(6)(a) and (b) and 3(7)(a) and (b).

been brought for an offence in connection with the cash,[104] though there are provisions for appeal.[105]

Freezing assets to protect the UK economy or residents

The ATCS Act also empowers the executive to protect the British economy or residents by freezing assets. Part 2 allows Her Majesty's Treasury (HM Treasury or Treasury) to temporarily freeze property if satisfied that a foreign government or resident has taken, or is likely to take, action to the detriment of the UK economy or which constitutes a threat to the life or property of UK nationals or residents. Part 2 has been described as a means for the UK government to unilaterally impose sanctions where multilateral organs have not responded to an urgent threat.[106] However, it was recently used in less dramatic circumstances to freeze Icelandic assets after British funds were caught in frozen Icelandic bank accounts.[107] As passed, Part 6 CT Act creates new appeal rights for parties, such as the Icelandic savers, whose assets were affected by the Part 2 orders.

4. Recovery pursuant to the UK's international obligations

The UN Orders

Finally, the UK government has implemented Britain's obligations under UNSC Resolutions 1267 and 1373 and the corresponding European instruments in the Al-Qaida and Taliban (United Nations Measures) Orders 2002 and 2006 (AQO) and the Terrorism (United Nations Measures) Order 2006 (TO). Each order enables the UK to recognise international lists, to designate persons on national lists and to prohibit financial transactions by and with designated persons, though recent

---

104 ATCS Act, s. 1(2).
105 ATCS Act, Schedule 1, para. 5 and 7; see also CT Act, s. 84.
106 Grote n 47, 603.
107 Paul Reynolds, 'Britain v. Iceland: Fish now finance' *BBC NEWS* (London 10 October 2008), available at http://news.bbc.co.uk/go/pr/fr/-/2/hi/uk_news/politics/7662827.stm, accessed on 11 March 2009.

legal challenges have created some uncertainty as to how they may apply in the future.[108]

The power to designate under the Orders

The power to designate persons as terrorists differs between the Orders. Under the AQO, HM Treasury is essentially limited to reproducing the UN list established under UNSC Resolution 1267, though it may add the names of persons it reasonably suspects of association with Bin Laden, the Taliban and al-Qaida by direction.[109] The power to designate persons under the TO is much broader, since it allows Treasury to direct a person be designated if it reasonably suspects he/she 'is or may be [someone who] [...] commits, attempts to commit, participates in or facilitates the commission of terrorism', as well as 'persons identified in the Council Decision' and 'persons owned or controlled by [...] or acting on behalf or at the direction of a designated person'.[110] Again, the breadth of this power reflects the breadth of the underlying UN and EC instruments and the policy objective of pre-empting as well as deterring and punishing terrorists.

The effects of designation under the Orders

The designation effectively places an embargo on financial transactions with and to the designated party. Once the designation is 'directed', others may not make any funds or economic resources available to the designated party, including funds and economic resources

---

108 *A, K, M, Q & G v. HM Treasury* [2008] EWHC 869 (Admin), Collins J, para. 49; Sean O'Neill, 'Freezing assets of terror suspects ruled unlawful by High Court', *The Times* (25 April 2008), available at www.timesonline.co.uk/tol/news/uk/article3806031.ece, accessed on 11 March 2009; 'Anti-terror asset-freezing order improperly made', *The Times* (5 May 2008) http://business.timesonline.co.uk/tol/business/law/reports/article3872678.ece, accessed on 11 March 2009.

109 'Listed persons' under the 2002 Order are 'person[s] designated by the Sanctions Committee in [its] list [...]': para. 2. Under para. 3 and 4 of the 2006 Orders, HM Treasury may issue a direction if it has reasonable grounds to suspect that a person is Usama Bin Laden, a person designated by the Sanctions Committee or is owned or controlled by, or acting on behalf of, or at the direction, such a designated person.

110 Terrorism Order, para. 3 and 4.

that belong to, are owned by or are held by, that party or related parties.[111] In exceptional circumstances, Treasury may grant a licence allowing the discharge of funds.[112] But, in the absence of such a licence, it is an offence to knowingly and intentionally circumvent the embargo.[113] At least in the past, Treasury has used the broad definition of 'economic resources' to prevent family members from assisting the listed person in seemingly innocuous ways.[114]

Challenges to the UN Orders

A, K, M, Q & G v. HM Treasury[115] was a challenge to the legality of both UN Orders. Collins J, of the High Court, ruled in favour of the listed persons, though not on the basis that the Sanctions Committee's procedures were unfair.[116] Similar to the CFI in *Kadi*, he found that the UK was obliged, like other UN member states, to implement UNSC Resolution 1267, despite its procedural defects.[117] The High Court could, at most, require the UK government to 'pursue a delisting application to the Security Council' if it found that there was insufficient evidence for the listing.[118] In this respect, the decision of Justice Collins likens a series of decisions by the CFI handed down before the successful *Kadi and Al Barakaat* appeal.[119]

This was not enough to 'save' either one of the UN Orders, however, as the Judge also found that the AQO and the TO went beyond

---

111 Terrorism Order and Al-Qaida Orders, para. 7 and 8.

112 Terrorism Order and Al-Qaida Orders, para. 11.

113 Terrorism Order and Al-Qaida Orders, para. 10.

114 See also *R v. HM Treasury* [2008] UKHL 26 regarding the payment of social security benefits to the spouse of listed person.

115 *A, K, M, Q & G v. HM Treasury* n 108, per Collins J, para. 23 and 42.

116 *A, K, M, Q & G v. HM Treasury* n 108, per Collins J, para. 18.

117 *A, K, M, Q & G v. HM Treasury* n 108, per Collins J, para. 18 and 36.

118 *A, K, M, Q & G v. HM Treasury* n 108, per Collins J, para. 36.

119 Case T-306/01, *Ahmed Ali Yusuf and Al Barakaat International Foundation v. Council of the European Union and Commission of the European Communities* [2005] Court of First Instance, 21 September 2005; Case T-49/04, *Faraj Hasan v. Council of the European Union and Commission of the European Communities* [2006] Court of First Instance, 12 July 2006; Case T-253/02, *Chafiq Ayadi v. Council of the European Union Commission of the European Communities* [2006] Court of First Instance, 21 July 2006.

what was necessary and expedient to implement the underlying UNSC Resolutions.[120] In the first place, the TO went beyond what was 'necessary' to implement UNSC Resolution 1373 as it applied to a person of whom Treasury has *reasonable grounds for suspecting* is or *may be* (a) a person who commits, attempts to commit, [etc.] acts of terrorism' (emphasis added).[121] Then, the Orders were not 'expedient' as the Court was not in a position to consider whether the person met the criteria for listing established in the Orders and so to provide effective judicial review. In particular, there were no provisions allowing the Court to consider intercept material[122] or to appoint a special advocate to hear closed source material on the listed person's behalf.[123] Finally, Justice Collins found that the Orders were insufficiently certain as they did not make it clear when assisting a listed party was a criminal act and a measure of such breadth and severity should have been put to Parliament for consideration.[124] It followed that the Orders were probably invalid, though Justice Collins declined to quash the AQO and the TO before there had been a decision on the Government's appeal.[125]

---

120 *A, K, M, Q & G v. HM Treasury* n 108, per Collins J, para. 37 and 38–39.

121 *A, K, M, Q & G v. HM Treasury*, n 108, per Collins J, para. 40 citing AQO, Art. 4(2). UNSC Resolution 1373 applies to 'persons who commit, or attempt to commit, terrorist acts or participate in or facilitate the commission of terrorist acts': AQO, Art. 1(c) and (d).

122 *A, K, M, Q & G v. HM Treasury* n 108, per Collins J, para. 41. Intercept material is material obtained under a warrant issued by the Secretary of State of the Home Office under s. 5 of the Regulation of Investigatory Powers Act 2000 (RIPA). S. 17 and 18 RIPA prohibit any discussion of the fact that such a warrant has been applied for or issued in most legal proceedings.

123 *A, K, M, Q & G v. HM Treasury* n 108, per Collins J, para. 47. A special advocate is a lawyer who has been especially appointed by the court to represent a person during hearings at which neither she nor her legal representatives are present (closed hearings): CT Act, s. 68 and 73; *R (Roberts) v. Parole Board* [2005] UKHL 45, per Bingham LJ, para. 1; Dennis Keenan and Kenneth Smith, *Smith & Keenan's English Law: Text and Cases* (15th edn, Pearson Longman 2007), 107–108.

124 *A, K, M, Q & G v. HM Treasury* n 108, per Collins J, para. 42.

125 *A, K, M, Q & G v. HM Treasury* n 108, per Collins J, para. 49.

Challenges to the UN Orders – the High Court decision

The appeal in *A, K, M, Q & G v. HM Treasury*[126] was handed down on 30 October 2008, almost two months after the decision of the ECJ in *Kadi and Al Barakaat*. The majority of the English Court of Appeal[127] reversed Justice Collins' decision to quash the Orders, though, in the lead judgment, the Master of the Rolls, Lord Clarke MR, did not deny the problems identified at first instance. Rather, he attempted to construe the Orders – and the powers of the High Court on review – so as to mitigate the procedural flaws and allow the courts to decide the fairness of listings on a case-by-case basis.

Regarding the TO, Lord Clarke MR acknowledged both that it went beyond what is necessary or expedient to implement UNSC Resolution 1373 and that the offences were very broadly defined.[128] He even 'shared some of the concerns expressed [about] the operation of the licence system'.[129] Nonetheless, he found it was not necessary to quash the TO as a whole since the words 'or may be' could be severed from the Order and particular directions, which cited this criterion, quashed in this case.[130] Similarly, the fact that the High Court could not consider closed source and intercept material did not make the proceedings under the TO automatically unfair. The Court had inherent power to appoint special advocates and could restrict the use of intercept material so as to preserve the fairness of individual hearings.[131] In particular, HM Treasury would be prohibited from relying on inculpatory intercept material in any challenge to the listing and would be obliged to conduct its case consistently with any exculpatory intercepted material, 'in extreme cases', by abandoning its defence of

---

126 *A, K, M, Q & G v. HM Treasury* [2008] EWCA Civ 1187.
127 Per Clarke MR, with Wilson LJ concurring and Sedley LJ dissenting.
128 *A, K, M, Q & G v. HM Treasury* n 126, per Clarke MR, para. 87–91.
129 *A, K, M, Q & G v. HM Treasury* n 126, per Clarke MR, para. 87–91 and 96.
130 *A, K, M, Q & G v. HM Treasury* n 126, per Clarke MR, para. 32–50 and 54; Sedley LJ and Wilson LJ agreed on this point, para. 136–139 and 155–157 (respectively).
131 *A, K, M, Q & G v. HM Treasury* n 126, per Clarke MR, para. 55–59 and 60–78; per Sedley LJ, dissenting on the ability of the court to make detailed procedural rules, para. 132–133 and 140–141.

the listing.[132] As to the offences, he found they were sufficiently certain, especially when applied alongside a licensing scheme that was operated, 'fairly, expeditiously, [...] with good will [...] [and] lawfully' and so as to exclude very small amounts from the Orders.[133]

For these reasons, Lord Justice Clarke MR was also persuaded that the AQO was valid. In addition, he agreed with Justice Collins that persons listed under the AQO as a direct result of their listing by the UNSC had an implicit right to judicial review by the British courts.[134] If the Court found that there was insufficient evidence to justify the listing, it could require the UK government to support a delisting procedure before the Sanctions Committee.[135] As the Master of the Rolls explained, '[t]his will not be a challenge to the AQO itself',[136] though it would be a merits-based review, in which the listed person would be entitled to 'discover the case against [him/her], so that [he/she] may have an opportunity to meet it'.[137] Difficulties could arise if HM Treasury did not know the reasons for the UN listing, however, this was not the case here as the Sanctions Committee had listed the applicant in question at the UK's request.[138] At any rate, persons listed by the Sanctions Committee should have the same procedural rights as persons listed by HM Treasury.[139]

The government's response: changes under the CT Act

Following the High Court's decision in *A, K, M, Q & G v. HM Treasury*, the CT Act (then still a bill) was amended to provide for increased judicial supervision of decisions by Treasury in connection with the UN terrorism orders or a freezing order under Part 2 ACTS Act. It reflects many of the criticisms made by Justice Collins and Lord Clarke MR in the two *HM Treasury* cases. In particular, Part 6

132 *A, K, M, Q & G v. HM Treasury* n 126, per Clarke MR, para. 76.
133 *A, K, M, Q & G v. HM Treasury* n 126, per Clarke MR, para. 87, 92–99, 100–103.
134 *A, K, M, Q & G v. HM Treasury* n 126, per Clarke MR, para. 119–121; per Sedley LJ and Wilson LJ concurring, para. 146–150 and 157 (respectively).
135 *A, K, M, Q & G v. HM Treasury* n 126, per Clarke MR, para. 118.
136 *A, K, M, Q & G v. HM Treasury* n 126, per Clarke MR, para. 119.
137 *A, K, M, Q & G v. HM Treasury* n 126, per Clarke MR, para. 120.
138 N 137.
139 *A, K, M, Q & G v. HM Treasury* n 126, per Clarke MR, para. 120.

CT Act allows any person affected by such a decision (and certain other decisions)[140] to apply to the High Court or Court of Sessions to set aside the decision.[141] The Court will determine the application according to the principles applicable to judicial review proceedings[142] and may make orders or give relief as it would in such proceedings.[143] The Court is also given power to develop and apply special rules regarding the mode of proof, disclosure by Treasury and the appointment of special advocates, amongst other things.[144] In addition, Part 6 CT Act amends the RIPA to allow the discussion of intercept material in court, albeit in the absence of the listed party and their normal legal representative.[145]

5. Future developments

At the beginning of this section, we noted that UK counter-terrorism legislation has evolved since the 1970s in response to the changing terrorist threat to the UK. We have seen that it has been equally affected by developments in European law, the use of economic sanctions and international human rights law, particularly what may be called 'global administrative law'.[146] The challenge of harmonising these developments is evident in the High Court and Court of Appeal cases discussed above and no doubt will be seen in future appeals against listings and other measures against terrorist assets. In the meantime, the UK House of Lords EU Committee is considering 'the role of the EU and [its] member states in global efforts to prevent

---

140 In a subsequent revision, Part 6 was extended to decisions under CT Act, Schedule 7 (directions to financial institutions regarding terrorist financing, money laundering and certain other activities): see further, CT Act, s. 63(1)(c) and above, n 65.

141 CT Act, s. 63(1) and (2).

142 CT Act, s. 63(3).

143 CT Act, s. 63(4).

144 CT Act, s. 65–68.

145 CT Act, s. 69.

146 See e.g., Benedict Kingsbury, Nico Krisch and Richard B. Stewart, 'The Emergence of Global Administrative Law', 68 (2005) *Law & Contemporary Problems*, 15–61.

money laundering and terrorist financing'.[147] It is to be expected that the Committee will provide further insight into the impact of the *Kadi and Al Barakaat* within the UK and the apparent discrepancy between the ECJ and the Court of Appeal's decisions regarding the power of the courts to review executive acts implementing UNSC Resolution 1267.

VII. Conclusion: challenge and response in the law on terrorist financing

Almost two decades after the end of the Cold War, an array of 'hard' and 'soft' international laws demonstrate the increasing importance of asset recovery regimes in counter-terrorism law. Developed in relation to other transnational 'macro-crimes', asset recovery follows the logic of preventing, deterring and punishing crime by depriving criminals of the proceeds and instrumentalities of their offences. When used as a counter-terrorist measure, the preventative role of asset recovery has become more prominent next to the goals of deterrence and punishment, as was reflected in the two UN sanctions regimes against alleged terrorists and their associates. Though these regimes restricted procedural and property rights, they initially received strong support from states and international organisations. Recently, however, the consensus has shown signs of strain, as evidenced by the successful legal challenges in regional and national courts and the efforts at the intergovernmental level to prompt reform.

UK counter-terrorist financing and asset recovery laws have reflected the developments at an international and regional level. A party to all of the counter-terrorist conventions and a member of the UN, the EU and the FATF, the UK has enabled recovery of terrorist

---

147 UK Parliament, *Press Release: Lords EU Committee Launch New Inquiry into Money Laundering and the Financing of Terrorism* (19 December 2008), available at http://www.parliament.uk/parliamentary_committees/lords_press_notices/pn19 1208euf.cfm, accessed 24 March 2009.

property with and without a conviction – sometimes without an offence. And, as these laws have come under criticism and legal attack, so have the relevant British laws, as evidenced by *A, K, M, Q & G v. HM Treasury* and Parliament's initial rejection of the CT Bill (as it then was), At the same time, the decision in *A, K, M, Q & G v. HM Treasury* and the passage of the CT Act show that the UK executive wishes to retain its counter-terrorism powers and that the legislature and the judiciary will accept greater interferences with fundamental rights in the area of counter-terrorism. Debate surrounds the appropriate limits to those powers.

In short, if developments in the UN, the EU and the UK are any indication, states will retain significant powers in relation to terrorist assets, though subject to greater judicial supervision and more procedural guarantees for affected parties. These restrictions will, in turn, prompt national and international executive bodies to reform their procedures to accommodate previous and anticipate future judicial decisions. A similar process has already been observed between the European Court of Human Rights and the ECJ in cases concerning UN sanctions against the former Yugoslavia.[148] In relation to counter-terrorist 'blacklists', it can be seen *within* legal systems, in the legal challenges and responses to counter-terrorist financing laws in the EU and the UK. It could emerge *between* legal systems if the European judiciary is called upon to evaluate the efforts of the UNSC to reform its listing procedures. In any case, these parallel developments should be viewed as the maturation of the international consensus on counter-terrorist financing, rather than its dissipation.

---

148 Cathryn Costello, 'The Bosporus Ruling of the European Court of Human Rights: Fundamental Rights and Blurred Boundaries in Europe' (2006) *Human Rights Law Review*, 87–130.

MARK PIETH*, DANIEL THELESKLAF** AND RADHA IVORY***

The international counter-terrorist financing regime at the cross-roads

I. Introduction

The counter-terrorist financing regime, as we know it, crystallised around attacks by al-Qaida at the turn of the last century. Led by the United States and its allies in the 'War on Terror', the United Nations Security Council (UNSC) passed UNSC Resolution 1267, imposing sanctions on individuals and organisations deemed to be 'associated with' Usama Bin Laden, al-Qaida and the Taliban and, under Resolution 1373, called on states to take action against the funds and economic resources of other terrorists. The Financial Action Task Force (FATF), for its part, declared action in nine areas to form the 'basic framework' against terrorist financing and the Egmont Group of Financial Intelligence Units (FIUs) and the International Monetary Fund (IMF) expanded their mandates to include counter-terrorist financing. In 2002, the UN's International Convention for the Suppression of the Financing of Terrorism (1999) (Terrorist Financing Convention) also came into force.

*   Professor of Criminal Law, University of Basel, Switzerland.
**   Co-Executive Director, Basel Institute on Governance, Switzerland.
*** Research Fellow, Basel Institute on Governance, Switzerland.

II. The international consensus strained

After these initial developments, however, the apparent consensus on terrorist financing began to show signs of strain. Already in 2002, the Wolfsberg Group made it clear that financial institutions faced 'new challenges' in identifying the terrorists amongst their customers and distinguishing terrorist transactions from legitimate funds movements, concerns echoed by the authors in this volume. In 2004, the US commission established to investigate the attacks of 11 September 2001 stated that actions 'to designate terrorist financiers and freeze their money [...] appeared to have little effect [...]'.[1] More recently, the human impact of counter-terrorism financing measures has received more attention, national and regional courts quashing executive regulations implementing the UN lists and states, such as Switzerland, proposing reforms to the UNSC's procedures for listing and delisting.

III. Terrorist financing at the cross-roads

Hence, ten years after the passage of UNSC Resolution 1267, it is fair to say that the counter-terrorist financing regime, as we know it, is at the cross-roads. Governments and courts are not prepared to relinquish the goal of countering terrorism through the financial system, fearing, as GUIDO STEINBERG, that organisations, such as al-Qadia, remain a threat. At the same time, they are not prepared to see the counter-terrorist financing regime remain in its original form. How can it be restructured to maximise its contribution to the global effort against terrorism and minimise its strategic and human costs? The contributions to this volume and the discussions at the Giessbach II seminar in October 2008 generate some considerations on the way forward.

1 Thomas Kean and Lee Hamilton, *The 9/11 Commission Report* (National Commission on Terrorist Attacks upon the United States, Washington (DC) 2004), 381.

1. Reconsider the role of terrorist lists

There is a risk that the counter-terrorist financing regime is overly associated with, and reliant on, the counter-terrorism lists created pursuant to UNSC Resolutions 1267 and 1373. As discussed by SCOTT VESEL and MARK PIETH AND STEPHANIE EYMANN, the listing and delisting procedures used to administer the lists, particularly the Resolution 1267 list, are unfair in a number of ways. These deficiencies have made the lists controversial and, according to PIETH AND EYMANN, undermine the moral and political authority of the UN to criticise unlawful and oppressive acts. Moreover, for JACQUES RAYROUD, the lists make it more difficult for states to convict terrorists and impose criminal sanctions, such as confiscations and jail terms. In some ways, the lists meet the need they create, in that they facilitate indefinite extra-judicial asset freezes. This does not solve the ultimate problem, however. As SCOTT VESEL shows, unfair listing regimes are increasing vulnerable to legal challenge, with national and regional courts more willing than ever to strike down executive acts which proscribe individuals and organisations without due process.

2. Revisit criminal and civil mechanism for recovering terrorist assets

Given these difficulties, states and international organisations would be well advised to revisit criminal and civil mechanism for recovering terrorist assets. This raises three further questions. First, how should the act of terrorist financing be criminalised? The UN's Terrorist Financing Convention foresees the creation of an autonomous offence of terrorist financing. But, as YARA ESQUIVEL SOTO considers in relation to the Ibero-American states, supplying funds to terrorists can also be treated as an ancillary offence to other terrorist acts. Second, by what criminal and civil means should states enable the freezing, seizing and confiscation of the proceeds and the instrumentalities of terrorism? Answering this question will require an examination of national approaches, such as is undertaken by the FATF in its mutual evaluations and by RADHA IVORY in this volume in relation to the United Kingdom. Third, how effective are the current mechanisms for international cooperation in terrorist financing investigations and proceedings? JACQUES RAYROUD submits that many useful tools are indeed already provided in international instruments – if only states would ratify them.

3. Consider the role of financial institutions in counter-terrorist financing

The uncertainty surrounding the UNSC listing system also has implications for the role of financial institutions in counter-terrorist financing. It indicates that they will be less able to rely on the implementation of national and international lists to discharge their duties with regard to counter-terrorist financing. Instead, they will be increasingly expected to support, if not anticipate, law enforcement inquiries by detecting and investigating suspected terrorist finance. KRISTEL GRACE POH gives examples of how banks are already using their access to customer information to assist law enforcement authorities on an *ad hoc* basis. In addition, BOB UPTON, maintains, that financial institutions could increase their ongoing 'preventative' or 'detective' role if the public sector were to supply more meaningful and actionable intelligence. In his view, the UK's 'Vetted Group' is an example of how institutionalised consultative *fora* can facilitate such information exchange.

FIUs will play a key role in mediating this evolving relationship. They are already a conduit for information between public and private sector institutions and, as YEHUDA SHAFFER describes, they develop many of the terrorist financing typologies and information technology tools which private sector institutions use to analyse their transaction and account information. In designing such systems, HENRIETTE HAAS suggests that FIUs and banks should consider what information prosecutors could need in a subsequent investigation.

4. Work with developing states and communities to detect and detain terrorist funds

Comprehensive laws and efficient data management and analysis systems cannot be the preserve of rich states alone. KRISTEL GRACE POH and KILIAN STRAUSS discuss how some developing and transitions states may be 'soft targets' for terrorist finance due to a lack of legal powers to prosecute terrorist financiers and recover terrorist assets and information technology tools to detect terrorist funds. Increasing capacity is not as simple as drafting new laws or rolling-out the latest technology, however. There is a risk that efforts to improve their capacities in relation to counter-terrorist financing may be perceived as benefiting only developed (western) states – the stereotypical targets of terrorism. It will be important, therefore, that development agencies, international organisations and NGOs work with local governments and communities to design technical assistance programmes. It may be that counter-terrorist financing programmes are most effective when they are embedded in broader efforts to reduce financial crime (including organised crime and corruption) in developing or transition states. In any case, agencies should consider how local people experience terrorism and how counter-terrorist measures could impact on their social, political and economic activities, as ELIZABETH DIAW suggested at the Giessbach II seminar.

5. Guard against 'terrorist capital flight' by appropriately regulating vulnerable sectors

Even as we succeed in discouraging terrorists from using the formal financial system, we create incentives for them to channel their funds through other less regulated sectors. In thinking about ways to reduce the 'vulnerability' of these sectors we must avoid the temptation to reflexively apply the same responses as were successful in other areas. In some cases, the 'lessons learned' will be highly applicable. For example, the FATF recommends that states apply the same measures to alternative remittance service providers as they apply to bank and non-bank financial institutions. Similarly, looking at the contributions of KRISTEL GRACE POH, KILIAN STRAUSS and GIUSEPPE LOMBARDO, it is apparent that the measures needed to combat cross-border transportations of cash will, in many ways, mirror the measures needed to increase capacity in the financial sectors of developing states.

In other cases, different considerations will be germane. For example, the civic work and informality of some non-profit organisations may leave them inadequately supervised and/or attractive vehicles for moving terrorist funds. Yet, as PIETH AND EYMANN note, these qualities may make them essential service providers and/or important outlets for political and social expression. Similarly, the features which make the Internet an extraordinary tool for communication and commerce also enable terrorists to communicate with their donors and collect funds, as MARCO GERCKE illustrates in his survey of terrorist uses of the Internet. The same observations can be made again of trusts and other offshore financial services, as explained by STEPHEN BAKER.

How to discourage terrorist financiers from operating through these sectors whilst minimising the impact on legitimate service providers and users? In responding to perceived vulnerabilities, states and international organisations may need to depart from familiar governance models in the area of counter-terrorism. Is the state the most effective regulator? Indeed, is regulation the most appropriate tool? These and other questions remain as counter-terrorist financing engages with the risks and opportunities of reform.

IV. Outlook – challenge as an opportunity for renewal

The counter-financing regime, as we know it, has been challenged on numerous fronts. Already in 2004, US policy makers asked whether it was reasonable to try to prevent attacks by freezing funds. Since then, in the courts, listed parties have questioned the ability of the UNSC and UN member states to implement terrorist lists without customary guarantees for due process. The uncertainty surrounding the lists has implications for financial institutions, which use terrorist lists to vet their customers and transactions. They may be able to detect terrorist financing in other ways, though often only with help from law enforcement and intelligence agencies. In any case, there is good reason to believe terrorist money is being moved by other means through the so-called vulnerable sectors.

At first view, these challenges bode ill for the effectiveness of a uniform international regime against terrorist financing. Looked at again, they represent an opportunity for states and international organisations to ensure that the 'war on terrorist finance' is being conducted in keeping with its underlying and ultimate objective: to promote good governance and peaceful social change all around the world. From this point of view, it may be legitimate for states to take action against those who use violence to advance their social and political goals. However, those measures should not themselves disproportionately restrict fundamental rights, such as the right to due process or the freedoms of association and political communication. The goal of protecting the state against terrorists is, moreover, a moving target. Part of recalibrating the counter-terrorist financing regime is dispensing with the idea that one set of measures against one sort of actor can resolve the problem of terrorism or its financing for all time. Counter-terrorist financing is rather a process, in which we regularly reassess our response – and that of the terrorists.